The *Reformation Heritage Bible Commentary* is a unique series that promises to be a valuable resource for laity and preachers. The verse-by-verse commentary focuses on major topics, providing clear interpretation and devotional insight in keeping with how the Reformers approached Scripture, and emphasizing themes that were central in their teaching. Illustrative quotes from key Reformers and their heirs, including Lutheran, Calvinist, Anglican, and Wesleyan sources, provide insights in their own words, without trying to survey the range of views represented in this heritage. This focused approach gives a clear reading of the text which engages one's mind and heart.

—The Rev. Dr. Rodney A. Whitacre
Professor of Biblical Studies
Trinity School for Ministry
Ambridge, Pennsylvania

Busy pastors and teachers of the scriptures need commentaries that are biblical, theological, and practical. Fortunately, the Reformation Heritage Bible Commentary Series fulfills those requirements. The scholarship is reverent, demonstrating that the truths of the Reformation are relevant today just as they were in the 16th century. The volumes are accessible to a wide variety of readers, for it is written in a wonderfully clear way. I commend this work gladly.

—Thomas R. Schreiner, PhD
James Buchanan Harrison Professor of New Testament
The Southern Baptist Theological Seminary
Louisville, Kentucky

The Reformation Heritage series is a "Heritage of Reformation theology" now put at the fingertips of every serious Bible student, young or old.

This commentary helps anyone to dive deeply into the Scriptures, verse by verse, even word by word. I was blessed with its academic rigor in straightforward language, the sidebar articles explaining overarching Biblical themes, and the voices of the Reformers demonstrating again that this Good News of Jesus is a message for all times. If one yearns to know the unique message of the Scripture and its meaning for life, now and forever, then join me in having the Reformation Heritage Series in your library today.

—Rev. Gregory P. Seltz
Speaker, The Lutheran Hour

The *Reformation Heritage Bible Commentary* promises to be an asset to the library of serious Bible students, whether layman or clergy. This series exemplifies the reformers commitment to sola scriptura, that the revelation of God's saving purposes is in scripture alone, which is primarily about Christ alone. The blend of overviews and insights from our Protestant forefathers with exegesis and application from contemporary reformed theologians makes for an interesting read. Contemporary readers will also appreciate the devotional notes in these commentaries. Because the study of God's Word is not just an academic endeavor, it engages the mind, heart and will of those who trust Christ for their salvation. While many modern commentaries seem to focus on the application of the scriptures, the intent here is Gospel-centered interpretation, resulting in devotional application. This is a work of serious scholastic intent combined with theological scrutiny and integrity. I am grateful for such a work and confident that it will be profitable for years to come in aiding the church's effort to know Christ more fully as He is revealed in Holy Scripture.

—Kenneth R. Jones
Pastor of Glendale Baptist Church, Miami, FL
Co-host of nationally syndicated talk show—White Horse Inn
Contributed to *Experiencing the Truth, Glory Road,* and
Keep Your Head Up; all published by Crossway.
Contributed to *Tabletalk* and *Modern Reformation* magazines
Frequent conference speaker

The Reformation of the church brought with it biblical insights that revitalized churches and radically changed the course of theological studies as giants like Luther, Melanchthon, Calvin, Chemnitz, and Wesley commented extensively on Holy Scripture. The new *Reformation Heritage Bible Commentary* is a one-stop-resource where the observations of these and other distinguished Reformation leaders are brought together around specific books of the New Testament.

—The Rev. Dr. R. Reed Lessing
St. Michael's Lutheran Church
Ft. Wayne, IN
Longtime Professor of Exegetical Theology at Concordia Seminary, St. Louis, MO

Reformation Heritage
BIBLE COMMENTARY

PASTORAL EPISTLES

1 & 2 Timothy, Titus, Philemon

Also From Concordia

Biblical Studies

The Reformation Heritage Bible Commentary Series
  Mark, Daniel Paavola
  Luke, Robert A. Sorensen
  Galatians, Ephesians, Philippians, Jerald C. Joersz
  Colossians/Thessalonians, Edward A. Engelbrecht and Paul Deterding
  Hebrews, Steven P. Mueller
  General Epistles, Clinton J. Armstrong
  Revelation, Mark Brighton

The Living Word. An online Bible learning program, featuring studies on individual books of the Bible. www.OnlineBibleLearning.org

The Lutheran Study Bible, Edward A. Engelbrecht, General Editor

The Apocrypha: The Lutheran Edition with Notes, Edward A. Engelbrecht, General Editor

LifeLight Indepth Bible Study Series
  More than 50 studies available on biblical books and topics

Concordia's Complete Bible Handbook for Students, Jane L. Fryar, Edward A. Engelbrecht, et al.

Concordia Commentary Series: A Theological Exposition of Sacred Scripture
  Leviticus, John W. Kleinig
  Joshua, Adolph L. Harstad
  Ruth, John R. Wilch
  Ezra and Nehemiah, Andrew E. Steinmann
  Proverbs, Andrew E. Steinmann

Ecclesiastes, James Bollhagen
The Song of Songs, Christopher W. Mitchell
Isaiah 40–55, R. Reed Lessing
Isaiah 56–66, R. Reed Lessing
Ezekiel 1–20, Horace D. Hummel
Ezekiel 21–48, Horace D. Hummel
Daniel, Andrew E. Steinmann
Amos, R. Reed Lessing
Jonah, R. Reed Lessing
Matthew 1:1–11:1, Jeffrey A. Gibbs
Matthew 11:2–20:34, Jeffrey A. Gibbs
Mark 1:1–8:26, James W. Voelz
Luke 1:1–9:50, Arthur A. Just Jr.
Luke 9:51–24:53, Arthur A. Just Jr.
Romans 1–8, Michael Middendorf (forthcoming May 2013)
1 Corinthians, Gregory J. Lockwood
Galatians, A. Andrew Das
Ephesians, Thomas M. Winger
Colossians, Paul E. Deterding
Philemon, John G. Nordling
2 Peter and Jude, Curtis P. Giese
1–3 John, Bruce G. Schuchard
Revelation, Louis A. Brighton

Historical Studies

From Abraham to Paul: A Biblical Chronology, Andrew E. Steinmann

The Church from Age to Age: A History from Galilee to Global Christianity, Edward A. Engelbrecht, General Editor

History of Theology, 4th Rev. Ed., Bengt Hägglund

Reformation Heritage
BIBLE COMMENTARY

+ PASTORAL
EPISTLES

1 & 2 Timothy, Titus, Philemon

MARK W. LOVE

CONCORDIA PUBLISHING HOUSE · SAINT LOUIS

Library of Congress Cataloging-in-Publication Data

Love, Mark W.
    1 & 2 Timothy, Titus, Philemon / Mark W. Love.
        p.   cm. — (Reformation heritage Bible commentary)
    ISBN 978-0-7586-2772-8
    1. Bible. N.T. 1 Timothy--Commentaries. 2. Bible. N.T. 2 Timothy—Commentaries. 3. Bible N.T. Titus—Commentaries. Bible NT. Philemon—Commentaries. I. Love, Mark W.- II. Title. III. Title: 1 & 2 Timothy, Titus, Philemon.
  BS2715.53.E54   2015
  227'.077--dc23   2011044778

1 2 3 4 5 6 7 8 9 10   24 23 22 21 20 19 18 17 16 15

Contents

About This Series

The great reformers' influence upon the Bible's interpretation and application could not help but revitalize our churches. This is as true today as it was 500 years ago. This renewal happens in part because the reformers drew upon the insights of the Renaissance, which linked the medieval church back to her earlier roots in the ancient world. There the biblical texts sprang up. The reformers were among the earliest students to pursue classical studies, not only due to personal interest but especially due to the benefits such study brought to the study of the Bible. By reading the New Testament Scriptures in their ancient languages and context, the reformers dispelled many misunderstandings.

Second, the fires of controversy, which followed Luther's proclamation of justification by grace through faith on account of Christ alone, served to refine the study of Sacred Scriptures. So many ideas that medieval people took for granted or that were accepted based on human authority alone were tested and retested, leading to more careful study of God's Word.

Third, the reformers themselves taught with special insight due to their constant reading, study, translating, and preaching of the Sacred Scriptures. Their approach to the Scriptures and the insights they gained have continued to inform biblical studies even to the present day. For all of these reasons, Concordia Publishing House wished to produce a readable commentary series that would serve the current generation by sharing with them (1) insights from the reformers and (2) commentary that stemmed from their heritage.

In preparing this commentary, we drew upon the insights of the following reformers and heirs to their evangelical approach to teaching the Scriptures:

John Hus (c. 1372–1415)

Martin Luther (1483–1546)

Thomas Cranmer (1489–1556)

Philip Melanchthon (1497–1560)

John Calvin (1509–64)

John Knox (c. 1513–72)

Martin Chemnitz (1522–86)

Johann Gerhard (1582–1637)

Johann Albrecht Bengel (1687–1752)

John Wesley (1703–91)

Not every commentary in this series will include quotations from each of these reformers or heirs of the Reformation since these authors did not all comment on Books of the Scriptures with equal frequency. Other reformers may be included, as well as citations of Reformation era confessional documents such as the Augsburg Confession and Westminster Confession. Readers should not conclude that citation of an author implies complete endorsement of everything that author wrote (heaven knows, these were fallible men as they themselves acknowledged). The works of other significant Reformation era commentators are less available in English. We have intentionally stayed away from more radical reformers such as Andreas Bodenstein von Karlstadt, Ulrich Zwingli, Thomas Münzer, etc.

The commentary is not simply a compilation of sixteenth century views but a thorough verse-by-verse commentary built from the reformers' approach of *Scripture interprets Scripture* and supplemented from their writings. Along with quotations from the reformers and their heirs, readers will also find quotations from some early and medieval Church Fathers. This is because the reformers did not wish to overthrow the earlier generations of teachers but to profit from them where they were faithful in teaching the Word.

Some readers will note that the writers listed above represent different branches in the Protestant family of churches, and they may wonder how compatible these writers will be alongside one another. It is certainly the case that the reformers held different views, especially concerning the Sacraments, biblical authority, and other matters. Some authors for the series may at times describe differences between the various reformers.

However, while it is true that these differences affect the fellowship and work of the churches of the Reformation, it is also true that the reformers shared significant agreement. For example, the great historian Philip Schaff noted, "Melanchthon mediated between Luther and Calvin" (*History of the Christian Church* vol. VII, second revised ed. [New York: Charles Scribner's Sons, 1894], 260). Early Reformation works like Melanchthon's *Commonplaces* and the Augsburg Confession served as models for the various traditions of Protestant confession and doctrine. What is more, as the writers focused on a particular biblical text for interpretation, they often reached very similar conclusions regarding that text. The text of Scripture tended to lead them toward a more unified expression of the faith. This is something I have described as "the text effect,"[1] which illustrates for

---

[1]   *Friends of the Law* (St. Louis: Concordia, 2011), 136.

us a way in which the Bible brings us together despite differences and always remains the most important guide for Christian teaching and practice. In view of the 500th anniversary of the Reformation in 2017, I believe it is fitting for us to draw anew upon the time-honored insights of these great servants of God.

The Bible Translations

Among the translations for our commentary we have chosen, on the one hand, what many regard as the finest English translation ever produced: the King James Version. The KJV is a product of the Reformation era, and although it is now more than 400 years old, remains a most valuable tool for study. Along with the KJV we are pleased to present the English Standard Version, which has rapidly become one of the most widely used modern English translations. The success of the ESV is due in part to the translators' efforts to follow sound, classical principals of translation very like those used by the KJV translators. The result is a very readable English translation that also allows readers to grasp the biblical expressions and terms that appear repeatedly in the Bible. Due to this approach, we find the ESV an especially helpful translation for Bible study. Our notes are keyed to the ESV, but we have placed the KJV in parallel with the ESV for easy comparison. Since the ESV text is based on the broad consensus of biblical scholars who have consulted the early Greek manuscripts, it differs at points from the KJV text, which was produced when fewer manuscripts were available for study. Where significant differences between the translations appear, the notes include comment.

Our Prayer for You

The following prayer embodies the sense of study and devotion we wish to convey to all who take up these commentaries:

Blessed Lord, You have caused all Holy Scriptures to be written for our learning. Grant that we may so hear them, read, mark, learn, and inwardly digest them that, by patience and comfort from Your holy Word, we may embrace and ever hold fast the blessed hope of everlasting life; through Jesus Christ, our Lord. Amen.

Rev. Edward A. Engelbrecht, STM
Senior Editor for Bible Resources

PREFACE

Unlike the rest of St. Paul's Epistles, the four Letters in this volume are written to individuals. All are addressed to church leaders: two to Pastor Timothy, one to Pastor Titus, and one to Philemon, whose home hosts a congregation. Yet these Letters are also for the entire Church. We read counsel for pastors and for all Christians. What can we expect of, and from, our ministers? We hear God's guidance for those in various stations in life: old and young, male and female, slave and free—all are to live in response to the Gospel and in service to their neighbor.

As these Letters provide God's Word, their teachings are, at times, counter-cultural. They have sometimes been viewed with suspicion or skepticism. But they are indeed the Word of God and they are written in love for all who read them. Paul writes to Timothy and Titus with fatherly love, calling them his spiritual children. We see Paul's love and concern for Onesimus, a runaway slave, but also for Philemon his owner. Their common faith in Jesus will transform their relationship. We, too, can hear God's loving-care for us in these writings.

Above all, these Epistles point to Jesus. As God's inspired Word, they join the rest of Scripture as being "able to make you wise for salvation through faith in Christ Jesus," and through their words of teaching . . . reproof . . . correction, and . . . training in righteousness," we will be "complete, equipped for every good work" (2Tm 3:15–17).

Steven P. Mueller, Ph.D.
General Editor

ABBREVIATIONS

AD	*anno Domini* (in the year of [our] Lord)	NT	New Testament
		OT	Old Testament
BC	before Christ	p.	page
c.	circa	pp.	pages
cf.	confer	St.	Saint
ch.	chapter	v.	verse
chs.	chapters	vv.	verses

Canonical Scripture

Gn	Genesis	Dn	Daniel
Ex	Exodus	Hos	Hosea
Lv	Leviticus	Jl	Joel
Nu	Numbers	Am	Amos
Dt	Deuteronomy	Ob	Obadiah
Jsh	Joshua	Jnh	Jonah
Jgs	Judges	Mi	Micah
Ru	Ruth	Na	Nahum
1Sm	1 Samuel	Hab	Habakkuk
2Sm	2 Samuel	Zep	Zephaniah
1Ki	1 Kings	Hg	Haggai
2Ki	2 Kings	Zec	Zechariah
1Ch	1 Chronicles	Mal	Malachi
2Ch	2 Chronicles		
Ezr	Ezra	Mt	Matthew
Ne	Nehemiah	Mk	Mark
Est	Esther	Lk	Luke
Jb	Job	Jn	John
Ps	Psalms	Ac	Acts
Pr	Proverbs	Rm	Romans
Ec	Ecclesiastes	1Co	1 Corinthians
Sg	Song of Solomon	2Co	2 Corinthians
Is	Isaiah	Gal	Galatians
Jer	Jeremiah	Eph	Ephesians
Lm	Lamentations	Php	Philippians
Ezk	Ezekiel	Col	Colossians

1Th	1 Thessalonians	1Pt	1 Peter
2Th	2 Thessalonians	2Pt	2 Peter
1Tm	1 Timothy	1Jn	1 John
2Tm	2 Timothy	2Jn	2 John
Ti	Titus	3Jn	3 John
Phm	Philemon	Jude	Jude
Heb	Hebrews	Rv	Revelation
Jas	James		

The Apocrypha

Jth	Judith	2Macc	2 Maccabees
Wis	The Wisdom of Solomon	Old Grk Est	Old Greek Esther
Tob	Tobit	Sus	Susanna
Ecclus	Ecclesiasticus (Sirach)	Bel	Bel and the Dragon
		Pr Az	The Prayer of Azariah
Bar	Baruch	Sg Three	The Song of the Three Holy Children
Lt Jer	The Letter of Jeremiah		
1Macc	1 Maccabees	Pr Man	Prayer of Manasseh

Other Books

1Esd	1 Esdras	Ps 151	Psalm 151
2Esd	2 Esdras	1En	1 Enoch
3Macc	3 Maccabees (Ptolemaika)	2En	2 Enoch
4Macc	4 Maccabees	Jub	Jubilees

Abbreviations for Commonly Cited Books and Works

ANF   Roberts, Alexander, and James Donaldson, eds. *The Ante-Nicene Fathers: The Writings of the Fathers Down to AD 325*, 10 vols. Buffalo: The Christian Literature Publishing Company, 1885–96. Reprint, Grand Rapids, MI: Eerdmans, 2001.

Chemnitz   Chemnitz, Martin. *Chemnitz's Works*. 8 Vols. St. Louis: Concordia, 1971–89.

Church   Huss, John. *The Church*. David S. Schaff, trans. New York: Charles Scribner's Sons, 1915.

Concordia   McCain, Paul Timothy, ed. *Concordia: The Lutheran Confessions*. 2nd ed. St. Louis: Concordia, 2006.

ESV   English Standard Version.

FC   Formula of Concord. From *Concordia*.

Gerhard   Gerhard, Johann. *Theological Commonplaces*. Richard J. Dinda, trans. Benjamin T. G. Mayes, ed. St. Louis: Concordia, 2009–.

H82   *The Hymnal 1982, according to the Use of The Episcopal Church*. New York: The Church Hymnal Corporation, 1985.

KJV   King James Version of Scripture.

LSB   Commission on Worship of The Lutheran Church—Missouri Synod. *Lutheran Service Book*. St. Louis: Concordia, 2006.

LW   Luther, Martin. *Luther's Works*. American Edition. General editors Jaroslav Pelikan and Helmut T. Lehmann. 56 vols. St. Louis: Concordia, and Philadelphia: Muhlenberg and Fortress, 1955–1986. Vols. 56–75: Edited by Christopher Boyd Brown. St. Louis: Concordia, 2009–.

SA   Smalcald Articles. From *Concordia*.

SD   Solid Declaration of the Formula of Concord. From *Concordia*.

SLSB   Eales, Samuel J., trans. and ed. *Some Letters of St. Bernard, Abbot of Clairvaux*. The Complete Works of S. Bernard, Abbot of Clairvaux 1. London: John Hodges, 1904.

TPH   *The Presbyterian Hymnal*. Louisville, KY: Westminster/John Knox Press, 1990.

TUMH   *The United Methodist Hymnal*. Nashville, TN: The United Methodist Publishing House, 1989.

Wesley   Wesley, John. *Explanatory Notes upon the New Testament*. 12 ed. New York: Carlton & Porter, 1754.

TIMELINE FOR THE NEW TESTAMENT

Anatolia, Greece, and Rome	Egypt and Africa	Dates	Syria, Canaan, and Israel	Mesopotamia and Persia
		4 BC	Angel appears to Zechariah (c. Nov 15; Lk 1:8–22)	
		3 BC	The Annunciation (inter Apr 17–May 16; Lk 1:26–38); John the Baptist born (Aug; Lk 1:57–66)	
	Holy family in Egypt	2 BC	Jesus born (mid Jan to early Feb; Mt 1:25; Lk 2:1–7); Magi visit; flight to Egypt (mid to late in the year; Mt 2)	
		1 BC	Death of Herod the Great (after Jan 10; Mt 2:19); return to Nazareth (Mt 2:19–23)	
		AD 6	Judas the Galilean leads revolt against Rome; Judea, Samaria, and Idumaea combined to form the Roman province of Judea	
		c. 10	Rabbi Hillel dies	
		11	Jesus in temple before the elders (c. Apr 8–22; Lk 2:42)	
Tiberius, Roman emperor		14–37		
Revolt in Gaul; grain shortages cause unrest in Rome		21		
		29	Baptism of Jesus (fall; Lk 3:1–2)	
		30	Jesus at Passover (c. Apr 8; Jn 2:20)	
		32	Jesus at Passover (c. Apr 15; Jn 6:4); Jesus arrives at Feast of Booths (c. Oct 14; Jn 7:14); Feast of Booths (Oct 17 or 18; Jn 7:37)	

Anatolia, Greece, and Rome	Egypt and Africa	Dates	Syria, Canaan, and Israel	Mesopotamia and Persia
Roman senators unable to pay debts; subsidized by Emperor Tiberius		33	Triumphal entry (Sun, Mar 29); Last Supper (Thurs eve, Apr 2); crucifixion (Fri, Apr 3); resurrection (Sun, Apr 5); ascension (May 14; Lk 24:51; Ac 1:9); Pentecost (May 24)	Jews of Parthia, Media, Elam and Mesopotamia travel to Jerusalem for Pentecost
	Ethiopian eunuch baptized, returns home (Ac 8:26–39)	c. 35		
		35–42		Revolt of Seleucia on the Tigris against Parthian rule
		36	Paul's conversion (Ac 9:1–31)	
Caligula (Gaius), Roman emperor		37–41	Josephus, Jewish historian, born	
	Philo of Alexandria leads Jewish delegation to Rome	c. 39	Caligula attempts to place statue of himself in Jerusalem temple	
		41	Martyrdom of James (late Mar; Ac 12:2); Peter in prison (Apr; Ac 12:3–4); Passover (May 4; Ac 12:4); Peter leaves Jerusalem (May; Gal 2:11)	
		41–44	Herod Agrippa I rules Judea	
Claudius, Roman emperor		41–54		
Peter on mission in Asia Minor (spr/sum; 1Pt 1:1–2); [in Corinth (fall); at Rome (mid Nov)]		42	Peter in Antioch (May 41–Apr 42; Gal 2:11)	
		44	Herod Agrippa at festival in Caesarea (Mar 5; Ac 12:19); death of Herod Agrippa (Mar 10; Ac 12:21–23)	

Anatolia, Greece, and Rome	Egypt and Africa	Dates	Syria, Canaan, and Israel	Mesopotamia and Persia
		47–48	Paul's 1st missionary journey (Ac 13:1–14:28)	
Paul goes to Macedonia; Barnabas and John Mark go to Cyprus (mid May; Ac 15:36–16:10)		49	Conference in Jerusalem (Ac 15:1–35); Peter goes to Antioch (Feb; Gal 2:11); Paul confronts Peter (Apr; Gal 2:11)	
		49–56	[Peter in Antioch (seven years)]	
Paul's 2nd missionary journey (Ac 15:39–18:22)	Philo of Alexandria leads second Jewish delegation to Rome	49–51		
Paul's 3rd missionary journey (Ac 18:23–21:17)		52–55		
Nero, Roman emperor		54–68		
		55–57	Paul imprisoned in Caesarea (Ac 23:23–26:32)	
Paul's journey to Rome (Ac 27:1–28:16)		57–58		
Paul in custody in Rome (Ac 28:17–31)		58–60		
		62	Martyrdom of James, the Lord's brother	
Paul assigns Titus at Crete (Ti 1:5)		64–65		
Paul in Ephesus, where he leaves Timothy (spr–sum; 1Tm 1:3)		65		

Anatolia, Greece, and Rome	Egypt and Africa	Dates	Syria, Canaan, and Israel	Mesopotamia and Persia
	Tiberius Julius Alexander, of Jewish descent, appointed Roman prefect of Egypt	66		
		66–70	Jewish revolt against Romans	
Peter and Paul martyred		68		
Emperor Vespasian		69–79		
		70	Titus destroys Jerusalem temple; Rabbon Yohanan ben Zakkai at Yavneh Academy	Jerusalem Jews settle in Babylonia, which becomes the new center of Judaism
		c. 73	Fall of Masada	
Emperor Titus		79–81		
Emperor Domitian		81–96		
		c. 90–115	Rabbon Gamaliel II at Yavneh Academy	
Jews revolt in Cyprus	Jews revolt in Egypt and Cyrene	115–17		Trajan captures Mesopotamia; Jews revolt
	Founding of Antinoöpolis by Emperor Hadrian	130		
		132–35	Bar Kokhba revolt; death of Rabbi Akiva, Yavneh Academy leader who hailed Bar Kokhba as the messiah	

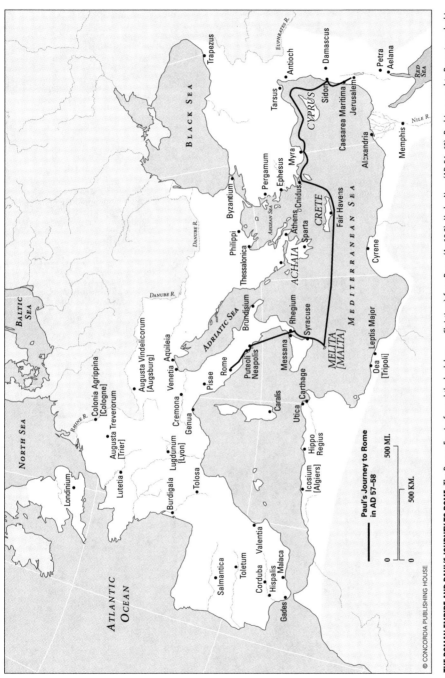

THE ROMAN EMPIRE AND PAUL'S JOURNEY TO ROME. The Roman Empire formed the backdrop for the ministries of Jesus and the apostles. Jesus was born during the reign of Caesar Augustus (27 BC–AD 14; Lk 2:1). He carried out His earthly ministry, was crucified, and rose from the dead during the reign of Tiberius (AD 14–37; Lk 3:1). Claudius (AD 41–54) expelled Jews (and Jewish Christians) from Rome (Ac 18:2). Under Nero (AD 54–68), Paul journeyed to Rome to make his appeal to Caesar and bear witness to Christ there (AD 57–58; Acts 27–28). Later, Nero persecuted Christians, and in AD 68, Paul and Peter were martyred in Rome.

© CONCORDIA PUBLISHING HOUSE

xxi

1 TIMOTHY

INTRODUCTION TO
1 TIMOTHY

Overview

Author
Paul the apostle

Date
AD 65

Places
Ephesus; Macedonia

People
Paul; Timothy; Hymenaeus; Alexander

Purpose
To encourage and instruct Timothy as he called the Ephesians to be faithful to God's Word

Law and Sin Themes
Charged/appointed with service; threat of false teachers; management

Grace and Gospel Themes
The glorious Gospel; salvation through Christ, our Mediator; hallowed by God's Word/grace

Memory Verses
Chief of sinners (1:15–16); one mediator (2:5–6); the mystery of godliness (3:16); contentment (6:6–8)

Reading 1 Timothy

"My lord," the chief servant explains, "the granary is full, though the harvest is not yet complete." The head of the household excuses himself from his guests, crosses the mosaic floor of the men's quarters (Gk *andron*), and enters the family courtyard. His wife sits in the shade of the women's quarters. She spins thread while watching the progress of the young women. Their children and the slaves' children race clay horse figurines around the beaten-earth courtyard. The lord (Gk *kyrios*) passes into the street, encouraging his chief servant as they walk through town on the way to the fields.

In 1 Timothy, the apostle Paul speaks as Timothy's father (1:18). Paul compares Timothy's service in the Church at Ephesus with the service of a father in a typical Greek household. The overseer must manage his household, commanding and teaching the members (4:11), seeing that care is distributed to all. Each member must fulfill a role and a calling in service to the Lord of all.

Luther on 1 Timothy

This epistle St. Paul writes in order to provide a model to all bishops of what they are to teach and how they are to rule Christendom in the various stations of life, so that it may not be necessary for them to rule Christians according to their own human opinions.

In chapter 1 he charges that a bishop keep true faith and love and resist the false preachers of the law who, beside Christ and the Gospel, would also insist on the works of the law. In a brief summary, he comprehends the entire Christian doctrine concerning the purpose of the law and the nature of the Gospel. He offers himself as an example to comfort all sinners and those with troubled conscience.

In chapter 2 he charges that prayer be made for all stations of life. He also commands that women are not to preach or wear costly adornment, but are to be obedient to men. [For Luther's intent, see Eph 5:21–33 where it is clear that spouses honor their God-given responsibilities in marriage by looking out for each other's interests.]

In chapter 3 he describes the kind of persons that bishops, or priests, and their wives ought to be, and also the deacons and their wives. He praises those who desire to be bishops of this kind.

In chapter 4 he prophesies of false bishops and the spiritual estate which is opposed to that spoken of above, who will not be persons of that kind, but instead will forbid marriage and foods, and with their doctrines of men inculcate the very opposite of the things Paul has described.

In chapter 5 he gives orders as to how widows and young women should be looked after, and which widows are to be supported from the common funds; also how godly bishops or priests are to be held in honor, and blameworthy ones punished.

In chapter 6 he exhorts the bishops to hold fast to the pure Gospel and to promulgate it by their preaching and living. They are to avoid senseless and meddlesome controversies which are only raised for gaining worldly reputation and riches. (LW 35:388)

For more of Luther's insights on this Book, see *Lectures on 1 Timothy* (LW 28:215–384).

Calvin on 1 Timothy

This Epistle appears to me to have been written more for the sake of others than for the sake of Timothy, and that opinion will receive the assent of those who shall carefully consider the whole matter. I do not, indeed, deny that Paul intended also to teach and admonish him; but my view of the Epistle is, that it contains many things which it would have been superfluous to write, if he had had to deal with Timothy alone. He was a young man, not yet clothed with that authority which would have been sufficient for restraining the headstrong men that rose up against him. It is manifest, from the words used by Paul, that there were at that time some who were prodigiously inclined to ostentation, and for that reason would not willingly yield to any person, and who likewise burned with such ardent ambition, that they would never have ceased to disturb the Church, had not a greater than Timothy interposed. It is likewise manifest, that there were many things to be adjusted at Ephesus, and that needed the approbation of Paul, and the sanction of his name. Having therefore intended to give advice to Timothy on many subjects, he resolved at the same time to advise others under the name of Timothy. (*Commentaries*, p. xiii)

Gerhard on 1 Timothy

At one time the Donatist Petilianus considered Paul's disciple Timothy to be a layman, according to Augustine (Contra liter. Petiliani, bk. 3, c. 106). It is evident from the Epistles written to him, however, that he was a distinguished light of the Eastern Church, the bishop of Ephesus for forty years, as some think. The apostle had put this disciple of his in charge of the congregation at Ephesus that he [Paul] had planted. In this Epistle, then, [Paul] is instructing [Timothy] how he ought "to conduct himself in God's house" and how he must perform his duty correctly.

It consists of six chapters and is entirely of teaching, for he is instructing Timothy regarding ecclesiastical duties, persons, and virtues. (E 1.266)

Bengel on 1 Timothy

The epistles sent to Timothy, Titus, and Philemon, as being addressed to individuals, have some things which are rather sealed, than explicitly set forth, for example [1Tm 1:18]. If there were no epistle to Timothy extant, we should have particularly wished that there was one, in order that we might see what Paul would chiefly recommend to Timothy; now, since there are two [epistles to Timothy], we ought the more earnestly to turn them to use. (Bengel 239)

Wesley on 1 Timothy

The mother of Timothy was a Jewess, but his father was a Gentile. He was converted to Christianity very early; and while he was yet but a youth, was taken by St. Paul to assist him in the work of the Gospel, chiefly in watering the churches which he had planted.

He was therefore properly (as was Titus) an itinerant evangelist, a kind of secondary apostle, whose office was to regulate all things in the Churches to which he was sent; and to inspect and reform whatsoever was amiss either in the bishops, deacons, or people.

St. Paul had doubtless largely instructed him in private conversation for the due execution of so weighty an office. Yet to fix things more upon his mind, and to give him an opportunity of having recourse to them afterward, and of communicating them to others, as there might be occasion; as also to leave Divine directions in writing, for the use of the Church and its ministers in all ages; he sent him this excellent pastoral letter, which contains a great variety of important sentiments for their regulation.

Though St. Paul styles him his own son in the faith, yet he does not appear to have been converted by the apostle; but only to have been exceeding dear to him, who had established him therein; and whom he had diligently and faithfully served, like a son with his father in the Gospel, [Php 2:22]. (Wesley 537)

Challenges for Readers

Paul's Authorship. The word choice in 1 Timothy differs somewhat from that in Paul's earlier letters. As a result, critics have concluded that Paul did not write this Letter to Timothy. However, authors often adapt their writing style based on the recipient. Paul also typically worked through a scribe, which could affect the letter's style (cf. Rm 16:22). The Early Church unanimously received 1 Timothy as a letter from Paul.

Relation to Titus. Many features of 1 Timothy correspond with those of the Letter to Titus. Like administrators today, Paul likely adapted his letter for one pastor to meet the needs of another pastor. Luther wrote about other examples, "Just as the Epistle to the Galatians resembles and is modeled on the Epistle to the Romans, comprising in outline the same material that is more fully and richly developed in Romans; so this epistle resembles that to the Ephesians and comprises also in outline the same content" (LW 35:386).

Service in the Churches. Paul strongly distinguishes the roles of men and women in the family and in the life of the Church. His distinction is consistent with typical Jewish and Greek cultures in the first century. However, Paul does not appeal to culture as a basis for his instruction. Rather, he appeals to God's orderly creation (2:11–15) and specifically restricts some offices in the Church based on gender (3:2, 12). Some radical expressions of modern feminism have sought to either dismiss or reinterpret these passages.

Blessings for Readers

In 1 Timothy, Paul offers sound teachings for young and old, for men and women. As you read this letter, look for passages about your particular calling in order to learn more about your service and the service of others. Be encouraged to pray for those who serve in your congregation and nation.

God's Word and prayer hallow our good works offered in thanks to our "blessed and only Sovereign" (6:15). Although He has challenged us to serve well, He has also equipped us with sound teaching (6:3) so we may pursue righteousness, godliness, faith, love, steadfastness, and gentleness (6:11).

Outline

   I. The Power of the Pure Gospel (ch. 1)
   - A. Greeting (1:1–2)
   - B. The Task at Hand (1:3–11)
   - C. The Power of the Gospel (1:12–17)
   - D. Some Opponents of the Gospel (1:18–20)
   II. The Church's Organization (chs. 2–3)
   - A. Good Order in the Church (ch. 2)
     1. Good order in public worship (2:1–7)
     2. Good order in the Church's ministry (2:8–15)
   - B. Qualifications for Offices (ch. 3)
     1. The pastoral office (3:1–7)
     2. Deacons and deaconesses (3:8–13)

PART 1

THE POWER OF THE PURE GOSPEL (CH. 1)

Greeting (1:1–2)

ESV	KJV
1 ¹Paul, an apostle of Christ Jesus by command of God our Savior and of Christ Jesus our hope, ²To Timothy, my true child in the faith: Grace, mercy, and peace from God the Father and Christ Jesus our Lord.	*1* ¹Paul, an apostle of Jesus Christ by the commandment of God our Saviour, and Lord Jesus Christ, which is our hope; ²Unto Timothy, my own son in the faith: Grace, mercy, and peace, from God our Father and Jesus Christ our Lord.

Introduction to 1:1–2 Although Timothy had long been an assistant to Paul in his ministry, he was alone now in his pastorate in Ephesus. He will have to act there without Paul's presence. This letter gives Timothy authoritative instruction on how to faithfully carry out his pastoral charge for his own sake and that of his hearers (1Ti 4:16). Even though Paul references his apostleship in this letter, as in his others, here he directs both Timothy and his hearers back to the ultimate source of authority, Jesus Christ. The referencing of God and of Jesus Christ is not redundancy, but a confession of where all true ministry comes from, who it comes through, and through whom it is carried out.

1:1 *apostle.* Paul uses this term in the narrower sense of those whom the Lord Jesus Christ Himself personally called and sent with His full authority. The very meaning of the word ("sent one") excludes any idea that it is an office one takes on themselves and of their own authority. *Christ Jesus.* Paul speaks of Jesus first according to His office as Christ, or Messiah, and then according to His name: Jesus. While this is not the usual order, the word change serves to emphasize the authoritative nature of Paul's calling to the office of apostle, and indirectly, to Timothy's office as a pastor. This emphasis on authorization serves to provide the pastoral office with both authority to speak and the limitations of what can be spoken authoritatively. *command.* It is very likely that Timothy will share this letter with other pastors and congregations beyond the churches in Ephesus. Having had to defend his apostolic authority before with other congregations, Paul steps up his terminology here to stress his apostolic charge from God the Father and God the Son (Ac 26:15–18). *God our Savior.* Paul speaks of God as "Savior" to stress that the author of the letter was not himself but God, and that it was written for the purpose of God furthering His saving work. Paul isn't piling on the titles of God, he is simply stating the truth that, as the source of our salvation, God is our Savior. This designation would have been familiar to the Jewish readers in Ephesus. This is how the prophet Isaiah refers to God (Is 12:2; 45:15). Paul identifies God this way later in this letter and in Ti 1:3; 2:10; 3:4. *our hope.* As God is the source of our salvation, Jesus is that salvation in human flesh and thus, the hope of all those born of the flesh. Jesus is our hope, gives us hope, and fulfills our hope. While Paul has been called to the high office of an apostle, he attributes everything relating to God's saving work for us to Christ Jesus.

1:2 *Timothy.* He grew up in the town of Lystra which was set at the center of the tri-regional area of Pisidia, Pamphylia and Cilicia (modern Turkey). His father was Greek (Ac 16:1) and his mother Eunice and his grandmother Lois, who were devout Christians, likely first introduced him to the teachings of the Gospel (2 Tm 1:5). *true child.* Though this was a common expression in both Jewish and Roman writings, Paul harkens back to his first missionary journey where he first met Timothy. Paul speaks of Timothy as his child because the Holy Spirit had called Timothy and brought him to faith through Paul's faithful preaching of the Gospel. There is no mistaking the tender regard Paul has for this young pastor. Having experienced the trials and troubles that can accompany faithful ministry, Paul is concerned for him and the congregations he serves. Holding such a special status with him, Paul expects Timothy to follow the instructions as a faithful son would obey his father. In Jewish tradition, the son of a prophet would seek to be just like his father the prophet. *mercy.* When Paul writes to the churches, his greeting is "grace to you and peace"; writing to Timothy, he adds "mercy." Having mercy follow in the wake of grace, Paul emphasizes the tender quality of grace, especially toward the unconverted and hostile. Only by being a constant recipient of God's mercy is anyone able to faithfully carry out the ministry of the Gospel.

1:1–2 in Devotion and Prayer Whenever the Church is struggling, be it on a national, regional, or local level, there is always a temptation to reinvent it so that it might be saved from its struggles, and finally achieve success. To do this is to confess a belief that the Church is a human creation and that is it built, maintained, and grown by the words and works of humanity. In the Greco-Roman world of Paul and Timothy's day, every one of the pagan religions was created, built, and maintained by the people. Paul's opening confesses the Church to be a totally different creation, with a completely different means by which it is built, maintained, and grown. Everything it has—its servants (apostles, pastors, etc.), its means (the Word and Sacraments), and its works—are from God in Christ Jesus. The Church's message is from God alone, centering in Christ Jesus, and this message, faithfully proclaimed and administered, is the sole God-given means by which He continues to build, nurture, and grow His Church. • Preserve Your Word and preaching, The truth that makes us whole, The mirror of Your glory, The pow'r that saves the soul. Oh, may this living water, This dew of heav'nly grace, Sustain us while here living Until we see Your face. Amen (*LSB* 658:4).

The Task at Hand (1:3–11)

ESV	KJV
³As I urged you when I was going to Macedonia, remain at Ephesus so that you may charge certain persons not to teach any different doctrine, ⁴nor to devote themselves to myths and endless genealogies, which promote speculations rather than the stewardship from God that is by faith. ⁵The aim of our charge is love that issues from a pure heart and a good conscience and a sincere faith. ⁶Certain persons, by swerving from these, have wandered away into vain discussion, ⁷desiring to be teachers of the law, without understanding either what they are saying or the things about which they make confident assertions. ⁸Now we know that the law is good, if one uses it lawfully, ⁹understanding this, that the law is not laid down for the just but for the lawless and disobedient, for the ungodly and sinners, for the unholy and profane, for those who strike their fathers and mothers, for murderers, ¹⁰the sexually immoral, men who practice homosexuality, enslavers, liars, perjurers, and whatever else is contrary to sound doctrine, ¹¹in accordance with the Gospel of the glory of the blessed God with which I have been entrusted.	³As I besought thee to abide still at Ephesus, when I went into Macedonia, that thou mightest charge some that they teach no other doctrine, ⁴Neither give heed to fables and endless genealogies, which minister questions, rather than godly edifying which is in faith: so do. ⁵Now the end of the commandment is charity out of a pure heart, and of a good conscience, and of faith unfeigned: ⁶From which some having swerved have turned aside unto vain jangling; ⁷Desiring to be teachers of the law; understanding neither what they say, nor whereof they affirm. ⁸But we know that the law is good, if a man use it lawfully; ⁹Knowing this, that the law is not made for a righteous man, but for the lawless and disobedient, for the ungodly and for sinners, for unholy and profane, for murderers of fathers and murderers of mothers, for manslayers, ¹⁰For whoremongers, for them that defile themselves with mankind, for menstealers, for liars, for perjured persons, and if there be any other thing that is contrary to sound doctrine; ¹¹According to the glorious Gospel of the blessed God, which was committed to my trust.

1:3 *remain at Ephesus.* Timothy had come to Ephesus to meet and join Paul, who had just set out from Rome on his fourth missionary journey. Paul was heading to Macedonia as he promised in

Php 2:24. Seeing the situation, Timothy believed they both needed to stay and stifle the false teachers and, further, to teach the faith and spread the Gospel. In all his missionary journeys, Paul had stayed the longest at Ephesus. Led by the Holy Spirit and his familiarity of the situation, Paul has Timothy stay. Through the exercise of his pastoral office, Timothy is to stop those who were teaching false doctrine, devotion to myths, and other such things that obscure the Gospel and lead to speculation. The key to this was a clear and constant proclamation of both God's Law and His Gospel. There is nothing to suggest that Timothy did not want to stay and take the charge when Paul initially gave it to him. Now something has changed, and Timothy believes that he is able to move on. Whether it is to go and be with Paul, or to pursue some other missionary endeavor, we do not know. Paul learns of this and turns Timothy back to his initial calling given to him in Paul's charge to remain. False teachers and perverters of the Gospel persist, and Timothy must continue in his calling to stop them with biblical doctrine for the sake of the elect. *Ephesus*. Located on the west coast of modern Turkey where the Cayster River meets the Aegean Sea. It had what was considered to be one of the great wonders of the ancient world: the Temple of Artemis. A silversmith named Demetrius, who made miniature silver shrines of Artemis, gathered workmen in the same type of business, warning them that the ministry of Paul and the Christian Church was a direct threat to their wealth. They believed that the Gospel, if allowed to go unchallenged, would bring Artemis and her temple to nothing (Ac 19:23–27). *charge*. While the term seems to carry a stern tone, the basis and the aim of it is love (v. 5). What the Lord says has absolute authority (1Co 7:10). This authority is the basis of Paul's charge, and it is the basis of both Timothy's charge (1:3–4) and the charge he as pastor would give to the false teachers, the widows, and the rich. *different doctrine*. The false doctrine likely took many forms, with the mixture of Jewish tradition, early forms of Gnosticism, and other teachings, none of which conformed to the teaching of Christ or godliness (6:3). These teachers were trying to set forth their heresies in such a way so as to make them just as valid as sound Christian doctrine. Many today, as then, still argue for a mingling of teachings so as to provide for a supposedly better hybrid form of Christian doctrine that is more inclusive; yet in truth any such mergers only create something that is completely non-Christian. Whenever anything is added to Jesus Christ, He ceases to be Jesus Christ, God's Son, who was sent to save mankind. The same is true when anything is added to the Word of God; it ceases to be the Word of God and becomes, by its additions, the mere word of man that has no power beyond the man who added it. Knox wrote about this, saying: "Mark well, the Spirit of God calls all which is added to Christ's religion, the doctrine of the devil, and a deeper invention of the adversary Satan" (127).

1:4 *myths.* While we tend to think of the Greeks when it comes to mythology, Paul refers to myths that are Jewish in origin in Ti 1:14. In rebuking the Pharisees and scribes for teaching false doctrine, Jesus explains why their teachings were nothing but myths. **"You have a fine way of rejecting the commandment of God in order to establish your tradition . . .** thus making void the word of God by your tradition" (Mk 7:9; 13a; cf. Mk 7:5–13). These myths were a type of eclectic syncretism which married modified Mosaic Law with Greek philosophies and Gnosticism. Jesus identifies the motive for these myths in the days of Timothy and in our day, "in order to establish your tradition!" *endless genealogies.* This refers to more than simply someone's family tree. Many of the Jewish myths arose from the expansion and embellishment of the actual biblical genealogies. As most all teaching was oral in nature, there were no written accounts with which to check the credibility of these genealogies. A large part of the apocryphal book Philo is dedicated to establishing the genealogical link between the leading families of the time and their forefathers of the OT, especially Noah. During the intertestamental period, there was a great power vacuum, and these genealogies served as a basis for authority and gravitas on the part of leaders. The practice was so common that if one mentioned genealogies, they were understood as some kind of mythical history. As you had multiple teachers using the same set of genealogical characters, endless questions were created, as their embellished accounts clashed with one another. None of the questions could be answered and, even if they were, the answers did nothing toward furthering the work of the Gospel. The practice of genealogical embellishment proved useful to would-be teachers, because it had the appearance of establishing their authority and influence in a community. Such teaching and mythical spinning could do nothing but diminish, and even deny, the Gospel and its preachers and teachers. It took the eyes of the saints off Christ and the Gospel, and fixed them on the individuals and their pedigree. *stewardship from God.* Everything in the Church is to be directed toward distribution of God's two great words: the Word of the Law and the greater Word of the Gospel. The purpose for this faithful distribution is for the salvation of all: those in the Church and those yet to be converted. Christ Himself gave this stewardship to the Church in the Great Commission (Mt 28:19–20). These false teachers and their mythical embellishments take the eyes and the energies of the Church off the Great Commission. They attempt to have the Church take up matters and agendas not given them by Christ or the Gospel. Whenever people, even in the Church, take to themselves responsibilities and teachings not given to them by God, they will only get in the way of the work God has given them to do.

1:5 *our charge.* Their charge has a purpose totally other than themselves and their welfare. The fact that everything they were to do had *love* as its goal was entirely bound up in the eternal benefit and blessing of others. This is no mere romantic or emotion-based care and concern. The word for "love" in the Greek used here is "agape." It is a love that flows from God in Jesus Christ and aims all things toward the eternal welfare of those in need. Having given them this charge with the aim of love, God gives them the means of reaching their aim of love by giving them His Word, which is God's expression of love, and thus God's work of love. Their goal was the conversion of the lost and the building up of the saints. The only means to this is, as Paul says in Ephesians, "speaking the truth in love" (4:15) in Baptism, Absolution, the Lord's Supper, preaching, and teaching. Paul contrasts their selfless, love-for-neighbor mission and ministry with the self-seeking and self-aggrandizing ways of individuals whose motive is love of self. What follows in this letter is an exposition of this charge and its aim—love. *from a pure heart . . . sincere faith.* We know what it is to have a guilty conscience, as well as a want to ease our conscience by doing something good in the hope that we might "make up for our wrong." Paul is making it clear that everything he says and does has no such self-serving motive. Every pastor is to preach the Gospel from such a clean conscience, cleansed in the forgiveness of Christ to teach, preach, speak, and serve for the good and eternal welfare of the Church and the world. Such purity and sincerity of faith can come only through faith in Jesus Christ. Of some who would argue that Paul places greater emphasis on love than on faith, Calvin wrote: "They who are of that opinion reason in an excessively childish manner; for, if love is first mentioned, it does not therefore hold the first rank of honour, since Paul shews also that it springs from faith" (27).

1:6 *Certain persons.* Paul narrows the group of those Timothy is to stop to those who have departed from the three things Paul lists in v. 5, love (*agapē*), a pure heart, and a sincere faith. To be dedicated to, and do all things for the eternal welfare of others would require a denial of self they were unwilling to make. This insertion of self into the ministry taints the conscience that must justify and serves to justify or clear the conscience. To achieve this tainted and impure end, they have to trust in tainted and impure teachings. *vain discussion.* When the Gospel is modified for any reason, it ceases to be the Gospel, the pure gift of God and His complete and total means of saving the sinner. It may sound good, even godly, and its goal may be lofty and holy, but, having become the word of man, it becomes vain because its goal is not love; its means is not the love and grace of God and neither is it a faith in Christ alone. Such talkers become like some of the friends of Job with whom the Lord said: "My anger burns against you and against your two friends, for you have not spoken of Me what is right, as My servant Job has" (Jb 42:7).

1:7 *teachers of the law.* A nonofficial title of those who had been schooled in Mosaic Law as found in the first five books of the Old Testament. In an attempt to be seen as such, these former Jews and pupils of Jews (Ti 1:10, 14), were making bold assertions about all kinds of things. All of their assertions, those of their own imaginations and those made on their shallow knowledge of Mosaic Law, were without any understanding of what they were saying. Neither Paul nor Timothy were opposed to the Law, as long as it was used and taught according to the Law, but these would-be teachers were without any real knowledge of the Law, its fullness, nature, or purpose. They were certainly among those puffed up with conceit yet lacking any understanding (6:4). Paul warned the Colossian congregation of such people who were captive to a sensuous mind (Col 2:18).

1:8–10 This passage is the source of the "uses of the Law," which became so important to the Reformation theology of Law and Gospel. Chemnitz wrote:

> Luther in a very learned way sought the foundations of this doctrine in the Epistle to the Galatians, and divided the use of the Law

into one aspect which was civil and one which was theological. Likewise in Galatians 5 there is one use of the Law in justification and another for those who have been justified. From this Luther constructed the threefold division of the uses of the Law. (8:805)

1:8 *the law is good.* This statement is not one of mere opinion on the part of Paul. Paul is speaking of God's Law, which is good in and of itself because it is the divine will of God. While one's use of the Law cannot take away from its intrinsic goodness, one can use it in a way that is contrary to God's purpose in giving it. The Law of God is always in service of the Gospel, to lead people to a realization of their sinfulness and prepare them for the Good News in Christ. For Christ came not to get rid of the Law, but to fulfill the Law for us and for our total salvation (Mt 5:17–19). Timothy was going to have to correct those who were using the Law in service of their own heresies and agendas. As pastors, Timothy and Titus were not to argue about the Law (Ti 3:9) but speak it in all its truth and fullness that it might make their hearers ready for the Good News of the Gospel.

1:9–10 What follows are six couplets corresponding to the Ten Commandments (Ex 20:1–17) that labeled a person according to his or her own sin. The first word of each is followed by its consequence. These couplets progress from the general to the more specific types of lawless persons. While the Law shows us God's holy will for us and our lives, it cannot show us this without also showing us where we are not right with His will. In this way, the Law serves as a mirror with which we examine ourselves and our doings. Where we are not right with the will of God as expressed in the Law, there is sin, and there is lawlessness. It is here that Law serves its intended purpose of working contrition (sorrow or regret) and repentance (a turning away from the sin) to the mercy and grace of God offered us in the Gospel of Jesus Christ.

1:9 *law . . . for just.* It is important to note that Paul speaks of the singular "just" denoting the individual who is justified by grace alone through faith in Jesus Christ (Eph 2:8–9). When Paul speaks of the "lawless," he uses the plural. Paul is instructing Timothy, and all pastors, in the fine art of applying the Law and the Gospel. Those justified through faith in Christ already have the fullness of the Law laid on them, even unto death, through Jesus Christ, who fulfilled the Law in all its requirements. They have been given a relationship with God through faith in Jesus Christ. Having been justified by grace through faith, they do not live without the Law but according to the Law already fulfilled in Christ for the sake of their neighbor. Since the Law has been removed as the basis of their relationships to God and to their neighbor, it does not coerce the justified on to good works. Instead, it guides them in the God-given ways of loving God and neighbor. *law . . . for the lawless.* Apart from Christ, the only basis for a relationship with God and one's neighbor is the Law. The only means of insuring a right relationship is by everything being measured, weighed, and checked. Where it is lacking in any detail, the relationship is not right (it is unrighteous), thus the person has been, and is, lawless. For the relationship to be saved, something has to be done to make every detail of the relationship right again. Having lost much of the Law and a right understanding of it due to the fall into sin, the Law is laid upon the lawless so that they might know themselves and their relationships to God and their neighbor according to the will and judgment of God. God's Word, both Law and Gospel, names everything as God names it, so that we might know ourselves as our Creator, our Redeemer, and our Sanctifier knows us. The lawless do not know themselves as God knows them, and the Law serves to show this to them. This is why Paul names them (vv. 9–11) and names the judgment upon them for being lawless. Only in this way will they be ready to hear the Gospel as the blessed good news of a new relationship with God, according to Christ rather than the Law.

1:10 *enslavers.* Literally those who take free people captive for the purpose of selling them into slavery. The Lord handed down a death sentence upon anyone doing this (Ex 21:16; Dt 24:7). When thinking of this kind of enslavement, we need to be mindful that there were various kinds of slaves and thus various means of enslavement. The coarsest kind would be literally stealing people from their life and family and selling them into slavery. There was a more subtle form that was often used where a person would become enslaved through debt and threat. While this may have happened because the person had no money, it was also the practice of driving prices or interest up so that the individual would be unable to pay those debts or basic necessities. Enslavement was often seen by some as the only means to provide for the basic needs of their families (Ne 5:7–11; Ezk 22:29; Am 8:4–5). *sound doctrine.* To refute and correct these false teachers, Timothy's teaching (doctrine), like that of all pastors, has to be sound (healthy). Only this way can false teachers be corrected and refuted in a manner that is aimed at their conversion and the further spiritual growth of the Church. Healthy faith, hope, peace, and trust all require healthy teaching. How does a pastor work to ensure that his doctrine (teaching) is sound (healthy)? By limiting his teaching to God's Word, and his exposition of God's Word, to the full testimony of Scripture in accordance with the Gospel (v. 11). Paul, Timothy, Titus, and all pastors, as undershepherds of Christ, are servants of His Word, not their own. John admonishes believers to "test" every spirit—that is, every word of teaching put forth as God's Word—because false prophets have gone out (1Jn 4:1). The only right way to test any teaching is to put it against the Word of God to see if it is of God. Timothy and every pastor preaches and teaches for the sake of sharing and strengthening the faith of their hearers. As servants of the Word, they are to take the lead in testing their teaching to ensure that what they teach and preach as God's Word in service of the Gospel is God's Word and not their own word or the word of another person.

1:11 *Gospel.* While the term means "good news," it is used here to refer to the totality of all that God, by His grace, has done through His Son, Jesus Christ, as the sole means of salvation for all from the condemnation of the Law. This was done as a free gift to all who would believe in Christ (Eph 2:1–10). Thus when it comes to the salvation of everyone, everything must constantly be only about what God has done, is doing, and will do for us in Jesus Christ. While the Gospel is the larger-than-life work of God's grace in Jesus Christ, it belongs to the yet-larger *glory* that is of the blessed God. What this means is that the awesomeness of the Gospel, the blessed work of God in Jesus Christ for our salvation, is but one aspect of the glory that belongs to God. *blessed God.* To grasp the wonder of this title, we begin with the name "God," which identifies Him as the source of all that is good, gracious, and right. In describing Himself as blessed, the Lord is revealing through St. Paul that freely out of Himself, He has been, is now, and ever shall be the Giver of these things to all who lack, that we might share in His goodness, grace, and righteousness. When the Lord blesses, He gives to us freely, out of Himself in Jesus Christ, what we lack to be good, gracious, and right. All this He gives and does to us through the sound (healthy) doctrine (teaching) of the Gospel. *entrusted.* While it may sound like Paul is pulling rank here, that is not what he is saying. Having been called and charged by God as His apostle, Paul seeks to be faithful to his charge, and he seeks that same faithfulness on the part of Timothy and all pastors according to their calling and office as servants of God's Word. Paul does this by humbly acknowledging that this calling and charge were not of himself but from God in service of the Gospel. All sound (healthy) doctrine (teaching) depends on faithfulness of the pastor in the exercise of the office, according to his divine call. Only in this way will believers have a sound (healthy) faith.

1:3–11 in Devotion and Prayer The Ephesian congregations were struggling with false teachers, who were all peddling their own man-centered teachings, promoting the welfare of the teacher to the detriment of the believers. While much they were saying sounded godly, it was wholly unhealthy to saving faith and the salvation of the hearers because it did not conform to the Word of God in service of the Gospel. Timothy, like every pastor, is charged with stopping such teachers by proclaiming the full Word of God in Jesus Christ for the salvation of all who believe, lest the hearers and their hearts be turned away from the saving Gospel. Every pastor is charged with preaching and teaching the whole Word of God in Jesus Christ for the sake of his hearers inside and outside the Church. To want or expect a pastor to be less than faithful to the whole Word of God is to want or expect him to be the very kind of false teacher that Paul charged Timothy to stop and silence. Jesus came not just to teach and preach the whole Word of God, but, being the Word of God in flesh, He came also to suffer the whole Word of God against us, so that we might be made just and blessed with new life in Christ according to His Word. • Blessed Lord, You are and have the words of eternal life. As You call men into the pastoral office to proclaim Your whole Word to the Church, grant that all their preaching and teaching may be sound in the Gospel of our Lord Jesus Christ, so that we might have a sound and healthy faith in Him as our only Lord and Savior. Amen.

The Power of the Gospel (1:12–17)

ESV	KJV
[12]I thank him who has given me strength, Christ Jesus our Lord, because he judged me faithful, appointing me to his service, [13]though formerly I was a blasphemer, persecutor, and insolent opponent. But I received mercy because I had acted ignorantly in unbelief, [14]and the grace of our Lord overflowed for me with the faith and love that are in Christ Jesus. [15]The saying is trustworthy and deserving of full acceptance, that Christ Jesus came into the world to save sinners, of whom I am the foremost. [16]But I received mercy for this reason, that in me, as the foremost, Jesus Christ might display his perfect patience as an example to those who were to believe in him for eternal life. [17]To the King of ages, immortal, invisible, the only God, be honor and glory forever and ever. Amen.	[12]And I thank Christ Jesus our Lord, who hath enabled me, for that he counted me faithful, putting me into the ministry; [13]Who was before a blasphemer, and a persecutor, and injurious: but I obtained mercy, because I did it ignorantly in unbelief. [14]And the grace of our Lord was exceeding abundant with faith and love which is in Christ Jesus. [15]This is a faithful saying, and worthy of all acceptation, that Christ Jesus came into the world to save sinners; of whom I am chief. [16]Howbeit for this cause I obtained mercy, that in me first Jesus Christ might shew forth all longsuffering, for a pattern to them which should hereafter believe on him to life everlasting. [17]Now unto the King eternal, immortal, invisible, the only wise God, be honour and glory for ever and ever. Amen.

1:12–17 While it seems that Paul is patting himself on the back, he is doing something much more significant. By naming himself for what he was in unbelief, prior to receiving mercy and grace in Jesus Christ, Paul radically differentiates himself from all the would-be teachers in the entire Ephesian Church. With regard to one's standing before God, Paul makes the case that he is the worst of sinners. In contrast, the would-be teachers made the case that they were the best of God's people. When identifying the basis of God's calling and charge to him as an apostle, Paul points to the same grace of God that saved him. The would-be teachers point to themselves, their experience, their ancestry, and their masterful eloquence. This radical difference points directly at the radically different nature of the God of the Gospel, against the god of the false would-be teachers. The living God—Father, Son, and Holy Spirit—doesn't save or call the qualified, He alone qualifies the lost in Christ. He does this so that they might be saved, thus giving them qualities for the service of the Gospel. All this God does out of the pure love and grace of our Lord Jesus Christ.

1:12 *judged me faithful.* Paul knows full well that he was not sufficient of himself for the faithful discharge of his calling as an apostle of the Lord. "Not that we are sufficient in ourselves to claim anything as coming from us, but our sufficiency is from God, who has made us sufficient to be ministers of a new covenant" (2Co 3:5–6). Since the Lord Jesus made Paul a new creation in Himself, He considered Paul to be faithful because of the faithfulness He gave him and would work through him. While there are many qualities that make for a good pastor, faithfulness to the whole Word of God is absolutely critical if the people those pastors serve are to know God and His salvation in Jesus Christ. *service.* Having called Paul to the office of apostle, the Lord Jesus was putting Paul in His own place, to speak what Jesus has given him to speak through the Holy Spirit. To be in the Lord's service is to be about the Lord's Word and work.

1:13 *formerly I was . . . opponent.* Paul leaves nothing out of his life's history prior to his conversion. Far more than merely being opposed to it, he was actively seeking to eradicate the message of the Gospel and the Church that is built upon it (Ac 7:58–8:3). Paul approved of the stoning of Stephen, the first martyr (Ac 8:1). Christ reveals the significance of this when He charges Paul with persecuting Him (Ac 9:4). In some ways, prior to his conversion, Paul was much like the would-be teachers in Ephesus who were total opponents of Jesus Christ and His Gospel. *received mercy . . . ignorantly.* Though Paul was such an evil man, note that the Lord first seeks him in mercy. The unique nature of mercy is that it is always given to one who lacks, and has no means to obtain that which one lacks, so that the person might not be lacking. Apart from Christ, Paul, like all unbelievers, is spiritually dead in the trespasses and sin in which merely earthly lives are lived. Everything he, or any unbeliever, does in terms of God is ungodly, or godless. This is so because, being spiritually dead, they lack the true God and are thus ignorant of Him. Being separated from Christ, spiritually dead, and ignorant, makes everything Paul did, and everything every unbeliever does, in opposition to the Gospel of Jesus Christ. By himself, Paul lacked Christ, and through Him the knowledge of God. Yet the Lord mercifully gives to Paul all that he lacks in righteousness, holiness, and understanding, thus converting him and causing him to become a new creation. Paul lived in this mercy every day of his life. This spiritual deadness and ignorance is widely disputed because the sinful mind is bound to what it sees and judges as godly, rather than to what God says and reveals as godly in Jesus Christ. It is a truth that is humbling because it puts to death any ideas we have of God, ourselves, and our righteousness before Him. Yet it is here alone that Christ stands ready to save and make known the true God: Father, Son, and Holy Spirit, so that one is made wise unto salvation through faith in Jesus Christ (2Tm 3:15).

1:14 When it comes to the salvation of the lost, God's mercy and grace might be likened to the two sides of the same coin. They are inseparable. Where God's mercy deals with us according to what is lacking, His *grace* undeservedly and freely does for us all we cannot do to be holy and right before Him. In light of the reality of Paul's past, it is undeniably clear that the motive and reason for God doing this to save him lay completely in God and His grace. *overflowed.* In his attempt to describe himself prior to his conversion, Paul lists his "big" sins. As one made alive in Christ, he has become more aware of the totality of his sinfulness. Every believer has some measure of his or her sinfulness, the seeming limitlessness of it in shape, size, quality, and quantity. We have this measure by revelation of the Word, and we know it in some degree because we have experienced it. In the face of his mountain range of sins that went beyond memory and sight, the grace of God is constantly given in an amazingly abundant manner to Paul and to every believer. This grace brings low every mountain of sin and goes beyond every range of sin to remove sin as far as the east is from the west (Ps 103:12). This is often doubted by many because the memory and awareness of actual sin lies heavy on the heart and mind. What is forgotten is that the grace of God is not a one-time gift but is an ongoing work of God alone in which we live every day through faith in Jesus Christ.

1:15 *The saying.* This points to the objective and therefore universal truth of the Gospel as stated in this verse, "Jesus Christ came into the world to save sinners." Because this is an objective truth, expressly stated as the salvation of all sinners of every race and nation,

it is worthy of *full acceptance*. Full acceptance refers to faith applying this truth to and for one's own life. *came into the world*. These
words reference all that Christ did from the moment He took human
flesh into God at His conception, through to His ascension in the
flesh to the right hand of the Father. Everything that Christ did as the
Son of God and the Son of Man, and now does ascended to the right
hand of the Father, was and still is given for the saving of sinners.
Here is the uniqueness of the Gospel in contrast to all other religions
of mankind. All other religions will tell you how they think you can
get to God, get in touch with God, or become God; only the Gospel
of Jesus Christ gives you God in His Son, who made Himself nothing
to meet sinners, who by our sin have made ourselves nothing. He
meets us, not to condemn us, nor to tell us what we need to do to
be saved, nor what we need to do to stay saved. He meets us in His
Word and Sacraments to always save us each and every day (cf. Php
2:5–8). *save sinners*. This states the purpose for Jesus Christ coming
into the world. What He comes to do, He does to save those who
are lost in sin. This an objective act because Christ does it universally
for all because all are lost in sin. Notice that there is no grading or
classification of sinners, because all have sinned and fallen short of
the glory of God (Rm 3:23). As stated here, every sinner is saved,
and remains saved, by His work alone, not ours. We are constantly
passive recipients of His saving work. When commenting on Christ's
saving "great and notable sinners," Bengel wrote:

> He saves also those whose sins have been not so aggravated; but
> it is much more remarkable that He saves so great sinners. I can
> scarcely happen, but that they who themselves have tasted the
> grace of God, should taste its universality, and, in like manner,
> from it entertain favour towards all men. (4:247)

I am the foremost. These words are true in and of themselves,
for Paul was a murderous persecutor of the Church. They state the
subjective truth that applies to Paul alone, according to his understanding of himself. Putting himself forth as the worst of sinners, and
backing it up with some measure of truth, would create only the
question in the hearers as to how he could possibly have become an
apostle and leader among the saints—a question that he will answer.

1:16 *I received mercy for this reason*. Paul is a living example of
the greatness of the love and mercy of God for all who are in Jesus
Christ. He is a living message that no one is beyond the power of

God's mercy. He can change sinners of all kinds, remaking them anew as saints in the one Lord Jesus Christ. Having described his radical sinful opposition to Christ and the Church (vv. 12–13a), Paul is confronted by something radically unexpected. Rather than receiving the justice he deserves for his sin and evil, Christ blesses Paul with what he does not and could never deserve: mercy. Not just any mercy, but radical mercy that works a radically complete change in Paul. He who was the worst sinner (v. 15) is changed into a holy saint, all by the power of God's mercy and grace in Jesus Christ. *display His perfect patience.* Paul is inspired to describe the patience God displayed in his life as perfect. He does this not so much to express the quality of God's patience but to express that God's patience achieved God's goal with Paul—his conversion. God's patience is perfect in itself because it is His; its perfection is displayed in us as we are converted. Thanks be to God that He does not give us what we deserve in the very minute we have earned it by sinning. Instead, God patiently allows time for each of us to come to the knowledge of our sin for the hearing of the Gospel, so that all might repent and believe in Jesus Christ (2Pt 3:9, 15). *example.* The radical change that Jesus Christ worked in Paul's life was living testimony as to how and what God will do for all who believe in the Lord Jesus Christ.

1:17 *King of ages.* While mankind has many ways of referring to time—eras, epochs, eons, periods, centuries, and the like—Paul rejoices that the Lord Jesus rules in and through all of these, from the moment time began through to its end. Even that age beyond time, known as eternity, shall be blessed under His kingship. This is a great comfort and encouragement to believers caught up in the trials and tribulations of each era and epoch. *immortal.* This is God's attribute of being imperishable. He is not subject to decay, corruption, or death. This also identifies God alone as the source of immortality. The Lord says "the dead will be raised immortal . . . and the mortal body must put on immortality" (1Co 15:52, 53), because they are no longer subject to sin and its decaying, corruptive, and deadly power. We shall not be subject to decay, corruption, or death. *invisible.* While Jesus is God, and in His humanity we see the image of God (Col 1:15), God is unseen by humanity in this world, as John states in Jn 1:18. Being Spirit (Jn 4:24), He is seen by faith alone (Heb 11:27). *only God.* Such declarations about God are based upon His nature, His being, and the attributes that reveal Him as the source of all that is good, gracious, and right. The psalmist concludes, "You alone are God" because He does great and wondrous things (Ps 86:10). Jesus states that it is eternal life to know God as the only true God, and Jesus Christ whom He has sent (Jn 17:3). It is God the Father and God the Son from whom proceeds the Holy Spirit (Jn 14:26; 15:26).

Some Opponents of the Gospel (1:18–20)

ESV	KJV
¹⁸ This charge I entrust to you, Timothy, my child, in accordance with the prophecies previously made about you, that by them you may wage the good warfare, ¹⁹ holding faith and a good conscience. By rejecting this, some have made shipwreck of their faith, ²⁰ among whom are Hymenaeus and Alexander, whom I have handed over to Satan that they may learn not to blaspheme.	¹⁸ This charge I commit unto thee, son Timothy, according to the prophecies which went before on thee, that thou by them mightest war a good warfare; ¹⁹ Holding faith, and a good conscience; which some having put away concerning faith have made shipwreck: ²⁰ Of whom is Hymenaeus and Alexander; whom I have delivered unto Satan, that they may learn not to blaspheme.

1:18 *charge.* What is given in v. 3, defined in v. 5, and expounded upon through v. 17. The charge will involve the rest of this verse and the first part of v. 19. *my child.* Paul is about to describe the challenges that will confront Timothy as a pastor who is faithful to the charge given him. He will liken these challenges to waging a war. Paul here returns to his close personal relationship to Timothy by again naming him his child. See exposition of v. 2. *prophecies.* This refers to the work of the Holy Spirit through Paul by which the Spirit set apart or identified Timothy as the one to be appointed to previous pastorates, and now to the pastorate at Ephesus. Each of these was a divine call mediated by Holy Spirit through Paul. Now at Ephesus, Paul, by the work of the Holy Spirit, administers to Timothy the divine call (prophecy) that he is to serve there as pastor. The same kind of prophecy happened in Antioch when the Holy Spirit set apart Barnabas and Saul for work the Lord had called them to do (Ac 13:1–3). Chrysostom explained: "What is 'by prophecy'? By the Holy

Spirit. For prophecy is not only the telling of things future, but also of the present. . . . To elevate him, and prepare him to be sober and watchful, he reminds him by whom he was chosen and ordained, as if he had said, 'God has chosen you'" (*NPNF1* 13:423). *by them.* Here, Paul speaks to the doubts that would arise in Timothy's heart about whether he was the right one to carry out the pastoral charge given him. These prophecies—this work of the Holy Spirit that called Timothy to the pastoral office—would answer such doubts and set Timothy free to focus on fighting the good fight of the faith, according to the divine charge, or call, given him. *good warfare.* Timothy's charge to stop false teachers, and those teaching, preaching, and practicing what is contrary to the Word of God, would involve much conflict. As pastor, Timothy would have to enter this conflict for the sake of his hearers, whether it be false teachers or those listening to them. The goal of the conflict is not defeat but conversion and salvation for all. How well Timothy, or any pastor, fares in such conflicts is not determined by the outcome but by the means he uses. There are two marks of such warfare that make the waging of it good. The first mark is that every aspect of it is fought for the sake of those it is waged against. The second mark, perhaps the most critical, is that the means of such warfare are limited to the means God has given to wage it: His Word and Sacraments. Such warfare and such means as God provides will include suffering. Where the war is waged without these, it is a personal fight waged in God's name, apart from His purpose.

1:19 *holding faith and a good conscience.* When waging this spiritual warfare seems to be unending, there is always a temptation to turn to other means than those that God has given for faith and salvation: His Word and Sacraments. As a pastor, Timothy would need to correct, rebuke, and stop false teachers by these God-given means. To do this would require that he have full faith in their ability to do God's will and work, when and where the Lord sees fit. To lose faith in God's means of salvation causes harm to one's own faith in God for personal salvation. When a person lets go of God's means of salvation in favor of any other means to wage spiritual warfare, that person sins against the conscience that God has made alive through His Word. Keeping faith in God's means (His Word and Sacraments), and using them to wage all spiritual warfare, provides for a good conscience. It is affirmed and strengthened through the use of God's means. *this*. God's means of waging the spiritual warfare, His Word and Sacraments. *a shipwreck of their faith*. Having rejected God's given means, a person becomes like a ship that has no rudder. Both they and their faith are "tossed to and fro by the waves and carried about by every wind of doctrine, by human cunning, by craftiness in deceitful schemes" (Eph 4:14). Having rejected God's Word and Sacraments, such people can only crash upon sin's shores and the rocks of sinful reality.

1:20 *handed over to Satan*. While thought of in terms of judgment, this is an exercise of spiritual discipline, with the goal of mercy. Hymenaeus and Alexander were examples of those who, while professing a faith in Christ, openly and unrepentantly taught and practiced what was contrary to faith in Jesus Christ. Their publicly unrepentant false teachings and practices were in open conflict and rejection of what they verbally confessed about Christ. This being the case, Timothy, on behalf of the Church, is to excommunicate these men. Excommunication does not condemn anyone, but it does declare to them that because of their persistent unrepentant teachings and practices, the Church can no longer assure them of their salvation. Such men have, by their own unrepentance, handed themselves over to Satan. Timothy is to confirm this to them in the hope that they will be awakened to the severity of their sin, and repent and thus be saved. Cf. 1Co 5:3–5, 9–13. *learn not to blaspheme*. Everything these two men, and all the other false teachers, were doing is defined as blasphemy. If these men were to be saved, they would have to learn the contents of the true faith, according to the Word of God alone, and put their full and undivided faith in it alone. The goal of their excommunication is not their damnation but repentance and true faith, that they might be saved and reclaimed for the kingdom of God. While this seems extreme, how much more extreme shall it be for that sinner who is left to eternal damnation in the name of compassion. This is perhaps the time when the warfare is the worst because the fight, for the pastor, is often within himself, and the conflict between ease for himself by letting the sin pass, and loving the sinner enough to suffer the long journey with them until they might come to repentance and faith (cf. 2Co 2:5–11).

1:12–20 in Devotion and Prayer Paul had given Timothy a challenging charge, as the pastor of Ephesus, to deal with and stop false teachers. Lest Timothy, or any pastor, think that faithful teaching and preaching of God's Word is useless in dealing with such false teachers, Paul holds himself out as example to the contrary. As Timothy accepted Paul, who was the worst sinner, Timothy would have to accept and trust in the fact that Jesus Christ came into the world to save sinners—sinners as bad as Paul. Paul was just such a false teacher and persecutor of the Church, yet by the mercies of God, he heard the Word of Christ and was converted from unbelief to faith, from death to life, from falsity to truth, from a persecutor of Christ to a preacher of Christ. It is easy to give up on false teachers and those opposed to Christ and all things religious. How often do we abandon the very mercy by which we have been saved, in order to save ourselves from the hard work of mercy? Is it easier to simply judge them to be beyond the power of God's mercy and grace, and deny them His Word through us? Paul doesn't want Timothy to adopt such an attitude lest he shipwreck his faith and the faith of those he is called to serve. Thanks be to God that having come to save sinners—all sinners—He who gave His Son on the cross still gives Jesus to us through His chosen means of the Holy Word and the Sacraments. Thanks be to God that His forgiveness and mercies are new to us each morning as we carry out the vocations and callings He has given through faith in Christ alone. • Blessed Lord, bless those You have called into the office of pastor with faithfulness to You and Your given means to shepherd the flock. Let not bias or doubt overcome them in sharing Your Word of truth, so that the erring might be turned to faith in Christ and the faithful be built up in one true faith unto eternal life. This we pray in faith through Jesus Christ, our Lord. Amen.

PART 2

THE CHURCH'S ORGANIZATION (CHS. 2–3)

Good Order in the Church (ch. 2)

Good order in public worship (2:1–7)

ESV	KJV
2 ¹First of all, then, I urge that supplications, prayers, intercessions, and thanksgivings be made for all people, ²for kings and all who are in high positions, that we may lead a peaceful and quiet life, godly and dignified in every way. ³This is good, and it is pleasing in the sight of God our Savior, ⁴who desires all people to be saved and to come to the knowledge of the truth. ⁵For there is one God, and there is one mediator between God and men, the man Christ Jesus, ⁶who gave himself as a ransom for all, which is the testimony given at the proper time. ⁷For this I was appointed a preacher and an apostle (I am telling the truth, I am not lying), a teacher of the Gentiles in faith and truth.	**2** ¹I exhort therefore, that, first of all, supplications, prayers, intercessions, and giving of thanks, be made for all men; ²For kings, and for all that are in authority; that we may lead a quiet and peaceable life in all godliness and honesty. ³For this is good and acceptable in the sight of God our Saviour; ⁴Who will have all men to be saved, and to come unto the knowledge of the truth. ⁵For there is one God, and one mediator between God and men, the man Christ Jesus; ⁶Who gave himself a ransom for all, to be testified in due time. ⁷Whereunto I am ordained a preacher, and an apostle, (I speak the truth in Christ, and lie not;) a teacher of the Gentiles in faith and verity.

Introduction to Ch. 2 Paul outlines the critical path for Timothy to follow if he is going to purge the churches of Ephesus of the corrupting and destructive false teachings ravaging the flock, and bring godly order to things. Paul reminded the Corinthians, "God is not a God of confusion but of peace" (1Co 14:33). So Paul begins by instructing Timothy and the Church on the primary means to bringing about both order and peace through an order of corporate worship that centers everything on Jesus Christ and the giving of Him to those gathered. As the Divine Service brings the Lord to those He has gathered, and gives to all equally of His gifts and grace, there is unity in the "one Lord, one faith, one baptism, one God and Father of all, who is over all and through all and in all" (Eph 4:5–6).

2:1 *First.* Whenever you hear someone use the word "first," you know there is a second and maybe a third to follow. Why prayer first? Because prayer is the simplest expression of faith. Where the heart is unwilling to bow in faith, to call upon the Lord according to all that He is and does through creation, Christ, and the Church (by the Holy Spirit), faith is fixed on something else, something less than the true God. Just as God so loved the whole world that He gave His only begotten Son, so the Church, the Body of Christ, loves the whole world by first giving it all back to God in corporate worship. *supplications, prayers, intercessions, and thanksgivings.* Paul's use of multiple terms in reference to prayer, drives home the force and confidence with which God is to be called upon. The four terms used to identify the content of our prayer symbolically point to bringing the full sweep of earthly life before the Lord. These are arranged in a progressive confidence in prayer that begins with seeking grace in desperate need (supplication), then moves on to larger and broader needs (prayer), and then being even more confident, moves on to intercede for the sake of others (intercessions), all for which gratitude and praise is offered (thanksgiving). *supplications.* A request that arises from a deep and humbling awareness of one's need for that which only God Himself is able to supply. Only God can meet this need. As a rule, this term is used in reference to those requests for God's works dealing with faith and salvation. *prayers.* While this is a common term, it refers to both requests and conversation with the Lord that are spoken in deep reverence, out of a recognition that the Lord is God, before whom all things must bow. *intercessions.* These are requests of God spoken out of a deep confidence and trust in the Lord to do that which He believes is most beneficial. The royal priesthood (1Pt 2:9) makes these requests on behalf of others. *thanksgivings.* Full acknowledgment of all God's blessings, physical and spiritual. The fact that this is plural testifies to the reverent reflection on all the unmerited gifts of God for the sake of the saints. To ponder on that which is given and the Giver Himself, is to look upon His promises fulfilled, by which faith is affirmed. *all people.* Prayer is a culture-crossing endeavor. As our Lord's love knows no bounds, neither ought the Church's prayers. As no nationality, no race, or no gender limits the bounds of His love and saving grace, neither can any of these serve to limit the hearing of our prayers. Through Christ, we have been united with the God who would have all men to be saved and come to the knowledge of the truth. Our prayers gladly embrace the wide sweep of God's desire, grace, and goal for salvation for every person (2:4). Cf. Mt 5:43–47.

2:2 *kings.* The term in the plural refers to all those who are in supreme positions of ruling authority. This embraces all kinds of kings, good and evil. If good, it is by the mercies of God, and they are in constant need of God's blessing to remain true. If bad or evil, they are in open rebellion and in constant need of repentance. Rebellious kings will likely deny the Church a peaceful and quiet life. The reality of this is that every king rules at the will of God. To refuse to pray for an evil ruler is to refuse to honor the one whom God has appointed to that office (Rm 13:1–7). *high positions.* These are persons holding offices of authority in service to the king, or ruler, for the sake of the monarch's governance. *peaceful and quiet life.* While the goal of these prayers might seem self-serving, these prayers are raised for the sake of society and the world as a whole. Conditions that provide for a peaceful and quiet life would be a blessing to all, but for the Church it would provide greater opportunities to share the Gospel. Though evil in many ways, Rome at the time of Christ and the Early Church had brought law and order to much of the Mediterranean world. Rome provided for a common language, and relative ease of travel and communication, thus allowing the Gospel to spread quickly. Paul states that governing authorities are God's servants, whom He has instituted for our good (Rm 13:4), and such is the goal of the Church's prayers. *godly.* Bengel included a long excursus on the meaning of the word "godly" or "pious," which the apostle often used: "Piety, in name at least never hitherto lightly esteemed, has at length been converted into a term of reproach, 'Pietist,' by an anonymous person of the worst character, whose death, as we are informed, was shocking" (554–55). It is not clear who the "anonymous person" was. Bengel perhaps referred to the strife that erupted in Halle, Germany, surrounding the rise of German Pietism, a holiness movement that had some helpful emphases but also theological problems. Bengel regretted that a proper understanding of biblical piety was lost or muted in the debate.

2:4 *who desires all people to be saved.* The few words simply express the reason that the Church is to be offering up all forms of prayer for all people. Since God is concerned with their salvation, we should be also. Paul affirms to the Church the desire of God, as expressed through the prophet Ezekiel: "As I live, declares the Lord God, I have no pleasure in the death of the wicked, but that the wicked turn from His way and live" (Ezk 33:11). Peter further expounds on this truth, affirming that the Lord does not wish that any should perish, but that all should come to repentance (2Pt 3:9). In each of these, there is no room for the notion that any person is exempt from God's desire that everyone be saved. Each of these echoes what God loved in Jn 3:16—"the world"—for which He gave His only begotten Son. No one is left out of God's desire in Jesus Christ. Hearing this glorious truth, and seeing the world, with so many who are unsaved, have you ever wondered why? Why are so many not saved; better yet, why do so many either reject Christ or wander away from Him? There are no easy answers to these questions. What God's Word and the life of His Son, Jesus Christ, tells us is that He would have all people to be saved, and that He has done everything necessary for all to be saved.

The best information on "why?" comes from God's Word as it tells us about ourselves. Being conceived in sin and born in iniquity (Ps 51:5), our hearts and minds are alienated from God (Col 1:21), and set on anything other than God and His Word. We are so alienated and set on earthly things that we cannot help but be hostile to God and His Word (Rm 8:7). Through His Word, God gives us the Holy Spirit, who makes us spiritually alive through His gift of faith so that we might be saved (2Th 2:13). So why do so many turn away and refuse this gift? Again, God's Word reminds us that within each believer there is a war going on with the desires of the flesh (the sinful nature). The desires and work of the Spirit are waging war against our flesh (Gal 5:17). Stephen told the high priest and the Israelites who had rejected Jesus that the reason they and others are not saved is that they "always resist the Holy Spirit" (Ac 7:51). If there is a cause as to why so many go unsaved, we cannot speculate on reasons beyond the bounds of what God reveals to us. To do so would be to take the seat of God and bind people's hearts to something God never said. Thanks be to God that no matter what, we can know God wants us to be saved, and that in Jesus Christ, everything has been done for us so that we might be saved.

2:5–6 Melanchthon wrote: "The Scriptures do not teach that we are to call on the saints or to ask the saints for help. Scripture sets before us the one Christ as the Mediator, Atoning Sacrifice, High Priest, and Intercessor [1 Timothy 2:5–6]. He is to be prayed to. He has promised that He will hear our prayer [John 14:13]" (AC XXI 2–3).

2:5 *one God.* Literally, "one (is) God" of all mankind. He is not the God of one group, nation, or race but the only God of all mankind. It is He who has revealed Himself to all through Jesus Christ and wants the Church to pray for all mankind. It is His desire to save through faith in the one mediator He has chosen and sent: Jesus Christ (cf. Rm 3:29–30). *one mediator.* Literally, "one (is) mediator" between God and all mankind, and that is Jesus Christ, the Son of God and the Son of Man. In the incarnation, "God our Savior" (v. 3) unites the one God and one mediator in one person. Calvin wrote:

> [The man Christ] gently invites us, and takes us, as it were, by the hand, in order that the Father, who had been the object of terror and alarm, may be reconciled by him and rendered friendly to us. This is the only key to open for us the gate of the heavenly kingdom, that we may appear in the presence of God with confidence. (58)

the man. While this seems obvious, it is essential to understand the great and blessed gift of His Son to be our substitute, so that He might take our place under the Law, under sin and its sentence of eternal wrath and death, that He might save us. Jesus is both "true God, begotten of the Father from eternity, and also true man, born of the Virgin Mary" (SC, Second Article). As a true man, His wondrous and gracious work of mediation was carried out on behalf of all humanity.

2:6 *ransom.* (Gk *antilytron*) means to pay a ransom or redeem something. As the mediator, Christ Jesus comes in our human flesh to be the promised Seed who would come and crush the serpent's head (Gn 3:15; Rm 16:20; Heb 2:14). Where do we find Jesus actually giving Himself as the ransom? As the first man and woman sold themselves to sin and Satan in a garden, so Jesus gives Himself as the promised ransom in the Garden of Gethsemane when He gave Himself up to His enemies so that He might die as the price of our freedom from our slavery to sin, death, and Satan. *for all.* These two words beautifully state the substitutionary role of Christ Jesus as our Savior for all mankind. (This is known as objective justification.) Christ offered Himself as a ransom for us all instead of all of us being left to pay our own debt of sin. We could never have paid our own ransom. Notice that Christ Jesus is not just a substitute for 90 percent, nor 99.9 percent but for all. Only by giving His life as a ransom for all could Jesus fulfill the desire of His Father that all be saved (v. 4). Cf. Mt 20:28. *testimony given at the proper time.* God's giving Christ His Son as the ransom on the cross for the salvation of the world and the preaching of this truth, are simply two phases or aspects of God's one saving work. Those who hear this testimony today receive the same saving work of God as those who heard it from Paul, or even from Jesus. Jesus is His Word, His testimony. He gives Himself and His saving work every time it is proclaimed. The proper time is when sinners are in need of this testimony of God's love and grace freely given in Jesus Christ. Every time a pastor teaches or preaches this testimony of Jesus Christ, you know it is a proper time for you to hear this glorious Good News. Every time you read the Word, you read the Good News. As Jesus Christ is and shall be the same until the end of time (Heb 13:8), His Word continues to accomplish God's saving work (Is 55:11).

2:7 *appointed a preacher and an apostle.* Having exhorted prayers for all, Paul references his mission and authority given to him by Christ (Ac 9:4–17), not as a power play but to show that such prayers are an essential part of the Church fulfilling the desire of God that all people be saved through the preached Word. Since faith comes from hearing, and hearing through the Word of Christ (Rm 10:17), Paul was called and appointed by God to teach and preach only God's Word. How often we would love to have our pastor say something more than the Word of God, so that this or that might be okay. Conversely, we would love to have our pastor not say all that God has to say, in the hopes that God's Word will not deny us something we want. Yet, if the pastor does this, he does it to the destruction of our faith, because none of it would be of Christ, and it would turn our hearts to believe something not of Christ. Pastors, like Paul, are called to be

God's preachers and heralds, not their own or anyone else's. *apostle.* See introduction to 1:1–2. *I am not lying.* By now, knowledge of Paul and His righteous rebukes of those teaching and living falsely, and the challenges to his authority, had reached the Ephesian congregations (cf. Gal 1; 1Co 9). Having affirmed not only his appointment as preacher and apostle as a part of God's desire and plan for the salvation of all (v. 4), he identifies those to whom he, as an apostle (which means "sent one"), has been sent: the Gentiles. Cf. Rm 9:1. *teacher of the Gentiles.* While Christ gave the twelve apostles the Great Commission to go into all the world, which was dominantly Gentile, Paul was uniquely sent to them (Ac 9:15; 22:21; 26:17, 18). This only serves to support his apostolic commission and authority.

Good order in the Church's ministry (2:8–15)

ESV	KJV
[8]I desire then that in every place the men should pray, lifting holy hands without anger or quarreling; [9]likewise also that women should adorn themselves in respectable apparel, with modesty and self-control, not with braided hair and gold or pearls or costly attire, [10]but with what is proper for women who profess godliness—with good works. [11]Let a woman learn quietly with all submissiveness. [12]I do not permit a woman to teach or to exercise authority over a man; rather, she is to remain quiet. [13]For Adam was formed first, then Eve; [14]and Adam was not deceived, but the woman was deceived and became a transgressor. [15]Yet she will be saved through childbearing—if they continue in faith and love and holiness, with self-control.	[8]I will therefore that men pray every where, lifting up holy hands, without wrath and doubting. [9]In like manner also, that women adorn themselves in modest apparel, with shamefacedness and sobriety; not with broided hair, or gold, or pearls, or costly array; [10]But (which becometh women professing godliness) with good works. [11]Let the woman learn in silence with all subjection. [12]But I suffer not a woman to teach, nor to usurp authority over the man, but to be in silence. [13]For Adam was first formed, then Eve. [14]And Adam was not deceived, but the woman being deceived was in the transgression. [15]Notwithstanding she shall be saved in childbearing, if they continue in faith and charity and holiness with sobriety.

2:8 *I desire.* Literally "I urge." The term "desire" tends to give the sense that Paul is using his apostolic authority to establish his preferences in the instruction that follows. As an apostle, Paul is authorized to instruct only according to the Word of God, as the Holy Spirit has inspired him. There can be no room for his desires or his preferences. To urge that the Church in every place do the following is based upon his apostolic responsibilities and authority to establish good order in the Church and in public worship. *every place.* Literally in every location where there is a congregation gathered together for public worship. *men.* Note the wording in the text. This is not just men in a general sense of people (which would be Gk *anthropos*), but males (Gk *andras*). This is emphasized by adding the article: "the" men. Based upon his apostolic responsibility, which provides for order in the Church according to the will of God, Paul here uses the article "the," found in the Greek text, to state that men alone are to publicly offer up prayers in the public worship services, and to teach the orderly way in which they are to act. *lifting holy hands.* When it comes to prayer in public worship, we are more familiar with the custom of hands folded in prayer, symbolizing that prayer is a time of putting away the busyness of life to converse with the Giver and Keeper of all life. In the time of this letter, praying with the palms of the hands turned up and raised was the custom of both the Jews (cf. 1Kg 8:22; Ezr 9:5; Ps 28:2; 63:4; 134:2; 141:2; Lm 2:19; 3:41; Is 1:15), and the pagan religions of the day. The lifting of open hands was an expression of offering up to God thanksgiving, petitions, and praise. While folded or uplifted hands are equally valid uses of the hands in prayer, the holiness of the hands is not optional. Holiness of hands arises from the heart made holy through faith in Christ. Such hands are raised or folded before the Lord in prayer with no *anger, quarreling,* or hostility toward others. Wesley wrote, "Wrath, or unholy actions, or want of faith in him we call upon, are the three grand hindrances of God's hearing our petitions" (554–55).

2:9 *respectable apparel.* While appropriate clothing was an issue among the women, Paul is aiming at their hearts. Dressing respectfully or humbly is an expression of a humble and respectful spirit before the Lord in all places, and especially with the fellow redeemed in the public worship. Ephesus was a very wealthy region, and the ability to dress extravagantly was within the reach of many. Such extravagant apparel was not the normal fashion. To dress beyond the fashion may be done to the glory of God, but it is conspicuous and draws attention to the individual rather than to God, and tempts others to envy. The apostle Peter echoes Paul's apostolic instruction saying, "Do not let your adorning be external—the braiding of hair and the putting on of gold jewelry, or the clothing you wear—but let your adorning be the hidden person of the heart with the imperishable beauty of a gentle and quiet spirit, which in God's sight is very precious" (1Pt 3:3–4). *modesty.* This is in reference to the type of clothing and how it can be used to reflect the godliness the people profess and the humility of repentant sinners living by faith in the Lord Jesus Christ. *self-control.* As then, so today, we clothe and adorn or make ourselves up for various reasons: for comfort, to make us look good, to hide some of our less flattering aspects, and the like. Yet self-control is to be exercised so that clothing is worn as an expression of humility and honor for being a new creation rather than an expression of self-gratification and glorification. *braided hair.* Braided hair was a common and useful means of arranging a woman's long hair. Here, Paul is addressing the more extravagant ways braided hair was interwoven with wreaths, gold or beaded moldings, and the like. Again, such extravagance still works against any sense of humility and meekness before the Lord or others. *costly attire.* Paul is not mandating a dull or drab dress code for all women, nor is he prohibiting the wearing of jewelry. He is calling for attire that expresses the reality of the communion of saints. Each woman, no matter her station or vocation, is equal to all other women in terms of sinfulness and salvation. No one is more sinful than another, and no one is more saved than another. No woman has any more of Christ than another, and all women's dress and attitude should reflect this humble communion with Christ and with one another.

2:10 *profess godliness.* Paul here turns women to their own public profession, or confession, of godliness in Jesus Christ on the basis of all dress and adornment. To profess godliness was to acknowledge reverence and awe before God in all things. *good works.* The adornment of good works displays the love of Christ for all people. They are a physical confirmation of professed godliness. Good works are done in faith and for the benefit of our neighbor. As such, the poorest woman can adorn herself with good works, as the richest woman. Such good works are not those identified as spiritual or holy, but they are all such works that arise from one's vocation according to the Law of God. The fact that they are done in faith makes them good works. The way one serves another is a true demonstration of love and beauty.

2:11 *learn quietly with all submissiveness.* The simplest way to understand this is that they were to be learners, not teachers in worship. Christianity elevated women to equality with men in regard to salvation and the learning of God's Word. Jewish tradition did not allow women to learn the Law. This learning was to be done passively, in the sense that women were not to publicly instruct and assist in the instruction or during the public worship service. As an apostle, Paul was sent to teach and preach the will of God as given to him in Christ. It is through Christ that the world was ordered and created. In His work of salvation, Christ did not do away with this order, but sanctified it and returned man and woman back to it (v. 13). While Christ would have a woman teach privately (Ti 2:3, 4; Ac 18:26), He would not have a woman do this publicly in worship. Therefore, she is to submit to the order that He has established for the public teaching and preaching of His Word in His Church.

2:12 *teach.* While this may seem like another personal preference on the part of Paul, the prohibition of women teaching publicly (i.e., in the worship service) is a matter of faithfulness to the Torah, as found in the order God gave in creation (v. 13). As man was formed before woman and given the responsibility of tending creation, and woman came forth from man, man has been given the responsibility to faithfully speak and teach God's Word to his family and the family of Christ. While this prohibition deals with the public teaching and worship of the Church, women ought to actively teach other women (Ti 2:3–5), children (2Tm 1:5), and other believers and unbelievers in private conversations (Ac 18:24–26). *exercise authority over a man.* Teaching is an act of exercising authority over those who are taught. Prohibited from teaching and preaching in the public worship service, a woman is therefore prohibited from publicly exercising the only authority the Church has, which is the Word of God. The exact opposite of teaching is being taught: learning. This is the meaning and purpose of being quiet.

2:13 *For.* Literally "because." You, like the people of the Ephesian region, might wonder why Paul, or the Lord, would restrict the role and responsibility of women in the Church of which they are equal members. What follows is not Paul's personal or cultural basis for this restriction, but rather the biblical basis found in the Torah (Gn 2–3) that is God's revealed basis for this. *Adam was formed first.* As God is a God of order, not chaos (1Co 14:33), He created everything according to His chosen sequence. While God was free to create both man and woman at the same time, He chose to create man first, and apart from woman. God chose to create woman out of man, not to make her less than man, but that man might understand his responsibility toward her as coming out of himself. The fact that she came from man, and was brought to the man, reveals that it was not God's intention that she exercise that same responsibility as man in the dominion God gave them. Since the Church is God's new creation in Christ Jesus, renewed in the purity of the first creation prior to the fall, Christ ordered the Church as the first creation. Salvation separates humanity from the fall into sin, not from the order of God's creation. As Christ restored humanity to our rightful place in the order of creation before God, Christ also restored the rightful places of man and woman. In none of this, be it in the first creation, in salvation, and now as a new creation in Christ, does this mean women are less or unequal to men in God's love, mercy, and grace.

2:14 *Adam was not deceived.* While this might seem like a slight of woman, Paul is merely revealing what happened when the woman listened to someone other than God's chosen servant of His Word to her (Adam). To understand the fullness of this, we need to look more deeply into Gn 3 and examine everything involved in the fall. The issue is not level of guilt, for both sinned. Yet because the woman was deceived (Gn 3:13), she not only listened to the serpent, but she took the role of teacher not given to her by God. Reversing the responsibilities given by God, she then exercised authority over her husband according to what she was told by the serpent. What was Adam's sin? "You have listened to the voice of your wife and have eaten of the tree of which I commanded you, 'You shall not eat of it'" (Gn 3:17). The guilt of both is equal; Eve was the victim of deception, and Adam sinned willfully. While God cursed the earth because of Adam's sin, God did not revoke his responsibility toward the exercising of authority over the woman in anything. Adam was to love his wife as himself and thus exercise his God-given authority for the blessing and benefit of his wife, just as Christ does for His Bride the Church (Eph 5). All men have this same responsibility! *transgressor.* This is understood as one who steps beyond a given boundary.

Having been deceived, Eve became a transgressor as she stepped beyond the boundary of her place and responsibility the moment she began to exercise authority over the man by teaching what the serpent said.

2:15 *she . . . they.* How sad that culture often robs these words of their real meaning. While childbearing is scorned by many, it is the blessed responsibility God gave to women. How glorious is woman that God chose her to cocreate all of humanity and to be the means by which His Son would become incarnate. Having listed the responsibilities that women were not to have in the Church, Paul speaks now of the responsibility that woman, not man, is uniquely created and blessed to fulfill: the conceiving, carrying, birthing, and raising of children. Outside of the Church, woman conceived children in sin and birthed them in iniquity (Ps 51:5). Now, though believing women still conceive children in original sin, in faith they bring infants to Christ that He might rebirth them to eternal life in Baptism. Such believing mothers teach and raise their children in the faith, so they might grow and increase in the faith unto eternal life in Christ. *saved through childbearing.* No woman is saved by giving birth to a child, neither is any woman condemned because she cannot bear a child. Having been saved by grace alone through faith in Christ alone, each woman is God's workmanship in Christ, created to do the good works God prepared in advance for her to do (Eph 2:8–10). Long before there was a corporate professional world, God created woman to be the mother of humanity. The woman who has been saved through faith in Christ will in faith fulfill the good works of motherhood God has given to her. To be a mother in the bonds of marriage is fulfilling God's order of creation; to reject this is to reject her Creator, Redeemer, and Sanctifier. *if.* Carries the idea of expectancy that a believing woman will not reject the good work that God has redeemed her to fulfill as her created responsibility. *faith . . . self-control.* While these qualities ought to be found in men and women, Paul highlights these for woman as the one charged with raising children from a young age. The mother who models these qualities will surely train her children well in these, and help them live the life of faith to which Christ calls them, and all believers.

Ch. 2 in Devotion and Prayer When hearing these words of the apostle with regard to the responsibilities of men and women in the Church, what kind of ears are you using? Ears tuned and filtered by cultural norms? personal preference? political correctness? Or do you hear these words of God given through the apostle with ears tuned and filtered by the full testimony of God's Word? Apart from faith, our ears are tuned and filtered by sin, sin that does not accept the things of God because they are spiritually discerned (1Co 2:14). Opposition to God's ordering of His chosen people is nothing new. Dathan and others became jealous of Moses and Aaron (Levites God chose to serve as priests), and rebelled against God's order. He caused the earth to open and swallow up Dathan and the company of Abiram, and fire to consume the wicked (Ps 106:16–18). The fact that God responded in this way to those who rebelled against His ordering of ministry reveals that the order of creation followed by Paul is not a matter of personal or cultural preference. The fall into sin came about because Eve rejected this order and Adam chose to allow her to do so. Thanks be to God that He sent Christ to redeem us from the fall into sin, with all its disordering of life, and caused us to be born again into a new creation. How blessed it is that, as we receive and live by the Holy Spirit, we are made wise unto God's saving order and live self-controlled in Christ's love. By His grace, each of us has been set free through faith to modestly, and with all self-control, do the good works He has prepared in advance for us to do. • Blessed Lord, You gather us together to one God and Father of us all. You do this as our one Lord, in one faith through one Baptism. Grant that we may be in the world but not of the world. Enable us through faith to rejoice in the vocations You have given us both in the Church and outside it. May Your Holy Spirit continue to enlighten us, and all the Church, in the reality that we are all members of Your Body, not our own. This we pray and live in Your holy name. Amen.

Qualifications for Offices (ch. 3)

The pastoral office (3:1–7)

ESV	KJV
3 [1]The saying is trustworthy: If anyone aspires to the office of overseer, he desires a noble task. [2]Therefore an overseer must be above reproach, the husband of one wife, sober-minded, self-controlled, respectable, hospitable, able to teach, [3]not a drunkard, not violent but gentle, not quarrelsome, not a lover of money. [4]He must manage his own household well, with all dignity keeping his children submissive, [5]for if someone does not know how to manage his own household, how will he care for God's church? [6]He must not be a recent convert, or he may become puffed up with conceit and fall into the condemnation of the devil. [7]Moreover, he must be well thought of by outsiders, so that he may not fall into disgrace, into a snare of the devil.	*3* [1]This is a true saying, if a man desire the office of a bishop, he desireth a good work. [2]A bishop then must be blameless, the husband of one wife, vigilant, sober, of good behaviour, given to hospitality, apt to teach; [3]Not given to wine, no striker, not greedy of filthy lucre; but patient, not a brawler, not covetous; [4]One that ruleth well his own house, having his children in subjection with all gravity; [5](For if a man know not how to rule his own house, how shall he take care of the church of God?) [6]Not a novice, lest being lifted up with pride he fall into the condemnation of the devil. [7]Moreover he must have a good report of them which are without; lest he fall into reproach and the snare of the devil.

Introduction to 3:1–13 Having conveyed God's will that men are to be the ones to teach and preach publicly within the Church, Paul now continues with the organization of the Church by addressing the kind of men God would have to serve in the offices of the Church.

3:1 *The saying.* Paul interjects this to affirm that what he has previously said regarding Church order, and what he is about to say regarding the qualifications of an overseer, has been sought out by other congregations and taught. Cf. 5:17–22; Ac 6:1–6; 14:21–23; Ti 1:5–16; 1Pt 5:1–5. *aspires.* Paul affirms aspiring to the office and service of overseer. Since such aspiration could be a mask for selfish gain or greed (6:10), Paul proceeds to check such aspirations against the qualifications that follow. *office of overseer.* The Greek term is *episkopē,* (from which we get the English word "episcopal"). It is often translated as "bishop." The term refers to the responsibility of spiritual oversight, and thus identifies the primary work of the office. The term "elder" is often used in the same way (Ti 1:5); it has its origin in Jewish tradition. The term "pastor" (shepherd) is also used as a synonym for this office, as it carries the oversight responsibilities as well. Knox published an account of the martyrdom of Walter Mill (d. 1558) that illustrated how differently the reformers thought about the office of bishop in contrast to the Roman Catholics. When charged with denying the office of bishop, Mill replied:

> I affirm that they whom you call bishops do not bishop's works, nor use the office of bishops, as Paul bids, writing to Timothy; but live after their own sensual pleasure, and take no care of the flock, nor yet regard they the word of God, but desire to be honoured, and called my lords. (234)

noble task. Paul refers to the work of a pastor in this way for two reasons. First, its purpose is devoted to the eternal welfare of those for whom it is done; second, because it is a labor dedicated to giving the gifts of God in Jesus Christ to the saints that they might abide in Christ and be equipped for work of ministry, for building up the Body of Christ—the Church (Eph 4:8, 12).

3:2 *above reproach.* In the Greek, this literally means that the man is "not able to be taken hold of" for failing to measure up to the attributes that Paul goes on to name. While there are several reasons for this, consider two of the most important. First, the pastor, by virtue of his office, is an example to the congregation and to any future pastors that the Lord might call from among the congregation. Second, and perhaps more important, the pastor deals in faith. As a servant of the Word, the pastor uses the Word of God so that the Holy Spirit might work, strengthen, enlighten, and grow faith. The congregation needs to be able to trust the pastor and trust that he believes what he preaches and teaches. This trust is strengthened as the congregant finds him living the faith. *husband of one wife.* As there were no seminaries and schools for the pastoral ministry, pastors were usually older men called from among the congregations, which were made up predominately of new converts. As such, their cultural and religious backgrounds permitted unscriptural divorces and the keeping of noncitizened women (slaves) for conjugal purposes. While all converts willingly forfeited this way of life upon conversion, one serving as pastor could not have this way of life as part of his past, lest it give the people of his past, or members of the congregation, reason to lay hold of him and accuse him of such a way of life. This would erode trust in the man holding the office. In no way does Paul mean that a pastor has to be married. This is a contrast to Jews who required a priest to both be married and have children so that he might learn mercy firsthand and thus be merciful. Wesley wrote:

> This neither means that a bishop must be married; nor that he may not marry a second wife [if the first died]: which it is just as lawful for him to do as to marry a first and may in some cases be his bounde[d] duty. But whereas polygamy and divorce upon slight occasions were common both among the Jews and heathen, it teaches us that ministers of all others ought to stand clear of those sins. (541)

sober-minded. While this might seem to refer to the use of alcohol (see v. 3), it is far more sweeping. At the heart of this term is the sense of "soundness" and "balanced" thinking in all things. A pastor's thinking has to rest first on the Word of God, and then on mercy. He cannot afford to so indulge himself, in anything, that his thinking becomes imbalanced in the carrying out of his office. *respectable.* In regard to how the pastor conducts himself as pastor, husband, father, and the like, everything must be well-ordered. *hospitable.* Far more than a kind word and cursory welcome, hospitality was about receiving, welcoming, and offering one's home and fare to strangers in need. This was especially important when ministering to exiles, to the poor, and to those fleeing persecution. While the pastor is to serve as the exemplar of hospitality, this is the responsibility of the whole Church (Rm 12:13, Heb 13:2, 1Pt 4:9).

3:3 *not violent.* The literal translation of the Greek is "not a striker," but the term connotes to far more. It means being "quick-tempered," and carries the sense of easily argumentative and combative when opposed or disagreed with. Such a characteristic would run contrary to the patience and mercy of God that the pastor proclaims and is to practice. That's why Paul immediately affirms the opposite quality of gentleness. *lover of money.* This does not demand a vow of poverty or forbid the enjoyment of God's blessings. Rather, a pastor should not consider his calling merely as a means to make an income or make his wealth and prosperity its goal. Congregations should faithfully support their pastors, but neither pastors nor those they serve should be dedicated to money (cf. 6:10; Heb 13:5).

3:4–5 *children submissive.* While it is not a requirement that a pastor has to have children, the pastor does need to father his children in such a way that they listen to, learn from, and obey him as God so orders the relationship in the Fourth Commandment. The dignity with which the father parents his children arises from him bringing up his children in the discipline and instruction of the Lord (Eph 6:4).

3:6 *recent convert.* In the Greek, Paul used a term to depict newly planted trees or vines (Gk *neophytos.* cf. Ps 144:12). While candidates for the pastoral office need to be baptized by the water and the Word of God, they need their new life of faith baptized in the real and humbling soul struggles of life that are common to those they will serve. Maturity is a requisite for any candidate, yet Paul's image begs a deeper understanding of what is needed. You see, without having been long schooled in the daily confrontation with his nothingness in temptation, sin, sickness, and suffering that drives him to Christ alone, such a man might easily lean on the reeds of his own understanding (Pr 3:5). How shall he be able to bring words of Christ's comfort to those confronted with such realities if he himself has not found life and been comforted by such words (2Co 1:3–4)? The greatest wisdom a pastor must exercise in carrying out his office is that in all things he is nothing, and his sufficiency in all things must come from Christ alone (2Co 3:5–6). This in no way excludes young men from the ministry, but like Timothy, they ought to have been raised in the faith. *condemnation.* While this sounds like pride might lead a young pastor to be condemned by the devil, this is not what is being said here. Paul warns that such conceit in a pastor is caused by the same sinful pride that led the devil to reject and rebel against God. The fruit of such sinful pride will bring the same condemnation that the devil received from God.

3:7 *outsiders.* Jesus identifies these as people who have not yet received the knowledge of the mystery of the kingdom of God (Mk 4:11), which is another way of saying those who have not yet been converted through the mystery of the kingdom of God, which is the Gospel. *snare of the devil.* As the pastor's only instrument is the Word of God, his use of the Word, in the application of the Law and the Gospel, will be used by hearers, both inside and outside the Church. If his teaching, preaching, or practice varies, depending on the situation or persons, he can easily be ensnared by his own words and actions, thereby undermining his credibility, and that of his office. The devil has many allies in laying such snares, as Jesus experienced when the Pharisees and the Herodians sought to entangle Him in His words (Mt 22:15–22). When the pastor faithfully speaks God's Word according to the Great Commission (Mt 28:19–20), he provides little or no opportunity for the laying of any snare.

3:1–7 in Devotion and Prayer As you read through the qualifications that God has set down for those who would serve in the Office of the Public Ministry, these might seem extreme, if not absurd, to our current culture. Having said that, the qualifications were not set forth for the approval of any culture, but for the sake of redeeming people in every culture. These qualifications were set forth not by those being redeemed, but by the God who has created and redeemed them. As Christ is the good and chief shepherd that has laid down His life for the sheep (Jn 10:11; 1Pt 5:4), it is His alone to set forth the qualifications of those who will speak and act in His stead. These qualification serve to encourage trust in the messengers by all hearers. If fault is found in any of the mentioned areas, such fault would be conferred to the office. It is the responsibility and privilege of every believer to support, encourage, and pray for their pastors to excel in these qualities that serve them and the Gospel. • Send, O Lord, Your Holy Spirit On Your servant now, we pray; Let him prove a faithful shepherd That no lamb be led astray. Your pure teaching to proclaim, To extol Your holy name, and to feed Your lambs, dear Savior, Make his aim and sole endeavor (*LSB* 681:1).

Deacons and deaconesses (3:8–13)

ESV	KJV
[8]Deacons likewise must be dignified, not double-tongued, not addicted to much wine, not greedy for dishonest gain. [9]They must hold the mystery of the faith with a clear conscience. [10]And let them also be tested first; then let them serve as deacons if they prove themselves blameless. [11]Their wives likewise must be dignified, not slanderers, but sober-minded, faithful in all things. [12]Let deacons each be the husband of one wife, managing their children and their own households well. [13]For those who serve well as deacons gain a good standing for themselves and also great confidence in the faith that is in Christ Jesus.	[8]Likewise must the deacons be grave, not doubletongued, not given to much wine, not greedy of filthy lucre; [9]Holding the mystery of the faith in a pure conscience. [10]And let these also first be proved; then let them use the office of a deacon, being found blameless. [11]Even so must their wives be grave, not slanderers, sober, faithful in all things. [12]Let the deacons be the husbands of one wife, ruling their children and their own houses well. [13]For they that have used the office of a deacon well purchase to themselves a good degree, and great boldness in the faith which is in Christ Jesus.

3:8–12 Paul addresses the qualifications of another office that was found within the church at Ephesus and Philippi (Php 1:1). As a servant of the Church and for the sake of the saints, the qualifications of a deacon corresponded similarly to that of the overseer/pastor (vv. 1–7). The fact that deacons were not required to have the ability to teach (v. 2), nor were they required to care for God's Church (v. 5), differentiated their office and responsibilities from that of the overseer/pastor. The fact that these were omitted immediately after naming them as requirements of the overseer means that these responsibilities were reserved for, and must be carried out through, the Office of the Public Ministry.

3:8 *Deacons.* The word "deacon" (Gk *diakonos*) refers to a "general servant" who could render service to others in many and various ways, for the sake of the Church. The likely origins of this office can be traced back to the appointment by the apostles of the seven who were to wait on tables, so that the apostles could devote themselves to preaching of the Word and prayer (Ac 6:1–6). Beyond the account in Acts 6, Scripture is silent on what exactly deacons did. Following the purpose of their appointment by the apostles, it can be concluded that whatever their service, it was as assistants to the overseers/pastors. The best way to understand the ministry of the deacon, as compared to that of the overseer/pastor, is in regard to the matters that each was given to attend to. The overseer/pastor attended to the spiritual needs and care of the church, while the deacon would attend to what would best be referred to as the business needs of the church (i.e., collecting and distributing alms; providing food and physical care for the poor, the sick, the orphans, and the refugees).

3:9 *mystery.* This does not refer to the personal faith of an individual but rather to the substance of *the faith.* The mystery of the faith refers to all the glorious acts and works of God centering on Jesus Christ, by which He has, does, and continues to save people through the preaching of His Word and the administration of the Sacraments of Baptism and the Lord's Supper (the Gospel). Paul refers to all this and more as a mystery because they are unknown apart from the Word of God and faith. While every person is born with some natural knowledge of God from the fragmented Law of God still written on our hearts, no one can know God's loving nature and saving work toward mankind apart from the revelation that He gives to us through His Word. A deacon must hold to contents of this revelation, so that he might serve according to the faith, and share that faith while serving. *clear conscience.* The deacon will need to believe and confess his belief in the fullness of God's revelation in Jesus Christ without any additions or deletions to the content of the faith. He cannot question the truths and teaching of the Christian faith as taught according to God's revelation. There can be no buffet approach to what is to be believed. Just as Christ could not have saved anyone by keeping His preferred bits and pieces of God's promises, but only by keeping all of them, so also, one is saved and serves according to all the promises kept for the deacon and any believer.

3:10 *tested.* As there are qualifications that the deacon must meet in order to serve, the character of any candidate for the office must be established through a formal examination. When the deacon is proven *blameless* (crimeless), by way of inquiry and investigation, then he is to serve. Having been rescued from the dominion of darkness and transferred into the kingdom of Christ, the deacon's character and conduct serve to give witness of this rescue, character, and conduct of the kingdom of Christ in which he now serves.

3:11 *wives.* This can also be translated "women must also be dignified." While this could refer to the wives of the deacons, who would have assisted their husbands in their diaconal work, it could also refer to women serving as deaconesses. An example of such a deaconess is Phoebe, whom Paul commends to the Romans as a servant of the church (Rm 16:1–2). While not holding the office of overseer (pastor), many such women have served the Church in this office to this day.

3:13 *gain a good standing.* The literal sense is that by their good service, the deacons and deaconesses move themselves in the hearts and minds of those they serve, and of the Lord, to a threshold, to a place where they could be entrusted with more or wider responsibilities. Being faithful in little would move others to trust them with much more in the administration of care and visitation of the poor and needy in the community. *confidence.* Faithful service would flow from a firm faith in Christ and would be devoid of timidity or hesitation when it comes to confessing that faith through faithful service. In the exercising of the faith, greater confidence would result.

3:8–13 in Devotion and Prayer In Micah 6:8, the prophet reminds the people of God of what He calls upon them to do as His redeemed, "to do justice, and to love kindness, and to walk humbly with your God." That the Body of Christ may pursue justice and kindness, the Early Church provided for the office of deacon and deaconess. As God is a God of order and not confusion, these offices serve in assisting the whole Church to humbly walk together with the Lord in works of service and mercy. Surely, you have seen such works of service that include, but are not limited to, speaking up for those who cannot speak for themselves (Pr 31:8) and providing for the poor, the hungry, the sick, and the like, according to their physical needs. By these servants, the Church is assisted in doing good to all, especially the household of faith (Gal 6:10). • Blessed Savior, You came not to be served but to serve and give Your life as a ransom for all. We thank You for the ministry of deacons and deaconesses throughout Your Church. Grant unto them Your Holy Spirit that they may be faithful to You as they serve the Church. Lead us to support them in their service through prayer and sacrifice that they might walk humbly with You for the sake of all. This we pray in the name of Christ, the Lord of the Church. Amen.

The Church: the community of faith (3:14–16)

ESV	KJV

[14]I hope to come to you soon, but I am writing these things to you so that, [15]if I delay, you may know how one ought to behave in the household of God, which is the church of the living God, a pillar and buttress of the truth. [16]Great indeed, we confess, is the mystery of godliness:
 	
He was manifested in the flesh,
    vindicated by the Spirit,
      seen by angels,
  proclaimed among the nations,
    believed on in the world,
      taken up in glory.
	[14]These things write I unto thee, hoping to come unto thee shortly: [15]But if I tarry long, that thou mayest know how thou oughtest to behave thyself in the house of God, which is the church of the living God, the pillar and ground of the truth. [16]And without controversy great is the mystery of godliness: God was manifest in the flesh, justified in the Spirit, seen of angels, preached unto the Gentiles, believed on in the world, received up into glory.

3:14 *come to you soon.* Paul was up in the region of Macedonia (Greece) where the churches at Thessalonica, Philippi, and Berea were located. A trip to Ephesus required hundreds of miles of difficult and often dangerous travel over land, and likely some of it by sea. Paul had written to Titus about the same time as this letter was sent to Timothy. In his Letter to Titus, Paul told Titus to meet him in Nicopolis (eastern shores of Greece), where Paul planned to spend the winter (Ti 3:12). It is likely that Paul hoped to get to Ephesus prior to arriving at Nicopolis. Paul promised to come to the Corinthians but was unable to get there as he had planned; this caused many to try to undermine his apostolic authority and teaching (2Co 1). Knowing that his plans were always subject to the will of God, Paul wanted to make sure that Timothy and the Church knew how the Church ought to be ordered for the sake of the Gospel.

3:15 *household of God.* While "household" is a collective reference to the body of believers (i.e., the Church), Paul refers to them as the "household of God," not so much because they belong to Him, but because God dwells in them. This also conveys the reality of all believers being joined in Christ. God has made them brothers and sisters of Christ and of one another. In this family household of God's making, Christ is the faithful one over the house of God for everyone in the house (Heb 3:6). *church of the living God*. While this refers to the assembly of believers in church of the firstborn (Heb 12:23), Paul uses this designation to identify the physical nature of the Church. It is not constructed of physical, dead material, but is built of living stones: those believers who have been made alive through the death and resurrection of Christ, who build upon Him, the living stone (1Pt 2:4–5). *pillar and buttress of the truth*. As the Church is a creation of God by means of the truth (that is, the Gospel), God has chosen it to serve as the support and foundation of the Gospel. Having sent the Church out into the world, it supports and bears the truth before the world so that others may be joined into this pillar and foundation of truth. Having been made a pillar and foundation by God through this truth, even though it be housed in the flesh of humanity, the gates of hell itself cannot prevail against it (Mt 16:18). Calvin wrote:

> If the instruction of the Gospel be not proclaimed, if there are no godly ministers who, by their preaching, rescue truth from darkness and forgetfulness, instantly falsehoods, errors, impostures, superstitions, and every kind of corruption, will reign. In short, silence in the Church is the banishment and crushing of the truth. (91)

3:16 *confess*. This means more than to merely say something. To confess is to state that which agrees with the truth (i.e., the Gospel of God in Jesus Christ, which is the mystery of godliness). It is through this faithful confession that the Church fulfills the commission that Christ gave her (Mt 28:19–20). Only by this faithful, continuous confession of the truth, does the Church remain a pillar and buttress of the truth (the Gospel). As we see the Church struggling, we are often tempted to look everywhere, and to anything that offers some kind of revival, yet the Church lives and grows by the confession of the Gospel. *mystery of godliness*. So how do you confess something that is a "mystery"? This godliness is not a mystery to the Church, for it is revealed, given, and lived in Jesus Christ (v. 16b) and known through faith. Paul refers to the godliness as a mystery because it cannot be known apart from faith. The mystery of this godliness deepens because it is not found or sustained through the thoughts, desires, words, or works of any person. It is totally the work of God for us in Jesus Christ. Because it cannot be grasped by the mind or heart of humanity, even after conversion, it must always be gladly and faithfully confessed and proclaimed. If you try to make sense of this love and grace that reside in God alone, you may have godly thoughts and ideas, but none of them will save you in the end. *He was manifested . . . up in glory.* While these six statements sound like a checklist of the events in Jesus' life as our Savior, it is much more. Greek usually places the verbs toward the end of any sentence. Here, Paul puts the verbs where we find them in the English, at the beginning of each phrase. This makes each of these emphatic statements an absolute truth about Jesus Christ for us that cannot possibly be changed or denied.

3:14–16 in Devotion and Prayer As Paul concludes this section on the organization of the Church and the offices within her, how do you hear this teaching? For many, this whole section sounds out of step with current thinking and organization. Yet what the apostle is organizing is no worldly organization. In these words, Paul is telling Timothy as a pastor, and the whole Church whom the pastor serves, that it is God's house, the Church of the living God. Its origin, organization, purpose, and life all come from the God who created it and set Christ over it as the Head (Col 1:18). In His Church, God's truth, that is His Word in Jesus Christ, is to be confessed and proclaimed as a witness to the world. Thanks be to God that His Holy Spirit has called us by the Gospel and enlightened us with His gifts, so that we abide in Him who is our Head, Jesus Christ. • Lord God, heavenly Father, thanks and praise to You we offer for having revealed the mystery of godliness in Jesus Christ. Grant that as You have made us members of Your household through the Gospel, we may abide and be faithful to the organization and purpose of Your House until the Head of the house, Jesus Christ, returns to gather us together with all the saints in glory. Amen.

PART 3

TRUE VERSUS FALSE TEACHING (CH. 4)

Doctrines of Demons (4:1–5)

ESV	KJV
4 ¹Now the Spirit expressly says that in later times some will depart from the faith by devoting themselves to deceitful spirits and teachings of demons, ²through the insincerity of liars whose consciences are seared, ³who forbid marriage and require abstinence from foods that God created to be received with thanksgiving by those who believe and know the truth. ⁴For everything created by God is good, and nothing is to be rejected if it is received with thanksgiving, ⁵for it is made holy by the word of God and prayer.	**4** ¹Now the Spirit speaketh expressly, that in the latter times some shall depart from the faith, giving heed to seducing spirits, and doctrines of devils; ²Speaking lies in hypocrisy; having their conscience seared with a hot iron; ³Forbidding to marry, and commanding to abstain from meats, which God hath created to be received with thanksgiving of them which believe and know the truth. ⁴For every creature of God is good, and nothing to be refused, if it be received with thanksgiving: ⁵For it is sanctified by the word of God and prayer.

4:1 *expressly says.* Paul's statement echoes Jesus as He spoke of the coming of the end of the age (Mt 24:10–11; Mk 13:22). Having received this already spoken truth by way of the Holy Spirit or one of the other apostles who had heard this from the Lord, Paul now states it as absolute fact. This shall happen and there is no turning it back. *later times.* While this would seem to point to the time just prior to our Lord's return, the use of the plural contradicts this. The plurality of time (seasons) refers to the ongoing movement of the Church through the various times or seasons of expansion, persecution, struggle, etc. We know these times were upon the Church in Timothy's day, as they are upon us in our day, because of the rebuttal Paul provides for these false teachers in what follows vv. 5–6 (cf. 2Ti 3:1ff). They began with the ascension of our Lord, and they will end when He returns again. *depart from the faith.* While this might seem to be addressing a departure from personal faith, it refers to a departure from the object of faith (the substance of what is believed in). It is a departure from the full biblical doctrine and teaching of the Gospel of salvation through Jesus Christ. This can happen by rejecting all of it, denying some part of it, or adding to it in a way that mixes human ideas with God's truth. Paul addressed this issue with several congregations, where false teachers were willing to acknowledge Jesus Christ in some part; but in regard to salvation, they were teaching that He alone, or faith in Him alone, was not sufficient for salvation. These false teachers taught their hearers that they needed to do some kind of additional work by which they could secure their salvation and be confident that they were right with God. Paul's letters to the Galatians and Colossians both address and refute these false teachings with the sole sufficiency of Christ for our salvation. *devoting.* This means that they literally held and dedicated their minds and themselves to the false and evil teachings of deceitful spirits and demons, by continuing to hear them and confessing them as truth. *deceitful spirits.* Those contrary to the Holy Spirit, the Spirit of truth. Such deceitful spirits speak through the false teachers (v. 2), and are identified as "deceitful" because they inspire the use of lies (false teachings) to deceive people. *teachings of demons.* Literally, the "teachings that come from demons." As "a liar and the father of lies" (Jn 8:44), all such teachings, though they be spoken by various individuals (v. 2), emanate from Satan and his legions. As these teachings come by deception, they rarely deny the totality of "the faith" (4:1a). The great danger for the Church in Timothy's day, as it is today, is that the falsity and error of these teachings, and their consequences, are often not recognized unless they openly deny the totality of "the faith" (cf. Gal and Col).

4:2 Like human flesh that has been deeply burned with a branding iron loses all sensitivity to touch, so the consciences of such liars have lost all sense of right and wrong, truth and life. Unable to know truth from error according to the author of truth (Jn 17:17), these liars are left to appeal to their own reasoning, which is bound in sin, and therefore in service to Satan. According to the Greek construct, this searing has been self-inflicted. This happens through a continuous hardening of the heart toward the Word of God, by their continued rebellion against the Word of God in thoughts, words, and actions.

4:3 *forbid marriage . . . abstinence.* Such mandatory sacrifices may have all the appearances of religious dedication, but they are contrary to the Word of God and the freedom won for us in the Gospel of Jesus Christ. The forbidding of marriage runs contrary to the command that it be honored by all (cf. Heb 13:4). To abstain from the foods that the Creator has provided to be received with thanksgiving and prayer is a denial of the Creator Himself, and of the freedom in Christ from being judged according to such things (Col 2:16). *received with thanksgiving.* Through faith, believers come to know and believe that every good and perfect gift has come down undeservedly to us from God the Father (Jas 1:17). Receiving and enjoying these blessings, believers confess this belief in God's undeserved goodness toward them through prayers of thanksgiving.

4:4–5 in Devotion and Prayer Having begun this letter with a warning against various false teachers, Paul begins to educate Timothy, and all overseers/pastors, regarding the source, the nature, and the practices of certain false teachings. In the midst of such a reality, Paul appeals to the truth and blessings of the Gospel for all who believe. Through such faith, the Lord has set believers free to enjoy and gladly give thanks for all God's blessings of body and soul. • Blessed Father in heaven, as we give thanks to You for Your blessed gifts to us for body and soul, even more so do we thank You for the freedom to enjoy them and share them through faith in Jesus Christ, our Lord. Amen.

True Godliness (4:6–10)

ESV	KJV
⁶If you put these things before the brothers, you will be a good servant of Christ Jesus, being trained in the words of the faith and of the good doctrine that you have followed. ⁷Have nothing to do with irreverent, silly myths. Rather train yourself for godliness; ⁸for while bodily training is of some value, godliness is of value in every way, as it holds promise for the present life and also for the life to come. ⁹The saying is trustworthy and deserving of full acceptance. ¹⁰For to this end we toil and strive, because we have our hope set on the living God, who is the Savior of all people, especially of those who believe.	⁶If thou put the brethren in remembrance of these things, thou shalt be a good minister of Jesus Christ, nourished up in the words of faith and of good doctrine, whereunto thou hast attained. ⁷But refuse profane and old wives' fables, and exercise thyself rather unto godliness. ⁸For bodily exercise profiteth little: but godliness is profitable unto all things, having promise of the life that now is, and of that which is to come. ⁹This is a faithful saying and worthy of all acceptation. ¹⁰For therefore we both labour and suffer reproach, because we trust in the living God, who is the Saviour of all men, specially of those that believe.

4:6 *these things.* This refers first to what Paul has just said in 4:1–5; and second, to all that preceded in the previous chapters. Paul would not have Timothy or any overseer/pastor put the false teachings before the Church (v. 1) and then not refute them, or withhold information about the false teachers (1:3–20). Paul does not want Timothy to teach prayers of thanksgiving (v. 5) and then be silent about his instruction on prayers for all people (2:1–8). Everything mentioned prior is for the sake of the Church (i.e., believers in Timothy's day), and for the sake of those who follow them. All these things have need to be constantly put before both pastor and people. *brothers.* This is Paul's usual designation for male and female believers when speaking of an entire congregation or collection of congregations. This reference echoes what Paul says of all believers, "in Christ Jesus you are all sons of God, through faith" (Gal 3:26). Those who have been led by the Spirit through the Gospel to faith are "sons of God" (Rm 8:14) and as such are heirs with Christ (Rm 8:17). *words* *of the faith*. The biblical texts that speak to both God's Law and the Gospel of salvation of sinners through faith in Jesus Christ alone. It is through these words of faith that faith is given (Rm 10:17). The "words of faith" do not stand in contrast to "good doctrine" but are the sum and substance of it. *good doctrine*. The full and faithful application of the "words of faith" through teaching and preaching to both believer and nonbeliever for the salvation of both.

4:7 *myths*. See exposition of 1:4. *train yourself for godliness*. As the evil spirits, like Satan, are always on the prowl, seeking whom they may devour by any means of deception or myth, both the overseer/pastor and the parishioner need to be constantly exercising themselves in the gifts of God (i.e., His Word and Sacraments). Only in this way shall they be preserved by the Spirit through these constant assaults of the evil one. To take to oneself a means of godliness that God has not given (myths and the like) is to weaken one's faith in the means of true godliness.

4:8 *bodily training is of some value*. Physical exercise and discipline are beneficial, but discipline, self-denial, and fasting do nothing to stop the desires and indulging of our sinful flesh. *value in every way*. Through true and faithful devotion to being trained in the "words of faith" and the faithful teaching of doctrine (godliness), there were promised blessings for this life and the life to come in eternity. The value of this godliness is held out in the promises given in it. This godliness offered these blessings to the believer, and to the whole Church, as together they exercised themselves in it, toward one another and the world.

4:9 *The saying*. Refers to all Paul has just said about godliness and its promises in vv. 7–8. This saying is identical to what Paul says in 1:15 regarding Christ. With this statement, Paul is making it clear that whether or not you believe it and accept it, it is, and will forever be, worthy of total and complete acceptance through faith.

4:10 *this end*. The pursuit of such godliness and its promises (vv. 7–8) for this life and the life to come. *hope set on the living God*. The confident expectation of the living God (cf. Mt 22:32) to fulfill His promises of godliness (v. 8). This hope is the reason for all the toiling and striving of Paul, Timothy, every believer, and the Church. *Savior of all people*. Such is the living God, who desires all people to be saved (2:4). To fulfill His desire, He sent His Son into the world to be the sacrificial Lamb who has taken away the sin of the whole world (Jn 1:29). Christ has come as the Savior of all people because He suffered once for all through His passion, death, and resurrection. *especially of those who believe.* While Christ came and accomplished the work of salvation for all people by dying and rising for all (objective justification), the work of the Savior benefits only those who receive it through faith (subjective justification/salvation). While many people strive and toil after God, it is the believer alone who has received these promises and strives after the godliness that has blessings for now and eternity.

Train Yourself for Godliness

Paul's admonition to Timothy garnered the special attention of Martin Luther as he lectured to his students in 1528 where Luther expounded a word that would become controversial in later centuries: godliness or piety. Luther said:

> The largest part of *eusebeia* ("godliness") is devoted to teaching. Whoever teaches the Word of God correctly should train himself for godliness. He does not lay the Word down in his napkin, as a lazy slave does (cf. Luke 19:20). He keeps it in use so that it may not rust or rot away. Rather, let him declare it every day. We read in John 15:2: "He will prune." For the man to whom God entrusts this word God stirs up enemies—his own flesh and the devil. God gives him many people that that gift of the Spirit may not lie idle but that the man may walk in the training of the Spirit. . . . You see, teaching, comforting, exhorting, praying, and writing are the exercising of godliness whose fruits stream over to other people. (LW 28:321–22)

Although Luther emphasized teaching as exercise in godliness, he also included other spiritual activities. Calvin commented similarly:

> [Timothy] ought to be employed in "godliness;" for, when he says, Exercise thyself, he means that this is his proper occupation, his labour, his chief care. As if he had said, "There is no reason why you should weary yourself to no purpose about other matters; you will do that which is of the highest importance, if you devote yourself, with all your zeal, and with all your ability, to godliness alone." By the word godliness, he means the spiritual worship of God, which consists in purity of conscience; which is still more evident from what follows, when it is contrasted with bodily exercise. (109)

Both reformers heartily commend the ideal of godliness. But by the end of the seventeenth century, talk of piety roused debate and anger. This can be seen in Bengel's comments on 1 Timothy 2:2. He included a long excursus on the meaning of the word "godly" or pious, noting how often the apostle used it. He then wrote:

> Piety, in name at least never hitherto lightly esteemed, has at length been converted into a term of reproach, "Pietist," by an anonymous person of the worst character, whose death, as we are informed, was shocking. (4:554–55)

It is not clear who the "anonymous person" was. Bengel perhaps referred to the strife that erupted in Halle, Germany, surrounding the rise of German Pietism, a holiness movement of the seventeenth and eighteenth centuries that had some helpful emphases but also theological problems. Bengel regretted that a proper understanding of biblical piety, as expounded by the reformers, was lost or muted in the debate.⚓

Paul's Charge to His Fellow Pastor Timothy (4:11–16)

ESV	KJV
¹¹Command and teach these things. ¹²Let no one despise you for your youth, but set the believers an example in speech, in conduct, in love, in faith, in purity. ¹³Until I come, devote yourself to the public reading of Scripture, to exhortation, to teaching. ¹⁴Do not neglect the gift you have, which was given you by prophecy when the council of elders laid their hands on you. ¹⁵Practice these things, immerse yourself in them, so that all may see your progress. ¹⁶Keep a close watch on yourself and on the teaching. Persist in this, for by so doing you will save both yourself and your hearers.	¹¹These things command and teach. ¹²Let no man despise thy youth; but be thou an example of the believers, in word, in conversation, in charity, in spirit, in faith, in purity. ¹³Till I come, give attendance to reading, to exhortation, to doctrine. ¹⁴Neglect not the gift that is in thee, which was given thee by prophecy, with the laying on of the hands of the presbytery. ¹⁵Meditate upon these things; give thyself wholly to them; that thy profiting may appear to all. ¹⁶Take heed unto thyself, and unto the doctrine; continue in them: for in doing this thou shalt both save thyself, and them that hear thee.

4:11 *these things.* As the apostle Paul's personal representative to the churches of Ephesus, Timothy is to command the things Paul has just said in vv. 6–10. The Greek word translated as *command* refers to the process of pounding something so that it stays in place. Timothy was to order, to drive these truths home to his hearers with all authority.

4:12 *youth.* In Jewish tradition at the time of the Early Church, anyone under the age of 40 was considered a youth. Paul's use of this term is not so much in regard to Timothy's age, but in regard to the office of overseer he held as Paul's authoritative representative. Because the voice of authority in the Jewish culture of this time resided in the more elderly men, listeners might despise, think little of, and reject Timothy's teaching and authority because of his "youth." *example.* By governing himself according to godliness according to the "words of faith" and "sound doctrine," Timothy's conduct testifies to his spiritual maturity. This would affirm both himself and the authority of his office of overseer/pastor. While it might not silence those devoted to the teachings of demons (cf. 4:1), it would deny them any grounds to accuse Timothy of hypocrisy, by which they might justify rejecting him or the authority of his office.

4:13 This is a shorthand version of what Paul describes to the Colossians as the ministry of overseers (Col 1:24–28). Here, Paul sets down three primary responsibilities of the Office of the Public Ministry. The call to be devoted to these things was not merely a personal exhortation. Timothy, serving in Paul's stead to the congregations of Ephesus, was to devote himself to making sure that, above all else, the ministry of the pastors and congregations was devoted to the public reading of Scripture, to exhortation, and to teaching God's Word. Cranmer wrote: "Resist with the Scriptures, when any man disputes. . . . [E]stablish a godly and a perfect unity and concord out of the Scripture" (2:17). *public reading.* This refers to reading of the Scriptures, the Old Testament, and those books which became the New Testament, as they came available. While this follows the fact that the Church rises and rests on the Word of God, the public reading and exposition of Scripture is the best way to refute those preaching themselves, genealogies, myths, and the like (cf. 1:4). This was not a new concept. The public reading of Scripture and exposition in the worship was the central part of Jewish synagogue worship (cf. Lk 4:16–21). *exhortation.* This is best understood as the teaching or sermon that would follow and be based upon the Scriptures that were read. Because it was an exhortation, it would include both the articulation and application of the Law (admonishment) and the Gospel (grace and encouragement) to their hearers. While this took place in the public worship service, this same pattern is followed in both public teaching and in the individual/personal application of the Word.

4:14 *gift.* In the Greek, the term is *charisma.* The gift itself is understood as prophecy, the ability to understand the true Gospel against the various and false teachers, and the ability to faithfully apply it to the lives of his hearers. This gift, or capacity to do this, was first and foremost the result of the Holy Spirit who had enlightened Timothy with His gifts. Whether Timothy was given something beyond his natural ability or used his natural ability is not the issue; either possibility would be sanctified and put to use by the Holy Spirit (v. 13) for the sake of the Church. *given you by prophecy.* Timothy's gift of understanding the Gospel and speaking it faithfully and contextually came from Paul's expounding of the Old Testament prophesies about the Christ. *council of elders.* These were fellow pastors in the region of Lystra who had examined Timothy, and finding him qualified for the Office of the Public Ministry, first placed him into the pastoral office. *laid their hands on you.* This is the visible sign to the congregation, by the elders or an overseer, which identified the man whom the Lord, through the Church, had chosen to serve as their pastor. This is a symbolical acknowledgement of God's will to the congregation, so as to establish the authority of the pastor in all things pertaining to the Word of God and doctrine. This apostolic practice continues today as pastors are trained, examined, ordained, and installed into their office by fellow pastors.

4:15 *these things.* Paul is referring to what he has just told Timothy and every pastor in vv. 6–14. Wesley revealed his ardor and a corresponding lack of interest in time-intensive hobbies when he wrote:

> True meditation is no other than faith, hope, love, joy, melted down together, as it were, by the fire of God's Holy Spirit: and offered up to God in secret. He that is wholly in these, will be little in worldly company, in other studies, in collecting books, medals, or butterflies; wherein many pastors drone away so considerable a part of their lives! (544)

In commenting on 5:12, he wrote in surprising fashion about "a holy resolution to walk in the highest degree of Christian severity." *progress.* Because Timothy traveled with Paul, the Ephesian congregations were acquainted with him at a younger age. Since Timothy had learned much from Paul and served as an overseer/pastor in other settings, his ongoing faithfulness to Paul's teaching in this letter would demonstrate to those in these congregations that Timothy had matured greatly in the faith (cf. Php 1:25).

4:16 *close watch.* This refers to the process of self-examination by Timothy, and every pastor, first in light of God's two words of Law and Gospel, then in terms of his divine call in accordance with the full testimony of God's Word. Paul gave this same charge to the Ephesian elders when he called them to him while he was at Miletus (Ac 20:28). The purpose of this close watch was to resist and overcome the various temptations common to all believers and to those particular to the Office of the Public Ministry (cf. Gal 6:1). *save both yourself and your hearers.* While it is God alone who saves, He is a God who saves through means (2:4). The personal faith, through which a person receives God's saving grace in Jesus Christ, comes from hearing the Word of Christ (Rm 10:17). The pastor is equal in his absolute need of God's saving Word, to those to whom he preaches and teaches that same Word. Thus, by faithfully applying God's Law and Gospel to himself according to the Word, his faith will be strengthened, and he will be better able to preach and teach that same saving Word to his hearers. Cf. 1Co 9:22; Jas 5:20; Jude 23.

4:6–16 in Devotion and Prayer Paul further prepares Timothy for the challenges he will face as an overseer/pastor. The only means Paul, Timothy, and any pastor has to refute the "teachings of demons" is the full testimony of God's Word. The key to any pastor's faithful use of the Word of God in care of His people is the pastor's faithful, day-by-day searching of His Word. It's only through such faithful study of the Word that the pastor's own faith is strengthened, enlightened, and encouraged in the care of God's people. In this way, the pastor will also be strengthened and enabled in Christ to stand firm on the Word of God against all errors from within the Church, or from without, in the culture and the world, and for the sake of those he serves. • Blessed Lord of the Church, bless us with faithful pastors who faithfully search Your Word in the fullness of its truth, so that they might faithfully teach and preach it for the sake of both the saved and the lost. Amen.

PART 4

EXHORTATION TO CHRISTIAN LIVING (CHS. 5–6)

Positions in the Church (5:1–6:2)

The shepherd (pastor) and various classes of sheep (Christians) (5:1–2)

ESV	KJV
5 ¹Do not rebuke an older man but encourage him as you would a father, younger men as brothers, ²older women as mothers, younger women as sisters, in all purity.	5 ¹Rebuke not an elder, but intreat him as a father; and the younger men as brethren; ²The elder women as mothers; the younger as sisters, with all purity.

Introduction to 5:1–6:2 Having given Timothy instruction and rules in regard to his personal conduct as an overseer/pastor, Paul now lays out how Timothy as a pastor, and as Paul's representative, is to handle certain cases and kinds of members in the Church. Thus, Timothy was to make sure that these rules were observed in all the congregations of Ephesus. Regarding Paul's method of instruction, Ambrose notes, "The first exercise in training the soul is to turn away sin, the second to implant virtue" (*NPNF2* 10:393).

5:1–2 *rebuke.* The Greek term refers to assaulting or striking with blows. Paul uses it metaphorically in the sense of verbally assaulting an older man so as humiliate him into submission. The only reason for rebuking someone is that something they are saying or doing is contrary to the will of God and thus a threat to their salvation and others. Though an older man may be in the wrong, he is to be treated with respect befitting his age (Lv 19:32). *father . . . brothers . . . mothers . . . sisters.* Christ Himself refers to believers as His mothers, brothers, and sisters (Mt 12:46–50). This familiar relationship is created within the Church through Baptism as we are born again in Christ. As such, any correction takes place within the household of God (3:15). When correcting members of Christ's family, Paul uses age and the vocational responsibilities within the context of a family to guide Timothy, and every pastor, in correcting those who have erred. *purity.* This refers not so much to how Timothy, and every pastor, is to deal with younger women, as to the state of these young women in Christ. While purity bespeaks their condition, it also is the goal in all a pastor's dealings with them.

The order of widows (5:3–16)

ESV	KJV

[3]Honor widows who are truly widows. [4]But if a widow has children or grandchildren, let them first learn to show godliness to their own household and to make some return to their parents, for this is pleasing in the sight of God. [5]She who is truly a widow, left all alone, has set her hope on God and continues in supplications and prayers night and day, [6]but she who is self-indulgent is dead even while she lives. [7]Command these things as well, so that they may be without reproach. [8]But if anyone does not provide for his relatives, and especially for members of his household, he has denied the faith and is worse than an unbeliever.

[9]Let a widow be enrolled if she is not less than sixty years of age, having been the wife of one husband, [10]and having a reputation for good works: if she has brought up children, has shown hospitality, has washed the feet of the saints, has cared for the afflicted, and has devoted herself to every good work. [11]But refuse to enroll younger widows, for when

[3]Honour widows that are widows indeed.
[4]But if any widow have children or nephews, let them learn first to shew piety at home, and to requite their parents: for that is good and acceptable before God.
[5]Now she that is a widow indeed, and desolate, trusteth in God, and continueth in supplications and prayers night and day.
[6]But she that liveth in pleasure is dead while she liveth.
[7]And these things give in charge, that they may be blameless.
[8]But if any provide not for his own, and specially for those of his own house, he hath denied the faith, and is worse than an infidel.
[9]Let not a widow be taken into the number under threescore years old, having been the wife of one man.
[10]Well reported of for good works; if she have brought up children, if she have lodged strangers, if she have washed the saints' feet, if she have relieved the afflicted, if she have diligently followed every good work.

their passions draw them away from Christ, they desire to marry [12]and so incur condemnation for having abandoned their former faith. [13]Besides that, they learn to be idlers, going about from house to house, and not only idlers, but also gossips and busybodies, saying what they should not. [14]So I would have younger widows marry, bear children, manage their households, and give the adversary no occasion for slander. [15]For some have already strayed after Satan. [16]If any believing woman has relatives who are widows, let her care for them. Let the church not be burdened, so that it may care for those who are truly widows.

[11]But the younger widows refuse: for when they have begun to wax wanton against Christ, they will marry;
[12]Having damnation, because they have cast off their first faith.
[13]And withal they learn to be idle, wandering about from house to house; and not only idle, but tattlers also and busybodies, speaking things which they ought not.
[14]I will therefore that the younger women marry, bear children, guide the house, give none occasion to the adversary to speak reproachfully.
[15]For some are already turned aside after Satan.
[16]If any man or woman that believeth have widows, let them relieve them, and let not the church be charged; that it may relieve them that are widows indeed.

5:3 *Honor.* This word is often understood in abstract concepts. Here, it is a concrete idea, meaning to literally "give preference to." Following Jesus' understanding of honor as including respect and material provision (Mt 15:4–6), widows who are qualified, according to what Paul goes on to say, are to be honored according to their spiritual and physical needs. Paul also uses this same word when quoting the Fourth Commandment (Ex 20:12) in his letter to the very people Timothy is serving as overseer/pastor (Eph 6:2). *truly widows.* These are those women who, upon the death of their husbands, are left without any family or financial means to support themselves (v. 5). As such, they qualify for the spiritual and material support of the Church (cf. Ac 6:1–6). To neglect these women would qualify as sin (Jas 4:17). Cf. Ex 22:22–23; Dt 14:29; 24:17; Jb 24:3; Ps 68:5; Pr 15:25.

5:4 *show godliness to their own household.* This refers to living the faith within the context of their earthly family. Having been made members of Christ's family, all believers' first mission and ministry field is their own family. As such, the love of Christ would compel any believing member of her family to provide for her needs. *some return*. This refers to giving back to one's parents or grandparents according to the good their parents gave to them as children. As their parents made provisions for them from birth through adulthood, so they ought to provide for their parents (widows) during their later years as they await death or the second coming of Christ.

5:5 *supplications and prayers night and day*. Paul here describes for Timothy the first and constant course of those believing widows who are destitute of family and financial means. Such a widow could not escape the reality of her lack, yet she believes in Christ, who, though being rich, became poor so that she might be made rich. Though she lacks earthly means, she knows that in Christ she is well provisioned. Such true humility in helplessness calls forth from other believers the very nature of Christ, and her needs are met.

5:6 *dead*. While still referring to widows, Paul now addresses a different kind of widow who lives to serve herself according to her own selfish ideas and desires. Though she is physically alive, she has made herself spiritually dead in her lifetime through her life's choices that cut her off from Christ. Even though these widows participate in church worship and feasts, they are referred to as "twice dead" (Jude 1:12).

5:8 *does not provide*. The physical, financial, and material support needed to sustain their family. *household*. This term was used to refer to everyone dwelling in the house. Thus a believer is to provide for the physical, financial, and material necessity of all those who live with them, be they family or servants. *denied the faith and is worse than an unbeliever*. This does not mean that the individual has no personal faith, but such a person has denied "the faith." Through the Gospel, Christ has saved us and set us free as new creations to love as He has loved us. Such a person may yet have some personal faith, but, by his or her actions, have spurned this freedom and the expression of faith's working through love (Gal 5:6). What makes this person worse than an unbeliever is that even unbelievers, as a rule, take care of their families. Cf. Lk 6:32; Rm 2:14. To persist in not providing for one's family is a rejection of the will of God, and therefore a hardening of the heart. When this takes place, personal faith is in grave danger.

5:9–10 *enrolled*. For a person to enroll in an educational class, that person must first register for the course. No widow could receive ongoing material and financial support from the church unless they were registered with the church according to the qualifications listed here (vv. 9–15). *sixty years of age.* Any reason for this particular age can only be inferred by the fact that at this age or older, such a woman would probably not be sought out for remarriage. This arose from the relatively short life span of people during this time period. At this age, such a woman, without any family or financial assets of her own, would not be able to support herself. *one husband . . . reputation.* Each of the things Paul lists give testimony to their faith in Christ working itself out in love and devotion for the sake of others. Such a widow would, in all likelihood, render service in the church and to the community on behalf of the church, and with such a beneficent lifestyle, she would serve as a model to other women in the church.

5:11 *younger widows.* These are those widows under the age of 60 who were still young enough to marry again in that culture. *passions.* This refers to the strong sexual desires that God created within women for men and men for women. The Lord said that woman's desire would be for her husband (Gn 3:16). Such desire is not wrong as long as it is satisfied within the bond of God's gift of marriage. *marry.* These widows would want to marry again to have and serve their own family.

5:12 *faith.* This refers to their personal faith in Jesus Christ as their Lord and Savior. Paul addresses a First Commandment issue. The desires of these widows could become so great that they would come to believe that having a husband was their greatest good, and be willing to marry an unbeliever and join him in his pagan beliefs and practices in order to get him (v. 15). The reason for this interpretation is based on the fact that getting married is not a sin. A widow getting married cannot bring condemnation; only unbelief can bring that. Though a widow may have pledged herself in service to the church, that pledge must yield to the vocation of wife. For in creation, the Lord established a woman's earthly vocation of wife first before all others and called it good.

5:13 *idlers . . . gossips . . . busybodies.* If these younger widows were enrolled so as to receive the support of the church, their lives would not be busied with trying to support themselves. With this free time/idleness, they would face great temptations to cast off spiritual restraint and busy themselves with the affairs of others rather than caring for their needs. Such sinful busyness served no one's welfare, least of all the one caught up in it; it only serves to create division within the Body of Christ.

5:14 *the adversary.* An "adversary" refers to one who is set against us in a battle or conflict. The definite article "the" serves to single out one "adversary," which can and likely does refer to Satan, who is mentioned in the next verse. This title also refers to any number of his agents who, with lies and distortions, perpetually attack the Church and all her members.

5:15 *strayed after Satan.* Literally "turned away after Satan." As a positive statement, this means that these have unrepentantly adopted ungodly lifestyles that follow the rebellious ways of Satan against Christ. No one can reject Christ, His ways, and His Word and not be following Satan. There is nothing in what Paul says here to indicate that such a person following Satan is ever aware of it. Such individuals, beguiled by the lies of Satan, in all likelihood believe to still be followers of Christ. Paul speaks of such a person in v. 6 as "dead even while living." While Paul is referring to some widows who had strayed after Satan, he began this letter identifying two men who were doing the same thing (1:20). Here, Paul explains the reason for the rules laid out. As much as these are for the sake of the Church, they are also for the sake of these women and their eternal salvation.

5:16 *believing woman.* Any woman who believes in the Lord Jesus Christ, whether she be widowed or still married. As women supervised the domestic care within their homes, Paul addresses them with their Christian responsibility to extend this care to any and all widows found within their family. These widows may or may not be believers; each one is a mission opportunity for the women to let their faith work through love (Gal 5:6) as a witness to the love of Christ for all. *care . . . burdened.* A widow who had family that could take care of her did not qualify as a widow that could be enrolled for support by the church. A believing woman would own her responsibility toward a widow within her family. When she takes up the burden of caring for a widow personally, it automatically eases the collective burden the church faces in caring for those who have no family.

Pastor Timothy and other pastors (5:17–25)

ESV	KJV
¹⁷Let the elders who rule well be considered worthy of double honor, especially those who labor in preaching and teaching. ¹⁸For the Scripture says, "You shall not muzzle an ox when it treads out the grain," and, "The laborer deserves his wages." ¹⁹Do not admit a charge against an elder except on the evidence of two or three witnesses. ²⁰As for those who persist in sin, rebuke them in the presence of all, so that the rest may stand in fear. ²¹In the presence of God and of Christ Jesus and of the elect angels I charge you to keep these rules without prejudging, doing nothing from partiality. ²²Do not be hasty in the laying on of hands, nor take part in the sins of others; keep yourself pure. ²³(No longer drink only water, but use a little wine for the sake of your stomach and your frequent ailments.) ²⁴The sins of some men are conspicuous, going before them to judgment, but the sins of others appear later. ²⁵So also good works are conspicuous, and even those that are not cannot remain hidden.	¹⁷Let the elders that rule well be counted worthy of double honour, especially they who labour in the word and doctrine. ¹⁸For the scripture saith, thou shalt not muzzle the ox that treadeth out the corn. And, The labourer is worthy of his reward. ¹⁹Against an elder receive not an accusation, but before two or three witnesses. ²⁰Them that sin rebuke before all, that others also may fear. ²¹I charge thee before God, and the Lord Jesus Christ, and the elect angels, that thou observe these things without preferring one before another, doing nothing by partiality. ²²Lay hands suddenly on no man, neither be partaker of other men's sins: keep thyself pure. ²³Drink no longer water, but use a little wine for thy stomach's sake and thine often infirmities. ²⁴Some men's sins are open beforehand, going before to judgment; and some men they follow after. ²⁵Likewise also the good works of some are manifest beforehand; and they that are otherwise cannot be hid.

5:17 *elders*. This refers to the overseers/pastors (3:1–7) in the various congregations in Ephesus. *rule well*. This is describing the pastoral responsibility of presiding over all matters regarding the Word of God and doctrine. The authority to do so is unique to the Office of the Public Ministry according to Christ, who instituted it. Cf. 4:13–14; 1Th 5:12; 1Co 12:28; Jn 20:23. *double honor*. As before, to "honor" is to give preference. To give double honor means to give a greater measure of preference. While the reasons for this greater honor are many, there are two that are foundational. First, the fact that these men were chosen by God through the Church, to fill the office Christ created for their sake as the Church, is essential to why they are worthy of double honor. They serve in an honorable office for the sake of the Church. Second, the fact that they are not merely teaching and preaching, but teaching and preaching the Word of God according to the needs of the saints for the sake of their salvation, makes them worthy of greater honor. The pastor has to be ever learning the Word of God and learning about the people he serves so that he is able to speak God's Word faithfully to them. This may be a call to repent, a word of forgiveness, comfort, exhortation, and the like. Such service is worthy of honor and support, as Paul goes on to state in the next verse (v. 18). *preaching and teaching.* This is the faithful application of God's two words of Law and Gospel to the lives of their hearers in worship, Bible study, or individual study. Pastors apply God's Word to both believers within the Church, to strengthen them in the faith, and to unbelievers, not yet a part of the Church, so that hearing the Good News of salvation in Christ, they might be saved. See v. 4:13 "exhortation."

5:18 Having said that pastors are worthy of double honor, Paul eliminates speculation about one of the ways this greater honor is to be expressed to pastors—compensation. He does this by first quoting Dt 25:4, regarding not muzzling the ox, which he also quoted to the Corinthians (1Co 9:7–14), and then by quoting Christ concerning the laborer and the wages he deserves (Lk 10:7; Mt 10:10). While affording the pastor double honor does not mean double compensation, it does include proper compensation. The most faithful rule to follow in terms of compensation is to be found in the words of Christ, "Whatever you wish that others would do to you, do also to them, for this is the Law and the Prophets" (Mt 7:12). As members would have their employers compensate them for their labor, so they, as believers in Christ, ought to compensate the pastor and other workers that the Lord has given them.

5:19 *evidence of two or three witnesses.* While this requirement for taking up any charge against a pastor may seem extreme, it was designed to protect pastors from spurious charges that may have been brought maliciously. The basis for requiring the evidence of multiple witnesses was the requirement the Lord set down for the Jews in handling criminal cases (Dt 19:15). This follows the very way the Savior said that we should handle the correction of one who is caught in sin (Mt. 18:16). Paul had the Corinthians follow this same rule in dealing with one another (2Co 13:1).

5:20 *persist in sin.* Aware of the fact that there were pastors who had done wrong, with credible charges of wrongdoing brought by multiple witnesses, Paul addresses how to deal with those who refuse to repent of their wrongdoing. Their lack of repentance was not due to ignorance but to willful persistence in the sin. *rebuke them in the presence of all.* The fact that there are multiple witnesses of the sin means that this sin is public rather than private. Since the accused person refused to listen to those calling him privately to repent, Timothy is to follow the command of Christ, which would bring the matter publicly before the whole church. The pastor's sin and his persistence in it had to be publicly rebuked in the sharpest of terms in this setting for two reasons. The first reason is that he might finally repent and receive Christ's blessed forgiveness and bring about an amending of his life. The second reason is for the sake of the Office of the Public Ministry and the pastors filling it. They must be made aware of the gravity of such sin, and the danger that persistence in it brings, and develop a proper godly fear of committing the same sin. *all.* As a rule, this refers to the members of the congregation. It can on occasion, depending on the situation, also refer to other elders. *fear.* Other pastors hold the same office, bear the same weakness of the flesh, and face the same temptations as the one who is being publicly rebuked. The public rebuking serves to foster a godly fear of succumbing to the same temptation in sin. Such fear is insufficient in and of itself. Such fear must include a right faith in Christ as their Lord and Savior if there is going to be any real check against such sin.

5:21 *presence.* A more literal understanding of this would be "in the sight of." While Paul's words might sound like a stern warning to Timothy, due to the importance of the issue, these words carry great encouragement and consolation to Timothy and every pastor. Paul has set before Timothy some difficult situations and issues that must be dealt with faithfully and impartially. Each of these brings its own baggage of hostility and temptations. What an assuring thing to know that in doing this work, no matter how difficult, it is done in the presence of God, who created Timothy and those he served; of Christ, who had redeemed them for Himself; and of the angels sent from God in service of Timothy and all the saints. *elect angels.* These are the angels that did not join Satan in his rebellion against God (2Pt 2:4; Jude 6). Their faithfulness to God means that they are faithful in service of God to the saints. *these rules.* These are the requirements Paul puts forth in dealing with charges against an elder/pastor in vv. 19–20.

5:22 *hasty in the laying on of hands.* Timothy was to take the greatest care in both selecting men to fill the office and making sure they had proved themselves qualified for the pastoral office (v. 3:10). In this way, it would serve to help prevent immaturity of life and faith leading a pastor into situations that would later require the aforementioned rebuke (v. 20). *pure.* This is understood in light of the words just prior, "nor take part in." To keep himself pure, Timothy would have to set himself apart from the sinful activities, lest he disqualify himself as pastor. Ultimately, purity is found in walking in the light, as Christ is in the light, so that His blood might purify Timothy, pastors, and all believers (1Jn 1:7).

5:23 *use a little wine.* In an attempt to avoid any grounds for a charge of drunkenness against himself, and to serve as an example to other pastors, Timothy had abstained from wine. Somehow, Paul learned of the stomach complications and ailments Timothy was having. He takes a moment to address Timothy personally about his need to drink some wine to medicinally deal with these issues. One of the frequent ailments that occurred to those who only drank water was dysentery from unclean water. Wine served to prevent such issues because it eliminated common problems brought on by bacteria and parasites.

5:24–25 Paul here returns to dealing with men who are considered for the pastoral office. Both the sins and the good works of some people could be readily seen. Paul also addresses the things that cannot be seen because the individual hides them. The evil one hides his sins to obtain that which his sins would deny him. At the same time, the faithful one hides his good works to the glory of God. What Paul assures Timothy is that nothing that is hidden will remain hidden because none of it is hidden to the Lord.

Slaves and their masters (6:1–2)

ESV	KJV
6 ¹Let all who are under a yoke as bondservants regard their own masters as worthy of all honor, so that the name of God and the teaching may not be reviled. ²Those who have believing masters must not be disrespectful on the ground that they are brothers; rather they must serve all the better since those who benefit by their good service are believers and beloved. Teach and urge these things.	6 ¹Let as many servants as are under the yoke count their own masters worthy of all honour, that the name of God and his doctrine be not blasphemed. ²And they that have believing masters, let them not despise them, because they are brethren; but rather do them service, because they are faithful and beloved, partakers of the benefit. These things teach and exhort.

6:1 *yoke as bondservants*. Paul uses the term "yoke," both to acknowledge and to describe the burden of being united to one while also under the control of another. The term for "bondservant" (Gk *doulos*) can also be translated as "slave." It carried a much broader meaning in the first century than the word connotes today. Slavery, in Paul's time, was not directed toward any particular race. There were three common ways in which a person came under the yoke of slavery. The most common was through conquest of war in which prisoners were relocated and sold. The second most common means of coming into slavery was being sold by parents or family to repay debts. The third most common follows the second, where individuals would sell themselves into slavery to pay their own debts. Slaves during this period could be, and often were, entrusted with great responsibilities and with the wealth of their masters (cf. the Book of Philemon). *masters*. Paul uses the Greek word *despotēs* from which we have the word "despot," instead of *kyrios* which means "lord" or "master." While both refer to "one who exercises domination," Paul uses the harsher term to indicate that these masters were likely unbelievers. Any sense of brotherhood among the slaves, and brotherhood of the master and his slaves, as is the case of those baptized into Christ, was seen as a threat to the Roman institution of slavery and suppression of conquered peoples. As such, these masters tended to treat slaves with a much more severe domination. *worthy of all* *honor.* Again Paul identifies someone else who is worthy of honor. In the first two (5:3, 17), it would be hard to dispute that those indicated were worthy of the honor they were to be given. Here, Paul is calling those bearing the yoke to honor—to give preference to—their masters, not according to what made sense to them, but according to faith. Every believer has been set free in Christ. They are not freed from serving, but rather are free to serve and love their neighbor. Being a slave, no matter how oppressive, is a vocation, not merely a status nor a state. Having been baptized into Christ and set free from the power of sin, death, and the devil does not set the believer free from their vocational responsibilities, but makes the doing of them holy (cf. 1Pt 2:18–19). Our Lord tells us to "love your enemies, do good to those who hate you" (Lk 6:27). Many find this puzzling, yet it follows what He has done for us. If we do not love our enemies, that is all they will ever be to us. Likewise for the slaves: if they do not honor their masters, there will be no opportunity for their masters to experience the free love of Christ, and become something more and better to the slave than a master—a brother. Cf. Ex 20:12; Lk 6:27–36.

reviled. Honor and obedience by any believer toward those over us—whether master, employer, teacher, or parent—is a living expression of love as found in our Lord's command to "honor your father and your mother" (Ex 20:12). It is a living expression of our faith in the Christ who lovingly honored His Father and the earthly authorities over Him. He did this on our behalf so that He might set us free in Himself to honor and serve them. This provides opportunities for evangelistic outreach, as one shows others what it means to have Christ as Savior and Lord. To refuse to do this means that Christ's teaching, our faith, and our new life in Christ are all nothing more than an exercise of words, rather than a living of new life, in which our actions follow our words and our words are those of Christ (cf 1Jn 3:18). Disrespect and disobedience by a Christian may well bring harsh treatment from those over us, but that is nothing compared to the harsh treatment they will give the name of Christ in their hearts and their conversations.

6:2 *believing masters . . . brothers.* Even though we are born again through Baptism, our sinful nature still adheres to us. This old nature loves to assume beyond what is given and move to conclusions beyond what is said. There would be a great temptation for a slave to believe that because their master was a believer, the slave could take greater liberties in serving their master. Being the Christian brother of the master was not an excuse to stop serving. Instead, it actually moves the slave to greater service born of mutual love and service (Phm 16). *they must serve . . . beloved.* If the slave was to honor an unbelieving master (v. 1) how much more the master who believes. Being fellow partakers of the free gift of God's grace in Jesus Christ with their masters, this honor would be returned to them by their believing masters in the mutual concern for the welfare of both (cf. Gal 6:10).

6:2 *Teach and urge.* Paul again reminds Timothy of his responsibility in regard to what Paul has just set forth in vv. 5:9–6:2a. Through the faithful teaching and urging or exhortation of these things, with those who preceded them, Timothy and every pastor serves to establish the ethical teachings of the Church in such matters. Cf. 5:7; 2Tm 2:14; Ti 2:15.

5:1–6:2 in Devotion and Prayer "Live as people who are free, not using your freedom as a cover-up for evil, but living as servants of God. Honor everyone" (1Pt 2:16–17a). These words of Peter echo what Paul is telling Timothy. Christians are free in Christ Jesus and are called to use their freedom in Christ-centered ways as they testify to the Gospel. Using this freedom for self-serving ends, at the expense of one's neighbor, the Church, or those who are over us in various relationships demonstrates a critical misunderstanding. It is, in fact, to be turned away from Christ and the new life He has given. Nothing in such selfish actions builds up the Church. In fact, such "self above all else" living empties the names "Christian" and "Christ" of any real meaning in the eyes of the world. Christ put Himself beneath and below all others that, honoring His Father, He could honor us with His sacrificial and saving service. Even now He honors us, interceding at the right hand of God (Rm 8:34). Through faith in Him, we have been exalted above all things, so that we can freely humble ourselves before all others in works of service and witness to the love Christ has for us and for all. • Blessed Lord, work in us by Your Holy Spirit so that all our works begun, continued, and concluded through faith in You might bring honor to those around us, and to You through Jesus Christ, our Lord, who honors us with His love. Amen.

True Godliness (6:3–21)

The importance of sound teaching (6:3–5)

ESV	KJV
³If anyone teaches a different doctrine and does not agree with the sound words of our Lord Jesus Christ and the teaching that accords with godliness, ⁴he is puffed up with conceit and understands nothing. He has an unhealthy craving for controversy and for quarrels about words, which produce envy, dissension, slander, evil suspicions, ⁵and constant friction among people who are depraved in mind and deprived of the truth, imagining that godliness is a means of gain.	³If any man teach otherwise, and consent not to wholesome words, even the words of our Lord Jesus Christ, and to the doctrine which is according to godliness; ⁴He is proud, knowing nothing, but doting about questions and strifes of words, whereof cometh envy, strife, railings, evil surmisings, ⁵Perverse disputings of men of corrupt minds, and destitute of the truth, supposing that gain is godliness: from such withdraw thyself.

6:3 *sound words.* The Greek term for "sound" is *hygiainō*, which means "whole, healthy." (It underlies our English word, "hygene.") Paul expressly has Timothy stay in Ephesus to deal with those who were teaching unsound, unhealthy words in regard to Christ and our free salvation through faith in Him. These false teachers may well quote and mention Christ, but the words they use deny and undermine Him and His substitutionary life, death, and resurrection for a salvation freely given to all through faith. Lacking the healthy and wholesome Word of Christ, Christ can become little more than a friend, a life coach, an example, or even a despotic master, demanding that you save yourself. Saving faith comes from hearing, and hearing from the whole Word of Christ (Rm 10:17). *accords with godliness.* The consequential goal and effect of teaching the sound words and life of Jesus Christ in a believer.

6:4 *controversy.* This word in the Greek is understood as "questionings." This type of person has a sick love for controversies for two primary reasons. First, they generate disagreement and quarrels. Second, only in this way does such a conceited individual have a chance in such quarreling, which was usually public, to gain possible notoriety and a following. The sad thing is that because it is all born of sin and a desire for self, it also separates and divides what Christ united. See the notes for 1:4.

6:5 *depraved*. This refers to thinking that is disconnected from the whole of God's Word, and therefore is corrupted by sensuality and deceitful desires that are self-serving. Paul addressed this same issue in his letter to the very people Timothy is to teach and admonish in these matters (Eph 4:19–22). *means of gain*. Rather than a lifestyle that flowed from having gained everything in Christ, such depraved individuals saw the practice of godliness as a way to obtain the financial and material things the world calls gain.

Contentment as a way of life (6:6–10)

ESV	KJV
6But godliness with contentment is great gain, 7for we brought nothing into the world, and we cannot take anything out of the world. 8But if we have food and clothing, with these we will be content. 9But those who desire to be rich fall into temptation, into a snare, into many senseless and harmful desires that plunge people into ruin and destruction. 10For the love of money is a root of all kinds of evils. It is through this craving that some have wandered away from the faith and pierced themselves with many pangs.	6But godliness with contentment is great gain. 7For we brought nothing into this world, and it is certain we can carry nothing out. 8And having food and raiment let us be therewith content. 9But they that will be rich fall into temptation and a snare, and into many foolish and hurtful lusts, which drown men in destruction and perdition. 10For the love of money is the root of all evil: which while some coveted after, they have erred from the faith, and pierced themselves through with many sorrows.

6:6 *contentment*. This does not refer to some kind of denial of wanting more, but rather a condition of being so satisfied with what one has that there is no desire to look elsewhere for it. This is a result of a faith that trusts in the care of God in Christ for all things physical and earthly. It is a necessary companion to true godliness, if one is to grow and increase in faith and sacrificial works of love and service. Without contentment, godliness will be quickly rejected or abandoned for the pursuit of whatever one believes to be of greater good or benefit to self than that of having and serving our loving God in Jesus Christ. Cf. Ps 37:16; Pr 15:16; 16:8; Php 4:11; Heb 13:5.

6:7 Here Paul reminds Timothy, his hearers, and us of a reality that everyone is bound up in. This truth is often confessed at the committal services of the dead in the words of Job: "Naked I came from my mother's womb, and naked shall I return. The LORD gave, and the LORD has taken away; blessed be the name of the LORD" (Jb 1:21). Such a reality check serves to remind believers that real and everlasting gain, like life, is to be found through faith in Jesus Christ that gives godliness and the contentment to enjoy and grow in both. St. Bernard of Clairvaux wrote, "Cease to pursue those things which it is misery to attain. . . . Will it be more prudent to yield them up for love of Christ than to have them taken away by death?" (*SLSB*, pp. 207–8). Cf. Ecc 5:15.

6:8 *food and clothing.* Paul uses a type of synecdoche in which he speaks of two parts of one larger thing to refer to the whole it. With these two words, Paul is referring to essential necessities for our bodies and life in this world, all of which come from God the Father, who is the "Maker of heaven and earth" (Apostles' Creed). Our Lord Jesus speaks the same way in the Lord's Prayer when He teaches us to use the words "daily bread" (Mt 6:11) to ask for everything we need for this body and life in this world.

6:9 *rich fall into temptation.* Our Lord likens such people to the seed that was sown among the thorns (Mt 13:22). The tense of the verb for "fall" in the Greek indicate an "ongoing falling." The desire to be rich brings with it countless temptations to turn a person to dishonest means of gain and the obtaining of riches. *snare.* This refers to a hidden trap. Many misquote the next verse (v. 10), claiming that "money" is the root of all evil. Money, in and of itself, is neither good nor evil; it is the love of it that causes blindness and allows one to become trapped by the illusion of what it can do for a person. *ruin and destruction.* Used together as Paul does here, these two terms indicate a condition in time and the consequence in eternity. Having ruined their faith and therefore their souls, and possibly their earthly lives, out of their love of money, they will suffer the destruction of soul and life in death throughout eternity.

6:10 *the love of money . . . evils.* This love of money is desiring it for its own sake or for selfish reasons, rather than for the sake of how it could be used in godly ways (e.g., to help the poor, to help one's neighbor, or to further the mission and ministry of the Church). This love is rooted in the sinful heart, and out of this heart it brings all kinds of evil thoughts, words, and actions that are bent away from all that is godly and good and toward self (Mk 7:20–23). While financial resources may be a blessing from God, the love of money turns His gifts into an idol. *wandered.* This refers to a gradual process that happened, and still happens, to lovers of money. No one intends to wander away, but such is what happens when attention and focus are diverted from the right course. While it is likely that none of those who had wandered would ever admit that they had departed from faith in Christ, their devotion and following after whatever teacher, teaching, and practices would help them obtain more money told the truth. The Pharisees were "lovers of money," and this love caused them to scoff at Jesus when He taught that "you cannot serve God and money" (Lk 16:13–14). *pierced themselves.* The Greek term Paul uses for "pierced" is used only here in the New Testament and had limited use in classical Greek. It's a simple verb that was used when referring to preparing a piece of meat to be put on a spit for roasting. As such, it does not simply refer to creating a hole, like the piercing of an ear, but to piercing into something so as to hold it in place. Through their love of money, they had inflicted themselves, their thoughts, their living, and the like with all manner of evil. These evils caused pain and held them captive in this pain.

6:2–10 in Devotion and Prayer Being conceived in sin and born in iniquity (Ps 51:5), our sinful nature is to covetously desire created things. We are equally prone to worship those things that do the most for us and provide us with what we believe to be our greatest good. Money is often seen as that which can do the most for us, and with it in our hands, we can choose the good we would have to be done. Therefore, it is easily loved and worshipped. Paul is warning Timothy, every pastor, and every believer to be on their guard because this sinful nature is still a part of every believer. While every believer is born again in Christ, until the day of death, we each live as a sinner and a saint. Each of these is in constant conflict; the love of money does battle in us against our faith and love of Christ. Christ has given us the victory over this love of money on the cross where He was sold for thirty pieces of silver. Christ has given us eternal riches that can never spoil, fade, or be taken away. Paul reminds us that we came into this world with nothing, and the only thing we can take with us are those things that Christ alone has given us through faith in Him. These are the eternal riches, and they are ours now and in eternity. • Blessed Father, fountain and source of all things good, gracious, and right, preserve us in Christ that we might treasure His true riches, be blessed with contentment, and rightly use all things for the sake of Your kingdom. Amen.

Personal note to Timothy (6:11–16)

ESV	KJV
[11]But as for you, O man of God, flee these things. Pursue righteousness, godliness, faith, love, steadfastness, gentleness. [12]Fight the good fight of the faith. Take hold of the eternal life to which you were called and about which you made the good confession in the presence of many witnesses. [13]I charge you in the presence of God, who gives life to all things, and of Christ Jesus, who in his testimony before Pontius Pilate made the good confession, [14]to keep the commandment unstained and free from reproach until the appearing of our Lord Jesus Christ, [15]which he will display at the proper time—he who is the blessed and only Sovereign, the King of kings and Lord of lords, [16]who alone has immortality, who dwells in unapproachable light, whom no one has ever seen or can see. To him be honor and eternal dominion. Amen.	[11]But thou, O man of God, flee these things; and follow after righteousness, godliness, faith, love, patience, meekness. [12]Fight the good fight of faith, lay hold on eternal life, whereunto thou art also called, and hast professed a good profession before many witnesses. [13]I give thee charge in the sight of God, who quickeneth all things, and before Christ Jesus, who before Pontius Pilate witnessed a good confession; [14]That thou keep this commandment without spot, unrebukable, until the appearing of our Lord Jesus Christ: [15]Which in his times he shall shew, who is the blessed and only Potentate, the King of kings, and Lord of lords; [16]Who only hath immortality, dwelling in the light which no man can approach unto; whom no man hath seen, nor can see: to whom be honour and power everlasting. Amen.

6:11 *man of God.* While this could be said of any believer born of God, Paul uses this title as it was used in the Old Testament to refer to men whom God chose to speak His Word to His people, (i.e., the prophets) (1Sm 2:27). This title simply refers to Timothy as the man that God has called into the Office of the Public Ministry that He created to preach and teach His Word to His people. As such, a pastor is understood as a "servant of the Word." *flee these things.* See vv. 2–10.

6:12 *Fight the good fight.* The image here is better understood as "contend" in the sense of competing in Greek athletic games, rather than "fight" in the sense of a battle scene. Paul is telling Timothy, and every other pastor, to continually contend for the substance of holy Christian faith against all competitors through the full and faithful teaching and preaching of God's Word, which is the sword of the Spirit (Eph 6:17). In this way, the Church herself does not win the victory, but through His Word, we have the victory already won for us, and for all who would believe in Christ. *Take hold of the eternal life.* The only way a victorious Greek athlete could obtain the crown of victory was to receive it. The victor never took the prize in his own hands and put it on his own head, but received it on his head by the hand of another. The same is true when it comes to the prize of eternal life. Paul is telling Timothy and every believer to be always receiving the free gift of eternal life through faith. Confessing this faith and contending for this faith are the results of having already received (believed) it. We do not contend for the faith in order to obtain it, but we contend for the faith because through it, we have already received the gift of eternal life from the One who has conquered for us, Jesus Christ. *called.* The work of the Holy Spirit through the Word of God that enabled Timothy, as He enables all believers, to hear and believe the glorious message of the Gospel as God's saving Word to and for him. This calling takes place through the Sacrament of Holy Baptism and the proclamation of the Gospel. *good confession.* As this confession is tied to his receiving the gift of eternal life, it refers to Timothy's public confession of faith in Christ according to the Word of God. Paul calls this confession good because it is the work of God the Holy Spirit to the eternal good of all who believe and confess Jesus Christ as Lord (cf. Mt 10:32).

6:13–16 As Paul begins to conclude his letter, the Holy Spirit has Paul remind Timothy that his calling and charge are from God, and are to be carried out according to the work and purposes of God the Father and God the Son.

6:13 *charge.* See exposition of 5:21. *God, who gives life.* Paul here names God and then identifies what God does. A better rendering of the Greek would be "God, who generates and sustains/preserves life." All of life and its continuance is solely the gracious work of God for the sake of the life He creates. Follow the sequence of His creating work in Genesis 1–2; everything He does, He does for the sake of what He is about to create. Even when Adam and Eve sinned and brought their lives to an end, the God of life steps in to preserve their earthly and eternal lives (Gn 3). Paul testified to this truth before the Areopagus in Athens (Ac 17:25). *testimony before Pontius Pilate.* This refers to what Jesus said as He stood before Pilate for judgment (Mt 27:11; Jn 18:33–37; 19:8–11). Unlike the Gnostics, who confessed a heavenly Christ, too spiritual to appear in human flesh, Paul proclaimed that Christ appeared bodily before a Roman governor. *good confession.* See notes on 3:16. What we believe, and confess that we believe, is the substance of what Jesus confessed, or bore witness to, before Pilate. Cf. Rv 1:5; 3:14.

6:14 *command.* This refers not to the Gospel but to the command given the apostles, and therefore the Church, to go and make disciples of all nations, baptizing them in the name of the Father and of the Son and of the Holy Spirit, teaching them to observe everything Christ has commanded them (Mt 28:19–20). *appearing of our Lord Jesus Christ.* This command is to be observed by the Church until the "end of the age" (Mt 28:20). This is when Christ will return visibly and every eye shall see Him, coming on the clouds (Rv 1:7).

6:15 *proper time.* As God, in His divine wisdom and love, chose the exact time for the coming of His Son in the flesh, as well as the hour of His crucifixion and resurrection, He will also choose the proper time for Christ's return (cf. Gal 4:4). *Sovereign.* While this refers to omnipotence or all powerful/mightiness, it carries with it an absolute freedom and ability to use and work His power when and where He will. This sovereignty is the foundation of the promise of Rm 8:28, that God is at work in all things for good. *King of kings and Lord of lords.* These names are written on the robe and the thigh of Christ at His return to judge (Rv 19:16). These names differentiate the supremacy of Christ from all other kings and lords (Rv 17:14). It could literally be said that He is the "King of those kinging/reigning and Lord of those lording/protecting."

6:16 *immortality.* The literal translation of this is "deathlessness." The only way Christ can have the attribute of deathlessness is if He has life in Himself (Jn 5:26). St. Ambrose wrote, "How could He not have immortality Who has life in Himself? He has it in His nature" (*NPNF2* 10:288). Christ shares His immortality with humanity through the Gospel (2Tm 1:10). Calvin wrote:

> The meaning is the same as if Paul had said, that God alone not only is immortal from himself and from his own nature, but has immortality in his power; so that it does not belong to creatures, except so far as he imparts to them power and vigour; for if you take away the power of God which is communicated to the soul of man, it will instantly fade away. (168)

dwells in unapproachable light. To grasp this, we need to first begin by understanding what Paul refers to by the term "light." This light is God (1Jn 1:7); it is therefore uncreated, eternal, and without any darkness. Some understand this in terms of God's glory. The psalmist tells us that God covers Himself with light like a garment (Ps 104:2), which means that God has chosen to dwell hidden in this light, making it impossible for anyone to approach Him. Yet as God is love (1Jn 4:8), He approaches creation and humanity through His Word, the Word He made flesh that dwelt among us (Jn 1:14). That Word is the light of the world—Jesus Christ (Jn 8:12). In the Nicene Creed, Christians confess that Jesus is "Light of Light," which means "Light out of Light." *no one has ever seen or can see.* Prior to the fall, we know that God spoke with Adam and Eve and walked in the Garden with them (Gn 2–3). There is nothing in Scripture that says whether they actually saw Him. After the fall, sinful humanity has not and cannot see God and live (Ex 33:19–23; Jn 1:18). We are blessed to see God in and through His Son (Jn 14:6, 9). *eternal dominion.* Paul here ascribes power to Christ, not just power that is everlasting, like it is merely a possession, but power that is being exercised forever (cf. Col 1:15–22).

A word to the wealthy (6:17–19)

ESV	KJV
[17]As for the rich in this present age, charge them not to be haughty, nor to set their hopes on the uncertainty of riches, but on God, who richly provides us with everything to enjoy. [18]They are to do good, to be rich in good works, to be generous and ready to share, [19]thus storing up treasure for themselves as a good foundation for the future, so that they may take hold of that which is truly life.	[17]Charge them that are rich in this world, that they be not highminded, nor trust in uncertain riches, but in the living God, who giveth us richly all things to enjoy; [18]That they do good, that they be rich in good works, ready to distribute, willing to communicate; [19]Laying up in store for themselves a good foundation against the time to come, that they may lay hold on eternal life.

6:17 *rich*. The fact Paul uses this title in context of the "present age" helps us understand he is speaking of those who have or shall acquire earthly wealth or possessions by honest means or inheritance. There is nothing wrong with having wealth. The issue for Paul is whether those who have it set their hopes on it or let it define them as better than those who are poor. Cf. Rm 12:3, 16. *present age*. A reference to time and everything found in time since the fall into sin. The present age speaks of the now; it denotes the age in which all things, like time, are passing away and will end. Any riches in this age are bound to the same curse and shall pass away, making them uncertain. *enjoy*. The Lord affirms over and over again that every good thing we have has been provided by God (Ps. 37:25; 145:15, 16; Ac 14:17; Jas 1:17). These He has provided for our use to enjoy the blessings of them with gratitude. He does not provide these things so that we may set our hopes on them or trust in them, for they are like the age passing away. Our sinful nature, which is hostile to God (Rm 8:7), would always work in us the worship and serving of what has been created and provided by God, rather than God the Creator and provider (Rm 1:25).

6:18 *rich in good works*. Good works neither earn nor maintain our salvation. They are the result of God's grace saving us through faith, for we have been born again in Christ to do good works God prepared beforehand (Eph 2:8–10). As such, good works are those responsibilities God has given believers to do in our various vocations or callings in life (i.e., father, mother, sister, brother, employee, employer, church member, neighbor, etc.). The fact that the Lord has chosen a person to be rich means that He has given him or her greater responsibility and opportunities to serve (do good works) by using these riches for the good and benefit of others, especially those in the Church (Gal 6:10). Cf. Ti 3:8, 14.

6:19 *storing up treasure.* The only treasure that will be there in the future is that which belongs to Christ. Through good works, the rich and the poor alike serve to bless those who belong to Christ, a family that will forever be true, forever be united and undivided, forever living for the blessing and benefit of one another. The striking thing is that those who do such good works of faith have no mind of what these will bring to them. The believer never considers good works as an investment for the sake of self; such is the way of the Law and the world. No, the believer born of God's grace considers all works in terms of mercy and charity for the sake of the one for whom they are done. Jesus reveals this when He speaks of the sheep who had done the slightest of things to others, totally unaware that they had done them to Christ Himself (Mt 25:34–40). Such works are truly treasured by the Lord Jesus. *take hold.* As before in v. 12, we lay hold of the life in Christ by receiving; we testify to the fact that we have received it (taken hold of it) as we respond verbally in confession of faith and physically by works of love and mercy.

A heartfelt farewell (6:20–21)

ESV	KJV
²⁰O Timothy, guard the deposit entrusted to you. Avoid the irreverent babble and contradictions of what is falsely called "knowledge," ²¹for by professing it some have swerved from the faith. Grace be with you.	²⁰O Timothy, keep that which is committed to thy trust, avoiding profane and vain babblings, and oppositions of science falsely so called: ²¹Which some professing have erred concerning the faith. Grace be with thee. Amen.

6:20 *guard the deposit.* The "deposit" is the same substance of "the faith" (1:2; 3:9, 13; 4:1, 6; 5:8; 6:10), and the "good confession" (v.

12)—the Gospel of salvation in Jesus Christ. The imagery of guarding this deposit likely tends to evoke, to a modern reader, the idea of a bank deposit safely locked away and guarded. But this interpretation runs contrary to how this deposit, how the Gospel, is guarded. The only way to "guard" or "protect" the Gospel is to proclaim it fully, faithfully, and without apology. The Gospel is Jesus Christ. He has met all attackers and detractors and has come out the victor. The Gospel is the power of God unto salvation, the only way to guard it, believe it, confess it, teach it, preach it, and share it faithfully in all its saving fullness. *irreverent babble and contradictions.* Paul began this letter telling Timothy to charge certain people to stop teaching myths, genealogies, and the like that promoted contradiction and speculation (1:3–4). Now he concludes the letter, telling Timothy not to get caught up in what they are saying by debate and the like; to do so would be to lend credence to their irreverence. The refutation of their babble comes from the fact that they contradict themselves, and this becomes evident to all. Cf. 1:6–7; 6:3–5. *knowledge.* This is used to refer to the sum of what someone has come to know. The means by which people come to know is through observation and speculation, based upon what has been observed and upon the fragments of God's Law still written on their hearts. What makes this knowledge false is that it lacks the knowing and knowledge of creation and mankind according to God's revelation through His Word in Jesus Christ. As such, this false knowledge will fall on itself (i.e., create its own contradictions as experiences change). When this happens, those who trust in this false knowledge move more and more into the realm of abstract and divorce the real from the spiritual. This is the heart of what became Gnosticism. Those who claim such "knowledge" remind me of know-it-alls. Such people will never claim that they know it all, but they do believe that all they do know is all there is to be known, and the babbling and contradictions begin.

6:21 *swerved from the faith.* Paul states the real consequences of trusting in these false teachers and their equally false knowledge. When a believer begins to trust in any kind of false knowledge, no matter how profound it may sound or seem, they have left the revealed knowledge God has given through His Word in Jesus Christ—which is the Gospel. Having left the Gospel, their salvation is in serious jeopardy. *Grace.* In short, "the favor of God." This word refers to God's merciful attitude toward undeserving people (Rm 5:12–21;

Ti 3:3–7), God's undeserved saving work in Jesus Christ for sinful humanity and His gift of the Holy Spirit who calls, enlightens, and keeps us in the true faith. *you.* In the Greek, this is plural and would be heard as "you all." While this letter was addressed to Timothy, the plural blessing indicates that Paul meant Timothy to share this letter with fellow pastors and believers in the various congregations in Ephesus.

6:11–21 in Devotion and Prayer Timothy must be centered on guarding the deposit entrusted to him as one whom God has called into the Office of the Public Ministry. The only way he and every pastor can guard it is to know this deposit, which is the Gospel, to preach and teach it, and to be guided by it alone in exercising the responsibilities of his office. As in the first century, so today we are awash in a sea of so-called (false) knowledge that is filled with its own contradictions. Every pastor, and believer for that matter, must be on their guard against such empty knowledge lest they wander away from the faith and their congregations with them. Thanks be to God, for He has brought us the knowledge of ourselves and our salvation in Jesus Christ. • Lord God, we give You thanks that You still preserve the Gospel to us in these latter days and call men to preach and teach it to us so that we might be saved and share in Your kingdom. Guard and keep every pastor in the one true faith and bless their teaching and preaching for the blessing of Your Church and those who do not yet know you through Jesus Christ, our Lord. Amen.

2 TIMOTHY

INTRODUCTION TO
2 TIMOTHY

Overview

Author

Paul the apostle

Date

AD 68

Places

Ephesus; Thessalonica; Galatia; Troas; Corinth; Miletus

People

Paul; Timothy; Lois; Eunice; Hymenaeus; Philetus; Paul's numerous co-workers

Purpose

To build up Timothy for service in the face of persecution and to appeal for him to visit Paul at Rome

Law and Sin Themes

Judgment Day; suffering for the Gospel; charges and commands

Grace and Gospel Themes

The appearing of our Savior; sound words of the Gospel; the gift of the Spirit; the good deposit; rescue

Memory Verses

God's purpose and grace (1:8–9); the value of Sacred Scripture (3:16–17)

Reading 2 Timothy

Seawater sprays over the ship's bow as it cuts through the Troas harbor on its way toward Corinth. Wobbly tourists grip their bellies, made sick by the September pitch of the Aegean Sea at the close of the sailing season. Travel-hardy merchants chuckle at the tourists. They slurp wine as a precaution against the illnesses that follow the trade routes. "We shall make Rome in a week," they declare, "if the weather holds."

The most famous traveler of the first century, the apostle Paul, was not on that ship, but lay in a Roman prison. He wrote this letter to request Timothy's comfort and companionship. Timothy had been guiding the congregation at Ephesus, but Paul sent a replacement (4:12) so Timothy, his son in the faith, could travel to him. This is Paul's last known letter, written with special emphasis on faithfully teaching the Word in opposition to false teachers and to rising imperial persecution.

Luther on 2 Timothy

This epistle is a farewell letter, in which St. Paul exhorts Timothy to go on propagating the Gospel, even as he has begun. This is quite necessary, since there are many who fall away; and false spirits and teachers keep springing up all around. Therefore it is incumbent upon a bishop always to be alert and to work at the Gospel. But he prophesies especially, in chapters 3 and 4, concerning the perilous time at the end of the world. It is then that a false spiritual life will lead all the world astray, with an outward show, under which every sort of wickedness and wrong will have its fling. Sad to say! we now see this prophecy of St. Paul all too amply fulfilled in our clergy. (LW 35:389)

Gerhard on 2 Timothy

With regard to time, this is the last Epistle of St. Paul. He wrote it to Timothy a few days before his blessed departure . . . from his captivity at Rome.

It consists of four chapters and falls into three parts. In the first, he encourages Timothy to guard the soundness of doctrine with great zeal and not to allow any perils to move him from his confession. In the second, he forewarns him of misleading spirits that already at that time were springing up in the Church. In the third, he explains his own situation to Timothy and asks Timothy to come to him, to bring Mark with him, and to bring some of his own things to him. (E 1.267)

Bengel on 2 Timothy

Paul wished Timothy to come to him in prison without fear, and he was about to deliver up to him before his decease the lamp (torch-light) of the evangelical office, [2Tm 4:5–6]. This epistle is the testament and last words . . . of Paul. It was written long after the first Epistle to Timothy, and yet the tone of both is very much alike. . . . Paul subserves the fulfillment of this promise in the discharge of his office. (Bengel 290)

Calvin on 2 Timothy

It cannot be absolutely ascertained from Luke's history [Acts] at what time the former Epistle [1 Timothy] was written. But I have no doubt that, after that time, Paul had personal communication with Timothy; and it is even possible (if the generally received opinion be believed) that Paul had him for a companion and assistant in many places. Yet it may readily be concluded that he was at Ephesus when this Epistle was written to him; because, towards the close of the Epistle, (2 Tim. iv. 19,) Paul "salutes Priscilla, and Aquila, and Onesiphorus," the last of whom was an Ephesian, and Luke informs us that the other two remained at Ephesus when Paul sailed to Judea, (Acts xviii. 18, 29.)

The chief point on which it turns is to confirm Timothy, both in the faith of the Gospel, and in the pure and constant preaching of it. But yet these exhortations derive no small weight from the consideration of the time when he wrote them. Paul had before his eyes the death which he was prepared to endure for the testimony of the Gospel. All that we read here, therefore, concerning the kingdom of Christ, the hope of eternal life, the Christian warfare, confidence in confessing Christ, and the certainty of doctrine, ought to be viewed by us as written not with ink but with Paul's own blood; for nothing is asserted by him for which he does not offer the pledge of his death; and therefore this Epistle may be regarded as a solemn subscription and ratification of Paul's doctrine.

It is of importance to remember, however, what we stated in the exposition of the former Epistle, that the Apostle did not write it merely for the sake of one man, but that he exhibited, under the person of one man, a general doctrine, which should afterwards be transmitted from one hand to another. (Commentaries, pp. 179–80)

Wesley on 2 Timothy

This epistle was probably wrote by St. Paul during his second confinement at Rome, not long before his martyrdom. It is, as it were, the swan's dying song. But though it was written many years after the former, yet they are both of the same kind, and nearly resemble each other. (Wesley 549)

Challenges for Readers

Paul's Authorship. See p. 6.

Blessings for Readers

In 2 Timothy, the Lord is calling you to cling faithfully to His precious Word. Paul praises the value of that Word most highly in

3:14–17, where he encourages teaching of the Word from childhood onward. In the Word, the Lord will grant you strength. No matter how you serve in the Lord's family, consider how God's Word guides your work and service.

Outline

I. Not Ashamed of the Ministry of the Gospel (ch. 1)
    A. Greeting (1:1–2)
    B. The Family of Faith (1:3–5)
    C. An Unashamed Ministry (1:6–14)
    D. Ashamed versus Unashamed (1:15–18)
II. Charge to Faithful Ministry in Hard Times (2:1–4:5)
    A. Laboring in the Truth (2:1–7)
    B. The Gospel of the Truth (2:8–13)
    C. Laboring for the Truth against Error (2:14–21)
    D. Laboring with the Truth for Those in Error (2:22–26)
    E. Opposition to the Truth (3:1–9)
    F. "Continue in What You Have Learned" (3:10–17)
    G. Final Charge to Timothy (4:1–5)
III. Paul's Farewell (4:6–22)
    A. Paul's Impending Martyrdom (4:6–8)
    B. Final Greetings and Requests (4:9–22)

PART 1

NOT ASHAMED OF THE MINISTRY OF THE GOSPEL (CH. 1)

Greeting (1:1–2)

ESV	KJV
1 ¹Paul, an apostle of Christ Jesus by the will of God according to the promise of the life that is in Christ Jesus, ²To Timothy, my beloved child: Grace, mercy, and peace from God the Father and Christ Jesus our Lord.	*1* ¹Paul, an apostle of Jesus Christ by the will of God, according to the promise of life which is in Christ Jesus, ²To Timothy, my dearly beloved son: Grace, mercy, and peace, from God the Father and Christ Jesus our Lord.

1:1 *an apostle.* Paul begins his second letter asserting his unique authority as one personally called and sent by Christ Himself. Paul writes this letter from prison and fully expects his life will end soon (4:6). As an apostle and with the authority of this office, he further addresses the proper way to exercise the pastoral office in reference to some difficult situation before his death. Everything he says cannot be taken as merely the word of some man, even a good man, but of one chosen by God to speak. *will of God.* Living in a community of would-be spiritual leaders, Paul authenticates his holding and exercising of his leadership in the office of apostle as the work or calling of God, not himself (cf. Ac 9:1–19). As such, what he says has Christ as the author and the fulfiller of it. *promise of the life.* Paul here identifies the purpose of his conversion: Christ calling him to serve as an apostle, his service as an apostle, and even the content of the letter that follows. Everything in it is service to giving the promise (Gospel) of eternal life in Jesus Christ. To have this promise of life in Jesus Christ is to have the life that is Christ's.

1:2 *Timothy, my beloved child.* While having spoken of Timothy as his true child in the first letter (1:2), here Paul speaks of Timothy in more endearing terms. While there is no stated reason for the change, Paul's situation (4:6) could have contributed greatly to his endearing thoughts of Timothy, who had been faithful to Christ and the ministerial charges Paul had given him. Paul is comforted in knowing that if the Lord calls him out of this world, the Lord has called a faithful one to follow after him in the pastoral ministry and the mission of the Church.

1:1–2 in Devotion and Prayer Paul begins this second letter using warm and affectionate words to address Timothy. While Paul's imprisonment and imminent death figure prominently in these words, his situation is further distressed by the fact that he was alone except for Luke. Demas had deserted him, Crescens was in Galatia, Titus was in Dalmatia, and Paul had sent Tychicus to Ephesus (4:10–12). In such a situation, those dearest to us seem all the more dear to us. Yet for all the emotional, physical, and spiritual issues he was dealing with, Paul did not let these interfere with the faithful asserting and exercising of his office and the apostolic instruction he brought. Thanks be to God that our Lord was with Paul, and is with us, as Savior, through such lonely times of faithfulness in service of the Gospel. • "In God, my faithful God, I trust when dark my road; Great woes may overtake me, Yet He will not forsake me. My troubles He can alter; His hand lets nothing falter." Amen (*LSB* 745 v. 1).

The Family of Faith (1:3–5)

ESV	KJV
³I thank God whom I serve, as did my ancestors, with a clear conscience, as I remember you constantly in my prayers night and day. ⁴As I remember your tears, I long to see you, that I may be filled with joy. ⁵I am reminded of your sincere faith, a faith that dwelt first in your grandmother Lois and your mother Eunice and now, I am sure, dwells in you as well.	³I thank God, whom I serve from my forefathers with pure conscience, that without ceasing I have remembrance of thee in my prayers night and day; ⁴Greatly desiring to see thee, being mindful of thy tears, that I may be filled with joy; ⁵When I call to remembrance the unfeigned faith that is in thee, which dwelt first in thy grandmother Lois, and thy mother Eunice; and I am persuaded that in thee also.

1:3 *my ancestors.* Contrary to the claims of other Jews in the region who had long since abandoned the Word of God in the Old Testament and the faith God gives through it, Paul here affirms that his service to God in Jesus Christ is in keeping with the faith of the ancient people of Israel. *clear conscience . . . prayers night and day.* This may seem like a rather arrogant thing for Paul to say. A "clear conscience"? Isn't this the guy who persecuted the Church (Ac 9:1–2), even watched approvingly as others stoned Stephen (Ac 7:54–60)? Yes, it is Paul who used to be called Saul, but he is not the same man. Having been forgiven in Christ, the blood of Christ cleansed him and his conscience of all sin (1Jn 1:7). A clear conscience for Paul, as for any believer, is cleared by God through repentance and faith in Jesus Christ alone. As such, Paul served the Lord and His Church according to Christ's work for him, in him, and through him. While his past might have given him no cause to pray, the mercy and grace of Christ had set him free to pray constantly to the Lord for Timothy and all people. Paul knew that God's reason to listen and to answer his prayers was in Christ alone, and this made him all the more bold to pray.

1:4 *tears.* These were the language of Timothy's heart that no words could express. Timothy's tears bore witness to the struggle within his heart. While these may have flowed at having to part company, they flowed from a pious love and attachment to Paul, who had been such a faithful teacher, preacher, mentor, and bishop to Timothy in the ministry.

1:5 *Lois . . . Eunice.* These women were Timothy's grandmother and mother. The fact that Paul mentions them by name, and that they had taught Timothy the Old Testament Scriptures in his childhood (3:14–15), means that it is likely that Paul knew these women well. Both these names are Greek, not Jewish, which would indicate that both of them, like Timothy, were raised in families that were dominated by Greek culture. Though Timothy's father was a Greek (Ac 16:1), his mother abided in the teachings of the Old Testament faith as set forth by the prophets.

An Unashamed Ministry (1:6–14)

ESV	KJV
⁶For this reason I remind you to fan into flame the gift of God, which is in you through the laying on of my hands, ⁷for God gave us a spirit not of fear but of power and love and self-control.	⁶Wherefore I put thee in remembrance that thou stir up the gift of God, which is in thee by the putting on of my hands.
⁸Therefore do not be ashamed of the testimony about our Lord, nor of me his prisoner, but share in suffering for the Gospel by the power of God, ⁹who saved us and called us to a holy calling, not because of our works but because of his own purpose and grace, which he gave us in Christ Jesus before the ages began, ¹⁰and which now has been manifested through the appearing of our Savior Christ Jesus, who abolished death and brought life and immortality to light through the Gospel, ¹¹for which I was appointed a preacher and apostle and teacher, ¹²which is why I suffer as I do. But I am not ashamed, for I know whom I have believed, and I am convinced that he is able to guard until that Day what has been entrusted to me. ¹³Follow the pattern of the sound words that you have heard from me, in the faith and love that are in Christ Jesus. ¹⁴By the Holy Spirit who dwells within us, guard the good deposit entrusted to you.	⁷For God hath not given us the spirit of fear; but of power, and of love, and of a sound mind.
	⁸Be not thou therefore ashamed of the testimony of our Lord, nor of me his prisoner: but be thou partaker of the afflictions of the gospel according to the power of God;
	⁹Who hath saved us, and called us with an holy calling, not according to our works, but according to his own purpose and grace, which was given us in Christ Jesus before the world began,
	¹⁰But is now made manifest by the appearing of our Saviour Jesus Christ, who hath abolished death, and hath brought life and immortality to light through the gospel:
	¹¹Whereunto I am appointed a preacher, and an apostle, and a teacher of the Gentiles.
	¹²For the which cause I also suffer these things: nevertheless I am not ashamed: for I know whom I have believed, and am persuaded that he is able to keep that which I have committed unto him against that day.
	¹³Hold fast the form of sound words, which thou hast heard of me, in faith and love which is in Christ Jesus.
	¹⁴That good thing which was committed unto thee keep by the Holy Ghost which dwelleth in us.

1:6 *gift of God . . . laying on of my hands.* See exposition of 1 Tm 4:14. Grammatically, Paul is not telling Timothy to start fanning the gift into flame, but to keep fanning the gift. Paul is about to share the news of his approaching departure (4:6). This is something that will surely distress Timothy, especially in light of the fact that his departure was because of persecution that arose against this gift. Paul's words are not a rebuke or correction, but an encouragement to keep the flame from burning lower and flickering in the face of distressing times and situations.

1:7 *a spirit.* The fact that Paul refers to "a" spirit excludes this from referring to the Holy Spirit. This refers to that gift of God that orients and animates a person's life and living. In creating mankind, God oriented and animated their lives with the power of love and self-control. When sin entered the picture, all our lives were reoriented by fear: a fear that weakened love so greatly that it limited love to self and the saving of self above all else. Having been born again in Christ, Timothy, like all the baptized, is reoriented and animated to God's original created order of life with God and our neighbor.

Bengel wrote, and Wesley nearly repeated these words in his own commentary:

> [Power, love, and self-control] operate in us, and animate us to the discharge of our duties towards God, the saints and ourselves. Power [strength] and sober-mindedness are the two extremes, but these in a good sense; love is in the middle, and is the bond, and as it were the check upon both, taking away . . . the two bad extremes, timidity and rashness. (Bengel 4:292)

1:8 *the testimony.* Here, Paul uses a form of shorthand to refer to the full witness to the Lord Jesus Christ as the Scriptures testify of Him, and as Paul and other faithful preachers bear witness to Him from those Scriptures. This word "testimony" is well chosen, for it identifies exactly what a witness gives to a jury. A true witness offers testimony only to what they actually witnessed. A preacher, teacher, or evangelist in service to Christ is to testify to Him, but only according to what they witnessed of Him in His Word. Any testimony offered only from personal experience would be a witness of self and not of Christ. If it is not rooted in the Word of God, it does not bear the Gospel, and it does not bear God's promise that it will work, feed, or build another person's faith. *His prisoner.* Paul was imprisoned in Rome under Nero during his general persecution of Christians. It would have been of particular importance to him to get rid of one of the most prominent and faithful witnesses to Christ. *share in suffering for the gospel.* The term "suffering" has a broad usage and meaning. Paul is more pointed, calling Timothy to be willing to share in, or accept, the same disgrace that Paul was dealing with for being faithful to the Gospel testimony. Paul was not ashamed of this testimony (the Gospel) because "it is the power of God for salvation to everyone who believes" (Rm 1:16), and it is at work in the hearts and lives of all believers (1Th 2:13). Any disgrace the believer faces comes from those who have no grace: from sinful mankind. Our faith is in the God of all grace, who is not ashamed to be called our God (Heb 11:16), and it is He who enabled Paul and us today to suffer whatever may come, and to live by the uninterrupted favor and victory of Christ.

1:9 *who . . . called us to a holy calling.* This refers to the Holy God who saved every person of every time through the life, death, and resurrection of Jesus Christ (objective justification), using His Holy Word spoken to us to give us the holiness of Christ through His gift of faith. This speaking of His Holy Word is not an exercise of omnipotence, but a free giving of divine love, mercy, and grace to all who receive it. It is referred to as a "calling" because prior to hearing these words, we are spiritually dead, and it is through these words that we are made alive in Christ (Eph 2:5). When Jesus raised His friend Lazarus from the dead, He called him from death to life (Jn 11:43). So in speaking the Holy Gospel to us, the Holy Spirit calls us and sanctifies us through faith (subjective justification). This calling is not irresistible; sadly many do reject it—to their own destruction. This holy calling is lived out in the life of each believer in the various vocational callings the Lord has brought to us. *not because of our works.* Here, Paul affirms what is perhaps the most offensive part of the Christian faith to the old Adam within us all. We have no part in our salvation, nor in our being called to receive it through faith. We are passive in our own salvation; it is purely the work of God's love, mercy, and grace (Eph 2:4–5, 8–10). We have no part in it, apart from simply receiving it. We can't even offer an "Amen" to this glorious work of God in Christ without first receiving it, so that we may be made alive to know it for the Good News it is for us. John explains this so well in the beginning of his Gospel account: "To all who did receive Him, who believed in His name, He gave the right to become children of God, who were born, not of blood nor of the will of the flesh nor of the will of man, but of God" (Jn 1:12–13). Cf. Ti 3:4–6. *purpose and grace . . . before the ages.* The motive, means, and accomplishment of our salvation, as well as our calling to salvation, all flow freely from God as a gift according to His nature, which is love (*agapē*; 1Jn 4:8). God's creating of heaven and earth and His creating man in His own image is an expression of Himself and His nature. While mankind's fall into sin changed us and our nature, God, according to His nature, is unchanged. His work of salvation is an expression of His nature that existed before time and sin. Knowing all things, even our fall into sin, God is still true to His nature, choosing not just to create mankind, but according to His love, also choosing to give His Son to save us so that we should all be holy and blameless before Him (Eph 1:3–5). The Lutheran reformers wrote, "Before we existed, yes, even before the foundation of the world was laid—when, of course, we could do nothing good—we were chosen by grace in Christ to salvation, according to God's purpose" (FC SD XI 43).

Knox wrote:

Neither are we called, neither yet saved, by works, much less can we be predestinate for them, or in respect of them. True it is, that God hath prepared good works, that we should walk in them; but alike true it is, that first must the tree be good, before it bring forth good fruit, and good the tree can never be, except the hand of the gardener have planted it. To use herein the plain words of St. Paul, he witnesses that we are elected in Christ, to the end that we should be holy and without blemish. Now seeing that good works spring forth of election, how can any man be so foolish as to affirm that they are the cause of the same? Can the stream of water, flowing from the fountain, be the cause of the original spring? I think no man will so hold or affirm. Even so it is in this matter; for faith and a godly life that [follow after] our vocation, are the fruits proceeding from our election, but are not the causes of the same. (322)

Calvin also wrote:

In the two words "purpose" and "grace" there is a figure of speech . . . as if he had said,—"according to his gracious purpose." . . . He chose to add "grace," that he might more clearly exclude all reference to works. And the very contrast proclaims loudly enough that there is no room for works where the grace of God reigns. (195)

1:10 *appearing*. While this refers to Christ coming into the flesh (incarnation), and becoming the Son of God and the Son of Man, it also refers to the totality of His bodily dwelling and actions among mankind, from His conception through His ascension to the right hand of the Father, as the Christ for the salvation of all mankind. *abolished death*. The Greek word (*katargeō*) might better be translated as "destroy" or "put an end to." Abolish is perhaps not the best word to describe what Christ has done to death since everyone, including Christians, tastes death. Christ gave Himself up to death with all our sins so that, through His death, He might fully atone and put sin to death. Since death lives off of sin, Christ put sin to death, and through His resurrection, death has lost its sting or victory (1Co 15:55–57). This does not prevent believers from tasting death, but it does prevent death from clinging to or having a grip on us, to hold us in it. So death becomes an event in Christ, not a destination or eternal state (cf. Jn 11:25–26).

1:11 *appointed*. See exposition of 1Tm 1:12. Paul asserted that both our salvation and our calling to it through faith in Christ are entirely the work of God. Here, he further asserts that all his service in this faith, be it as a preacher, an apostle, or a teacher, and even his suffering for this service, is also totally the work and appointment of God in Christ Jesus. *preacher . . . apostle . . . teacher*. Paul identifies not so much his titles as his responsibilities according to God's appointment. Each title, though it is a noun, arises from a verb; these were the divine appointed activities that God had given Paul. It is important to note the sequencing of these titles. Notice that "apostle," though it would seem to be the highest office, isn't set first. Paul places it between the two primary tasks of Timothy, and of every pastor: preaching and teaching. This was Paul's way of affirming that in their appointed service to the Lord, and the suffering that may come because of it, he and Timothy were on the same level. Paul doesn't do this as a gesture of self-abasement, but as a confession that, according to the appointment of God, they together were arm in arm in service of the Gospel.

1:12 *why I suffer*. Paul is imprisoned in Rome as a capital criminal, with the likely prospect he will be executed because he was faithfully serving as a preacher, apostle, and teacher of Jesus Christ.

While he describes his imprisonment as suffering, he in no way considers this suffering something to be avoided. Surely, Paul was not "gladly" suffering, but he was definitely okay with it because it afforded him an opportunity to fulfill God's mission of carrying Christ's name before the Gentiles and kings (Ac 9:15). *able to guard . . . entrusted to me.* Paul is referring to the Gospel ministry that had been entrusted to his service by God's calling of him to serve as a preacher, apostle, and teacher (v. 11). Because the Gospel ministry is God's work, Paul knew that it was not his, nor was it dependent upon him. It is God's to guard and perpetuate. Paul knew himself to be a sinner who needed constant rescue (Rm 7:15–25), yet God chose to call such a sinner into His service and entrusted him with the Gospel. As such, God "guarded" the Gospel and this ministry in such a way that He worked through this forgiven sinner to further His desire that all people be saved and come to the knowledge of the truth (1Tm 2:4). Paul knows that he is about to die and knows that God guarded the Gospel while entrusted to him, and He will continue to guard it in the hands of those who will follow after him in the pastoral office. Timothy is one of those in whom and through whom God was guarding the Gospel ministry. To this day, God is still guarding the Gospel ministry that He has given to the Church and entrusted into the hands of those He still continues to call into the pastoral ministry.

1:13 *pattern of the sound words.* Paul identifies that the substance of the sound or healthy words are those that he had spoken to Timothy. While we cannot know the totality of all that Paul had spoken to Timothy, we do know the substance contained in this letter and in 1 Timothy. Each of these contain both the Gospel and the doctrinal practice of the Gospel, order in the Church, and the care of the saints, both spiritually and physically. Timothy as a pastor, and all pastors, are to follow the substance of these apostolic and therefore divinely authorized words and patterns of the preaching and practice of God's Law and Gospel.

1:14 *dwells.* Through the Sacrament of Baptism, God gives us the gift of the Holy Spirit (Ac 2:38). It is the Holy Spirit, given by God through His Word and the water, who works regeneration and renewal, whereby we are saved and born again unto eternal life (Ti 3:5–6). As a result of this giving and work of the Holy Spirit, every believer is a dwelling place of the Holy Spirit (1Co 6:19), as He keeps us in the one true faith (1Jn 3:24, 1Pt 1:5). Paul knows, and reminds Timothy, that his following the pattern of sound words (v. 13) will happen only by the work of the Holy Spirit in and through faith. Cf. Rm 8:11; Gal 5:22–25. *guard the good deposit.* Paul here reminds Timothy that as the Gospel ministry was still entrusted to Paul, it is also entrusted to Timothy as God's called pastor. The only means by which Timothy or any pastor can rightly "guard" the Gospel, or the Gospel ministry, is by proclaiming the Gospel in all its fullness and following the pattern of practice that it lays out for the salvation of all. Like the Word of God, because it is living and active, the Gospel fully taught, believed, and trusted is its best defense. The ministry of the Gospel is the proclamation of all God's Word, which has two words: the Law (what I must do or be condemned) and Gospel (all Christ has done according to the Law because I could not, to save me). See exposition of 1Tm 6:20.

The Laying on of Hands

Issues of ministry naturally arose in the Reformation. On one hand, the reformers wanted to show that God did not institute monastic orders or the office of the papacy. On the other hand, they wanted to retain the office of pastor/priest as a divine institution. But was ordination—the laying on of hands—a sacrament? They gave different answers, even at different times. For example, in 1520 Luther wrote:

> Of [ordination] the church of Christ knows nothing; it is an invention of the church of the pope. . . . Who knows himself to be a Christian, be assured of this, that we are all equally priests, that is to say, we have the same power in respect to the Word and the sacraments. However, no one may make use of this power except by the consent of the community or by the call of a superior. . . . And therefore this "sacrament" of ordination, if it is anything at all, is nothing else than a certain rite whereby one is called to the ministry of the church. (LW 36:106, 116)

Yet in 1531, when Melanchthon wrote the Apology to the Augsburg Confession with Luther's approval, he wrote:

> If ordination is understood as carrying out the ministry of the Word, we are willing to call ordination a Sacrament. For the ministry of the Word has God's command and has glorious promises. . . . If ordination is understood in this way, neither will we refuse to call the laying on of hands a Sacrament. For the Church has the command to appoint ministers. (Apology XIII [VII] 11–12; Concordia 185)

In Luther's twilight years, when arguing against the Anabaptists, he could even say, "The imposition of hands is not a tradition of men, but God makes and ordains ministers" (LW 5:249). Ultimately, the Lutheran Church retained ordination as a worthwhile apostolic rite, though the Scripture does not specifically command ordination as a divine rite. The Scandinavian Lutheran state churches retained apostolic succession and ordination by a bishop.

Cranmer had the following in his *Corrections of the Institution by Henry VIII* (1538):

> As touching the sacrament of holy orders, we think it convenient, that all bishops and preachers shall instruct and teach the people committed unto their spiritual charge, first, how that Christ and his apostles did institute and ordain in the New Testament, that besides the civil powers

and governance of kings and princes . . . there should also be continually in the church militant certain other ministers and officers. (2:40–41)

Ultimately, the Anglican Church retained the rite of ordination by a bishop and the importance of apostolic succession, although they concluded that ordination was not a sacrament.

Calvin wrote decisively his view on the topic in the *Institutes* (1559):

See why [the papists] hold it necessary to be consecrated by sacraments, and to receive the Holy Spirit! It is just to do nothing. . . . Let them, at the same time, confess that there is not in the church, in the present day, any use or benefit of these sacred orders which they wondrously extol, and that their whole church is full of anathema. . . . All that we here proposed was to combat that novel invention of a sevenfold sacrament in ecclesiastical orders of which we nowhere read except among silly raving Sorbonnists and canonists. (4.19.24)

Reformed churches have continued to use a rite of ordination, typically conducted by presbyters.◌

Ashamed versus Unashamed (1:15–18)

ESV	KJV
¹⁵You are aware that all who are in Asia turned away from me, among whom are Phygelus and Hermogenes. ¹⁶May the Lord grant mercy to the household of Onesiphorus, for he often refreshed me and was not ashamed of my chains, ¹⁷but when he arrived in Rome he searched for me earnestly and found me—¹⁸may the Lord grant him to find mercy from the Lord on that Day!—and you well know all the service he rendered at Ephesus.	¹⁵This thou knowest, that all they which are in Asia be turned away from me; of whom are Phygellus and Hermogenes. ¹⁶The Lord give mercy unto the house of Onesiphorus; for he oft refreshed me, and was not ashamed of my chain: ¹⁷But, when he was in Rome, he sought me out very diligently, and found me. ¹⁸The Lord grant unto him that he may find mercy of the Lord in that day: and in how many things he ministered unto me at Ephesus, thou knowest very well.

1:15 *all*. The fact that Timothy, being in Ephesus, is in Asia, and Onesiphorus came from Asia to Rome, indicates that this "all" has to be qualified. To whom then does the "all" refer? To answer this, we must begin with the fact that Paul has been charged with a capital crime and will stand trial. He would need credible witnesses, Christian citizens of Rome, who could come and testify on his behalf. The fact that he says they "turned away" indicates that Paul had made some kind of an appeal to them to come to his defense. They likely ignored or refused his appeal, publicly or privately. Since Paul names Phygelus and Hermogenes, it's likely that they had denounced Paul publicly so as to save their own lives. So "all" refers to those Roman Christians in Asia who could have helped Paul in his trial before Caesar but refused to do so. *Phygelus and Hermogenes*. Nothing is really known of these two beyond the fact that they turned from Paul in his hour of need. Paul could rightfully have spoken condemningly of their actions. Yet by naming them according to their turning away from him, Paul, in meekness, does not revile them, but suffers it, entrusting both himself and them to the Lord who judges justly (1Pt 2:23). While it cannot be known with certainty why Paul singled out these two men, it is also reasonable to assume that their abandonment, and likely denunciation of Paul, was particularly unexpected and therefore hurtful.

1:16 *household.* Unlike our modern concept of this word, in the first century, this term referred to marital and blood relatives, as well as servants and staff that were in service to the master of the house. All these must have blessed and supported Onesiphorus in his mission of mercy to Paul. Based on what Paul says in v. 18 and 4:19, many speculate that Paul's prayer for the Lord to have mercy on Onesiphorus's family indicated that he was likely dead, yet there is no clear indication that this is necessarily true. Having come to refresh Paul, he might have been gathered up in the same, or subsequent, persecution of Christians that captured Paul, and was awaiting the same fate as Paul. The crucial thing in Paul's heart is that God be merciful to the household of one who had been so merciful to him in the face of likely imprisonment for doing so. *refreshed.* While the Greek term literally means "revived," refreshed better expresses the comprehensive effect of what Onesiphorus had done for Paul. The means and substance by which Onesiphorus did this for Paul cannot be known. It can be safely assumed that what he brought to Paul was of physical (food and drink) and spiritual (words of encouragement and prayer together) benefit. *chains.* See exposition of vv. 8, 12.

1:18 *on that Day!* This refers to Judgment Day. Paul echoes the description of Judgment Day as Jesus presents it in the separation of the sheep and the goats (Mt 25:31–46), especially when the Lord commends those saints who, having received mercy, were merciful (Mt 25:34–36). *Ephesus.* Onesiphorus was from Ephesus (4:19) and had likely provided Paul with lodging and support for him during his missionary journey and ministry there.

1:3–18 in Devotion and Prayer Paul is in prison charged with a capital crime that he believes will bring him a sentence of death. Virtually all his co-workers in the ministry have gone from him: the faithful to other fields of mission and ministry, and the unfaithful to the safety of unfaithful cowardice in the face of persecution. While he longs for the company and encouragement of Timothy, Paul is more concerned about Timothy standing firm in the faith and the faithful exercise of his office as pastor, and encourages him along these lines. Faithfulness is never an easy thing in the face of persecution or the seduction of pleasure, yet neither of these kept Christ from being faithful to God and to us so that we might be saved in

His faithfulness. • Blessed Savior, we thank You that in the face of persecution from mankind, and from God, You stayed faithful to us. Bless those whom You have called to faith, that in all times of persecution or pleasure, we may be kept faithful to You and to Your Church. Amen.

PART 2

CHARGE TO FAITHFUL MINISTRY IN HARD TIMES (2:1–4:5)

Laboring in the Truth (2:1–7)

ESV	KJV
2 ¹You then, my child, be strengthened by the grace that is in Christ Jesus, ²and what you have heard from me in the presence of many witnesses entrust to faithful men who will be able to teach others also. ³Share in suffering as a good soldier of Christ Jesus. ⁴No soldier gets entangled in civilian pursuits, since his aim is to please the one who enlisted him. ⁵An athlete is not crowned unless he competes according to the rules. ⁶It is the hard-working farmer who ought to have the first share of the crops. ⁷Think over what I say, for the Lord will give you understanding in everything.	2 ¹Thou therefore, my son, be strong in the grace that is in Christ Jesus. ²And the things that thou hast heard of me among many witnesses, the same commit thou to faithful men, who shall be able to teach others also. ³Thou therefore endure hardness, as a good soldier of Jesus Christ. ⁴No man that warreth entangleth himself with the affairs of this life; that he may please him who hath chosen him to be a soldier. ⁵And if a man also strive for masteries, yet is he not crowned, except he strive lawfully. ⁶The husbandman that laboureth must be first partaker of the fruits. ⁷Consider what I say; and the Lord give thee understanding in all things.

2:1 *my child.* Paul referred to Timothy as his "true child" in his first letter (1Tm 1:2). The basis of this title had not changed, but Paul's circumstances had, and referencing him in this way speaks of how dear Timothy was to Paul. The fact that this is preceded by "then" means that what Paul goes on from here to say is based upon his concern for Timothy, in the face of the same persecution and imprisonment he previously mentioned in ch. 1. The only way that Timothy, or any other pastor or believer, will be able to remain faithfully strong in the face of persecution is the same way a person is made a child of God: through the receiving of the grace of God in Jesus Christ. Cf. exposition of 1Tm 1:2.

2:2 *presence of many witnesses.* These are all the people to whom Paul consistently gave the grace of God in Jesus Christ, through his preaching and teaching, during his three missionary journeys. Timothy had accompanied him on these and had seen Paul's pattern and faithfulness in preaching and teaching the Word of God. This served as the pattern and practice of the pastoral ministry for Timothy and those to whom he would entrust that ministry as the Church moved forward, according to the Great Commission (Mt 28:18–20). *faithful men.* These refer to those men who meet the qualifications for the pastoral office that Paul set down in his first letter (3:1–7). In light of Paul's experience with the unfaithfulness of many in the face of persecution, he stresses the quality of faithfulness in those Timothy will prepare and likely appoint to be pastors.

2:3–6 In these verses, Paul uses three analogies to help Timothy and those who will follow him in the pastoral office understand what is involved in carrying out the responsibilities of their office.

2:3 *suffering as a good soldier.* Paul introduced the imagery of waging spiritual warfare in his first letter (1Tm 1:18). Here, he uses the analogy of an obedient soldier to further enlighten Timothy, and every pastor, to the potential consequences to one enlisted by God to fight the good fight of faith (4:7). The quality of "good" is determined by the pastor's willingness to share in the suffering that may come from faithfully fulfilling the charge and responsibilities of the pastoral office. The "good" pastor is the one who seeks no conflict in speaking and administering the Word of God for the sake of his hearers. At the same time, he does not shrink away from speaking and administering that Word, even if it may cause conflict or offense. It is spoken only and always for the sake of the hearers, whether they like that Word or not.

2:4 *civilian pursuits.* While Paul may have 1Co 7:26–34 in mind, he stresses the necessity of freedom from earthly agendas and occupations by which Timothy may have had to support himself prior to his enlistment in the Office of the Public Ministry. Paul seeks to have Timothy, and every other pastor, understand that he is to give himself wholly over to the work and will of God for him according to this office. This is a warning against any potential distractions of focus and conflicts between fulfilling their pastoral charge and earthly agendas. If pastors are drawn away from what they have been enlisted to do, they are less useful to those they serve and to the One who enlisted them. In emphasizing this, let it be understood that by these words Paul is not sanctioning the neglect of wife and family for the sake of the ministry. God created the office of husband and father before Christ instituted the Office of the Public Ministry. Paul's emphasis upon the importance of marital state on the part of any pastor or deacon makes this point most clear (1Tm 3:2, 12; Ti 1:6). *One who enlisted him.* When Christ enlisted the apostles, He did this immediately by personally calling each of them. When it comes to the Office of the Public Ministry, Christ enlists men by calling them through His Church. Whether a man was enlisted by the appointment of an apostle or his representatives (Ti 1:5) or by the local congregations, each man serves at the pleasure of Christ for the sake of His Body—the Church (cf. 1:1).

2:5 *crowned.* This refers to receiving the symbol of victory, such as that crown of laurels an athlete would receive for victory. Paul's point here is not as much about winning as it is about how one wins. If one does not compete according to the rules in any competition, that person may cross the line first but will lose the victory. In the pastoral ministry, all victories belong to Christ alone, who has won them for us all. The pastor is called not to win but to follow the course of the race Christ has run by the means He has given, so that along this course, the pastor is able to give Christ's victory to those who are fallen in sin along its narrow course.

2:6 *first share.* While this verse sounds rather proverbial with regard to hard work, it is a statement of fact in the matter of farming. By way of this third analogy, Paul uses the farmer and the harvest to illustrate not what ought to be, but what has to be in regard to the spiritual welfare of Timothy and every pastor. The farmer, no matter how hard he works, has to take the first share of the crop that's harvested if he is to survive. Notice it is the "first" share, not the largest. If he had said the "largest share," then the issue would be about how hard the pastor had worked. What Paul is telling Timothy and his fellow pastors is that when they are laboring to raise the harvest of spiritual food with which to feed those they serve, pastors must feed and nourish themselves with this same food. Any pastor who fails to preach and apply the Word of God to himself in all its fullness will be spiritually malnourished, become weak of faith, and ultimately, will poorly feed those he is called to serve.

2:7 *give you understanding.* Literally, "bring things together" for you. Just as the Lord had to bring the experiences of His apostles together with His Word, so that they could understand all these and Christ Himself (Lk 24:44–45), Paul affirms that the Lord will continue to give Timothy understanding. It is important to note that Paul does not promise that the Lord will give Timothy an "understanding of everything," but "understanding *in everything.*" The emphasis here is that neither Timothy nor any pastor is to lean on the reeds of his own understanding (Pr 3:5–6) but solely on the understanding the Lord provides through His Word. Working through His Word, God's Holy Spirit still opens our eyes (Ps 119:18; Ac 26:18) and our minds (Ps 119:34, 73, 104) to know Him, to know ourselves and our purpose in Him.

The Gospel of the Truth (2:8–13)

ESV	KJV
[8]Remember Jesus Christ, risen from the dead, the offspring of David, as preached in my gospel, [9]for which I am suffering, bound with chains as a criminal. But the word of God is not bound! [10]Therefore I endure everything for the sake of the elect, that they also may obtain the salvation that is in Christ Jesus with eternal glory. [11]The saying is trustworthy, for: If we have died with him, we will also live with him; [12]if we endure, we will also reign with him; if we deny him, he also will deny us; [13]if we are faithless, he remains faithful— for he cannot deny himself.	[8]Remember that Jesus Christ of the seed of David was raised from the dead according to my gospel: [9]Wherein I suffer trouble, as an evil doer, even unto bonds; but the word of God is not bound. [10]Therefore I endure all things for the elect's sakes, that they may also obtain the salvation which is in Christ Jesus with eternal glory. [11]It is a faithful saying: For if we be dead with him, we shall also live with him: [12]If we suffer, we shall also reign with him: if we deny him, he also will deny us: [13]If we believe not, yet he abideth faithful: he cannot deny himself.

2:8 *offspring of David.* This designation is the mark or qualification of Jesus as the Messiah promised in the Old Testament Scriptures who had come in the flesh. Paul reverses the sequence of Christ's life. He begins with His resurrection—His victory. By mentioning the need to keep remembering that Jesus was the offspring of David, Paul would have Timothy understand that the path to Christ's victory runs through the valley of fleshly life and through all of His suffering and death. It is, again, an attempt by Paul to make sure Timothy more fully faces the reality that faithfulness in the pastoral office will likely involve suffering and sacrifice in the flesh for the sake of Christ's Church. *my gospel.* Paul uses this same designation elsewhere (Rm 2:16; 16:25) to refer to his teaching, preaching, and writing of the Gospel of Jesus Christ. We tend to use the same kind of referencing when we refer to one of the four Gospels as "Matthew's Gospel" or "John's Gospel." In each case, it is understood as the account of the Gospel of Jesus Christ, according to Matthew, Mark, and the like. Paul likely uses this designation of the Gospel to differentiate between what he has preached according to his apostolic authority, and the so-called gospels that false teachers proclaimed (2Co 11:4; Gal 1:6, 9).

2:9 *bound with chains.* This phrase is to be understood figuratively, not literally. Paul says it this way to convey the degree of both the crime he is charged with and his imprisonment. Paul is facing a capital crime, which will bring him a sentence of death. Being so charged and imprisoned marked him as one of the worst of criminals. Having exhorted Timothy to be willing to suffer for the sake of the Gospel ministry, Paul testifies, through these few words, to the level of commitment it will take. *not bound!* Paul may be imprisoned for preaching the Gospel, but his imprisonment has not stopped his preaching and teaching of it. In his Letter to the Philippians, he testifies to this, that his imprisonment had actually served to advance the Gospel so that it had become known to the entire palace guard (Php 1:13–14). Paul does not say that the entire palace guard had been converted by the Gospel, but that they all knew the substance of the Gospel. Surely they spoke of it with one another and with their families, and whether they ridiculed or pondered, it was spoken and heard. This is the means by which God gives and works saving faith in all believers (Rm 10:17). Cf. Is 55:11; Heb 4:12.

2:10 *the elect.* The Church, the body of believers whom God the Holy Spirit has called by the Gospel, enlightened with His gifts, and still keeps in the one true faith. Notice that in his harsh imprisonment and the disgrace that has been heaped upon him, Paul's concern is not for himself but for the Church—the saints whom God has gathered into Christ. Again, Paul sets the focus of ministry for Timothy and every pastor. *eternal glory.* Our world tends to understand the word "glory" in terms of high praise, shouts of exultation, party, and celebration. The words that Paul wrote just prior to these words deny us such a worldly understanding of the term. The "glory" of God is rightly understood as the accomplishing of His good and gracious will. Christ's most glorious moment was also His darkest and most humiliating moment on the cross, when He was rejected by man and by God; in this moment, He accomplished God's good and gracious will that all mankind be saved from our sins and the wrath of God. God's good and gracious will is that all may obtain the salvation that is freely offered in Jesus Christ and through this, the "glory" that is the total fulfillment of His will, which is that we dwell in eternal life with Him (Jn 3:16).

2:11–13 To understand these verses, we need to begin with the little word "for." This is the equivalent of the word "because." Paul uses a series of condition-effect statements to set forth the same critical realities for Timothy and all the elect. Paul uses these to explain why he is willing to endure everything for the sake of the elect.

2:11 *If we have died . . . live with Him.* Paul begins with the dying of every believer in their Baptism, as each has been baptized into the death of Christ (Rm 6:3, 8). As a result, the baptized believer is also united with Christ in His resurrection, so that we live in newness of life (Rm 6:4, 8).

2:12 *if we endure . . . reign with Him.* As a result of our Baptism, this is a time of living by faith in which we must be prepared to endure temptations (Heb 2:18; 1Co 10:13), persecutions, afflictions (2Th 1:4), sufferings (Rm 8:17), and various trials (1Pt 1:6). As a result of abiding in faith, believers will reign with Christ (Rv 20:6; 1Pt 5:4). *if we deny . . . will deny us.* Here, Paul identifies the first negative reality, a reality taken almost verbatim from the promise that Christ Himself makes (Mt 10:33). He speaks of people who honor Him with their lips but are actually far from Him (Mt 15:8). Such a shock these same people will face when they are cast out of the kingdom of God due to their lack of faith in Him (Lk 13:25–30; Mt 25:41–46).

2:13 *if we are faithless He remains faithful.* Here, Paul refers to every and any sad occasion, no matter how, when, or where, in which we are false to our claim of faith in Jesus Christ. To be false to the faith we claim in Christ is to give up that faith, and thus, to become truly "faithless." While Christ is faithful to His Word, Paul's concluding words to this verse testify that he is referring to Christ's nature and His attribute of perpetual faithfulness (Dt 7:9–10). *He cannot deny Himself.* When we as believers sin, we are "faithless." In so doing, we deny ourselves as those redeemed in Christ. This happens because sin still adheres to us and often takes us captive (Rm 7:16–17, 22–23). Christ, as the Son of God, is also the love that is God (1Jn 4:8). As this is God's nature, being unfaithful would be a denial of the love that God is. For God to be unfaithful, He would have to change His nature, and that is impossible; "For I the LORD do not change" (Mal 3:6). This offers great comfort to the guilt-stricken as they seek the faithful love of God in Jesus Christ, freely offered to all who humbly repent of their sins and believe in the Lord Jesus Christ.

2:1–13 in Devotion and Prayer Paul's word, "I endure everything for the sake of the elect (i.e., the Church)," sums up the call of everyone who enters the pastoral ministry. Paul uses several different analogies to help Timothy, and every pastor, understand the nature and necessity of faithfulness in preaching the Gospel in the face of persecution and public disgrace. Paul provides the blessed assurance that in all of this, our Savior remains faithful, for He cannot disown Himself. This is a great comfort to the Church. Since Christ has united Himself to us in Baptism and will not deny Himself, neither shall He deny any member of His Body the Church. • Blessed Lord, as You endured all things in faithfulness to God the Father and us, grant us Your faithfulness that we may be forgiven and carry on to greater faithfulness in service of the Gospel and Your Church. Amen.

Laboring for the Truth against Error (2:14–21)

ESV	KJV
¹⁴Remind them of these things, and charge them before God not to quarrel about words, which does no good, but only ruins the hearers. ¹⁵Do your best to present yourself to God as one approved, a worker who has no need to be ashamed, rightly handling the word of truth. ¹⁶But avoid irreverent babble, for it will lead people into more and more ungodliness, ¹⁷and their talk will spread like gangrene. Among them are Hymenaeus and Philetus, ¹⁸who have swerved from the truth, saying that the resurrection has already happened. They are upsetting the faith of some. ¹⁹But God's firm foundation stands, bearing this seal: "The Lord knows those who are his," and, "Let everyone who names the name of the Lord depart from iniquity." ²⁰Now in a great house there are not only vessels of gold and silver but also of wood and clay, some for honorable use, some for dishonorable. ²¹Therefore, if anyone cleanses himself from what is dishonorable, he will be a vessel for honorable use, set apart as holy, useful to the master of the house, ready for every good work.	¹⁴Of these things put them in remembrance, charging them before the Lord that they strive not about words to no profit, but to the subverting of the hearers. ¹⁵Study to shew thyself approved unto God, a workman that needeth not to be ashamed, rightly dividing the word of truth. ¹⁶But shun profane and vain babblings: for they will increase unto more ungodliness. ¹⁷And their word will eat as doth a canker: of whom is Hymenaeus and Philetus; ¹⁸Who concerning the truth have erred, saying that the resurrection is past already; and overthrow the faith of some. ¹⁹Nevertheless the foundation of God standeth sure, having this seal, The Lord knoweth them that are his. And, let every one that nameth the name of Christ depart from iniquity. ²⁰But in a great house there are not only vessels of gold and of silver, but also of wood and of earth; and some to honour, and some to dishonour. ²¹If a man therefore purge himself from these, he shall be a vessel unto honour, sanctified, and meet for the master's use, and prepared unto every good work.

2:14 *them.* These are the faithful men who are able to teach others (cf. v. 2). Those called into the pastoral office and thereby entrusted with the Gospel ministry. *not to quarrel about words.* Understanding and teaching the meaning of certain words can be necessary for the sake of proper hearing and understanding of the faith of the hearers. The kind of quarrels Paul wants pastors to avoid are those that are begun by individuals seeking to use such quarrels to display how intelligent they are and to establish themselves as authoritative teachers. Their purpose is to glorify themselves, and is not for the sake of the hearers. They do not aid those who hear them in their life of faith. It's like wrestling in the mud with a pig. The problem is that, while the pig enjoys it, you get muddy. The proper understanding of words in the Scriptures cannot be drawn purely from their origins or merely from a dictionary meaning. The understanding must be informed from how the word is used elsewhere in Scripture. When its use is limited in the Scriptures, keys to rightly understanding that word can be found in how it was used in the common language and discourse of the time, as found in other documents. *ruins the hearers.* Such quarreling creates confusion and subverts the simple truths of God's Word. Uncertainty about the truths of God's Word serves only to cause doubt and disunity among the hearers. When we do not know the truth in such matters, there is a tendency to attach ourselves to personalities involved. As such, the source of faith is shifted from the Word of God to some person, and faith is quickly ruined. Paul's words here testify to the fact that such unprofitable quarreling does not take place privately, but publicly, as the self-appointed teacher seeks to establish himself among the hearers. Such quarrels are completely contrary to the responsibility of every pastor and church member to be "eager to maintain the unity of the Spirit in the bond of peace" (Eph 4:3) that Christ Himself has established among the saints.

2:15 *present yourself.* In contrast to the quarrelers who seek after the approval of the people to advance themselves and their agenda, Paul reminds Timothy that he, and every pastor, is to examine himself and his ministry according to what God approves. All pastors are to preach, teach, admonish, exhort, and administer the Sacraments in such a way that what they say and do, and how they say and do it, has the approval of God. How would Timothy or any other pastor do this? By letting their words and practice of the Gospel ministry flow from what God has said and from what Christ has done and commanded. This may not make Timothy or any pastor popular with the people, but it will be the words and practice that God approves of and blesses. *approved.* Timothy's young age led many to question both what he preached and his authority to do so. Paul is telling Timothy to preach, teach, and do all things as one whom God Himself has called into the pastoral ministry. In the face of opposition, Timothy, like many pastors, was tempted to doubt whether he still had God's approval as a pastor. Paul is telling him to jettison such doubt and get on with fulfilling his vocation of rightly handling the word of truth in love for the sake of the Church he served. *rightly handling the word of truth*. This describes the skillful application of God's Word, in which no provision is made to spare anyone or anything from it. How many people approach and handle the Word of God in such a way that they selectively apply it, so as to spare this person or that, even themselves and their own pet sins. It has to be handled for the salvific sake of the hearer. Can it be said mercifully? Yes, but it cannot be held back from the faithful and full application of it, lest the hearers obtain a false security in their sins. Bengel noted that a similar expression occurs in the Greek translation of Pr 3:6; 11:5: "Timothy may prepare a right course (may make ready a straight way) for the word of truth, and may himself walk straight forward according to this line, turning neither to the right nor to the left hand" (301). Melanchthon showed how this verse applies to the teaching of Law and Gospel, saying:

> We tell godly minds to consider the promises, and we teach about free forgiveness of sins and about reconciliation, which happens through faith in Christ. Afterward, we add also the teaching of the Law. It is necessary to distinguish these things aright, as Paul says in 2 Timothy 2:15. We must see what Scripture says about the Law and what it says about the promises. For it praises works in such a way that it does not remove the free promise. (Ap V 67)

2:17 *spread like gangrene*. The word "gangrene" is almost a transliteration of the Greek word *gangraina*. It refers to a fast "eating" or "consuming" type of incurable disease that can be counteracted only by removal or amputation of the area so affected. If left unremoved, it will quickly consume and kill the one who has it. It has all the qualities of a fast-moving form of cancer. The false teachings were of such a nature that they ate away at, or consumed, the faith and trust in Christ of many believers. *Hymenaeus and Philetus*. Paul identifies two individuals who were spreading this disease, both of whom he had Timothy remove from the church, so that they could no longer infect others. While both claimed a faith in Christ, what they unrepentantly taught and lived was contrary to that very faith. While this may seem like he is attacking the individuals, his purpose is to identify the type of false "talk" and lifestyle of those who taught it. As there were no textbooks, many teachings were identified by their teacher. Paul would have Timothy and the Ephesian churches know and avoid the gangrenous teaching of these men. See exposition of 1Tm 1:20.

2:18 *resurrection has already happened.* For those baptized in Christ, each is born again, spiritually resurrected in Jesus Christ to walk in newness of life (Rm 6:4; 8:11) as a new creation (2Co 5:17). Having been so resurrected in the Spirit, each believer looks forward to the final resurrection, when all flesh shall rise at the coming of Jesus Christ (1Th 4:16; Rm 6:5; 1Co 15:42). These false teachers sought to so spiritualize everything of Christ, so as to separate their faith from their living. In this way, the spiritual was everything, and the flesh and what you did in the flesh did not matter. According to this heresy, how you lived your earthly life had no effect on your spiritual life; therefore, immorality of the flesh could do nothing to harm your spiritual life. This teaching did not disappear, but became known as Gnosticism, and is resurging today.

2:19 *seal.* Based on what is inscribed on the seal, it is a guarantee of permanency on God's firm foundation that makes alteration of any kind impossible. *The Lord knows . . . His.* This is a quote from Nu 16:5 in the Septuagint (the Greek translation of the Hebrew Old Testament). The verb "knows" is not a progressive knowing, but a knowing all at once—prior to time—a knowing in eternity. This is what gives the seal its permanency. This particular quote is a reference to the elect, according to the foreknowledge of God (1Pt 1:2). Wesley described those who are the Lord's as "sealed with a seal, which has an inscription on each side," which are the two sayings cited in v. 19. In other words, the one side of the seal describes election, the other side the holy life of those who profess the faith (552). *Let everyone . . . iniquity.* As this is an inscription on the permanent seal, this is not something the elect, those whom God has known from eternity, are to do, but it is what they have already done in Christ. According to their regeneration (Ti 3:5), they confess to this command: "I have been made to stand away from sin."

2:20 *great house.* Here, Paul is referring more to a large dwelling place rather than to a house as a structure. He uses this image to describe the Church on earth. Paul limits the application of the house to the wide variety of vessels in the house.

Calvin wrote:

> Commentators are not agreed, however, whether the "great house" means the Church alone, or the whole world. . . . Paul's object is to shew that we ought not to think it strange, that bad men are mixed with the good, which happens chiefly in the Church. (229)

vessels. These are made of both the most precious of materials—gold and silver—and of the cheapest—wood and clay. The differentiation he makes goes further to distinguish between those vessels that endure because they retain their value due to their substance, and those that do not endure because of their worthless substance. Paul distinguishes between those members of the visible Church who have faith in Christ and those who, while being members of the visible Church, are only so in outward appearances. The true members of the Church are precious in God's sight, and in Christ they do endure. Thus, the true members of the Church are those who have been cleansed in Baptism and are set apart, holy and useful in God's house, the Church. The outward members of the visible Church refuse to be completely cleansed for the Lord's honorable purpose, and are useful only to themselves and Satan.

2:21 *cleanses himself.* Here, Paul changes his analogy slightly to illustrate the believer's life of daily repentance and faith in Jesus Christ for Timothy. This echoes the reality of God's promise, through John, that "if we walk in the light, as He is in the light, we have fellowship with one another, and the blood of Jesus His Son cleanses us from all sins" (1Jn 1:7). Only in this way is anyone, pastor or parishioner, able to be a vessel for honorable use. *set apart as holy.* Literally "consecrated by God for God's holy purposes." This again testifies to the fact that cleansing of the believers is solely the work of God in Christ, who has chosen and cleansed the believers (that is, made them holy) for His holy purposes. In this way, the true believer is useful to the Master because the Master has made him or her to be useful by His grace. *master.* This refers to God, who is the Head of the great house (v. 20).

Laboring with the Truth for Those in Error (2:22–26)

ESV	KJV
²²So flee youthful passions and pursue righteousness, faith, love, and peace, along with those who call on the Lord from a pure heart. ²³Have nothing to do with foolish, ignorant controversies; you know that they breed quarrels. ²⁴And the Lord's servant must not be quarrelsome but kind to everyone, able to teach, patiently enduring evil, ²⁵correcting his opponents with gentleness. God may perhaps grant them repentance leading to a knowledge of the truth, ²⁶and they may come to their senses and escape from the snare of the devil, after being captured by him to do his will.	²²Flee also youthful lusts: but follow righteousness, faith, charity, peace, with them that call on the Lord out of a pure heart. ²³But foolish and unlearned questions avoid, knowing that they do gender strifes. ²⁴And the servant of the Lord must not strive; but be gentle unto all men, apt to teach, patient, ²⁵In meekness instructing those that oppose themselves; if God peradventure will give them repentance to the acknowledging of the truth; ²⁶And that they may recover themselves out of the snare of the devil, who are taken captive by him at his will.

2:22 *flee*. Literally, "keep on fleeing." The simplest understanding of this word is the activity of moving quickly away from something. By this, Paul is telling Timothy that when it comes to the youthful passions, he is not to tolerate them, but move away from them and toward the Word. *youthful passions*. By this, Paul is not referring so much to sexual passions, but to the emotional escalation and rashness that less mature individuals are given to in disagreements or debates. When in the midst of such situations, Timothy, and every pastor, is to pursue the gifts of faith in Christ that serve to resolve conflicts and win hearts in debates. *Those who call on the Lord*. This is the response of faith. Stated collectively, as it is here, this is another way of describing the Church. Having been baptized and born again in Christ, these are those who call on the Lord in faith, according to His grace and mercy. *pure heart*. A heart that is free from sin and sin's corruption. The Church is made of those in whom God has created a clean and pure heart and given a right spirit (Ps 51:10).

2:23 *controversies*. Literally, "questionings." Paul tells Timothy to avoid the uninformed questions raised by those who lack even a basic understanding of the Christian faith. Those who raise such questions are not seeking any real kind of answer, but rather the opportunity to elevate themselves. They would bring their questions to Timothy seeking his support, and by it, validation of themselves as teachers and authorities.

2:24 *servant.* The Greek term is *doulos.* Paul uses this term to identify Timothy, himself (Rm 1:1), and every pastor as those who have been purchased by the blood of Christ (1Pt 1:18–19) and owe Him every allegiance and obedience.

2:25 *opponents.* Most immediately, Paul is referring to Hymenaeus and Philetus and those like them. See exposition of v. 17. These also include those who, by their questionings and babble, lead people into ungodliness (v. 16).

2:26 *escape from the snare.* These opponents were caught or trapped in their own words and their faith in these words. It would only be through patient and gentle correction with the Word of God that they have any hope of losing faith in their words and of coming to faith in the Word made flesh. See exposition of 1Tm 3:7. *captured by him.* Having abandoned the "pattern of sound words" (1:13), they lost the ability to rightly handle the word of truth (2:15). As such, they were captured physically alive but spiritually dead by Satan. They are held as willing prisoners to do his work. Martin Luther teaches how to guard against this when he writes:

> [The devil] hates to hear God's name and cannot remain long where it is spoken and called upon from the heart. Indeed, many terrible and shocking disasters would fall upon us if God did not preserve us by our calling upon His name. I have tried it myself. I learned by experience that often sudden great suffering was immediately averted and removed by calling on God. To confuse the devil, I say, we should always have this holy name in our mouth, so that the devil may not be able to injure as he wishes." (LC I 71–72)

2:14–26 in Devotion and Prayer In this section, Paul turns his attention and charge to rightly handling the word of truth (v. 15), which is the Word of God. Failure to do so leaves a pastor to converse in words that are nothing more than irreverent babble (v. 16) and ignorant questions that have no sure foundation or seal upon which the Christian's faith and hope rest. Only by rightly handling God's Word could Timothy, and any pastor today, build up the saints, who have the seal of God's knowing them, and correct opponents to this word of truth, so that they may escape the snare of Satan (vv. 25–26). It is only through the Word of God, rightly handled, that our Lord works repentance and faith, through which He guards believers in eternal life. • Speak, O Lord, Your servant listens. By Your speaking give me faith through which I may rightly believe and trust in Your Word. Amen.

Opposition to the Truth (3:1–9)

ESV	KJV
3 ¹But understand this, that in the last days there will come times of difficulty. ²For people will be lovers of self, lovers of money, proud, arrogant, abusive, disobedient to their parents, ungrateful, unholy, ³heartless, unappeasable, slanderous, without self-control, brutal, not loving good, ⁴treacherous, reckless, swollen with conceit, lovers of pleasure rather than lovers of God, ⁵having the appearance of godliness, but denying its power. Avoid such people. ⁶For among them are those who creep into households and capture weak women, burdened with sins and led astray by various passions, ⁷always learning and never able to arrive at a knowledge of the truth. ⁸Just as Jannes and Jambres opposed Moses, so these men also oppose the truth, men corrupted in mind and disqualified regarding the faith. ⁹But they will not get very far, for their folly will be plain to all, as was that of those two men.	3 ¹This know also, that in the last days perilous times shall come. ²For men shall be lovers of their own selves, covetous, boasters, proud, blasphemers, disobedient to parents, unthankful, unholy, ³Without natural affection, trucebreakers, false accusers, incontinent, fierce, despisers of those that are good, ⁴Traitors, heady, highminded, lovers of pleasures more than lovers of God; ⁵Having a form of godliness, but denying the power thereof: from such turn away. ⁶For of this sort are they which creep into houses, and lead captive silly women laden with sins, led away with divers lusts, ⁷Ever learning, and never able to come to the knowledge of the truth. ⁸Now as Jannes and Jambres withstood Moses, so do these also resist the truth: men of corrupt minds, reprobate concerning the faith. ⁹But they shall proceed no further: for their folly shall be manifest unto all men, as their's also was.

3:1 *last days.* This refers to the whole of time between Christ's bodily ascension into heaven and His bodily return, in which the Church carries out His Great Commission (Mt 28:18–20). It is within this time—the time in which we live—that there will occur difficult times and seasons, during which hypocrites within the Church, loving pleasure more than God, will bring all forms of evil upon the Church from within (vv. 3–5).

3:2–5 The types of people and kinds of behavior Paul describes here have sadly been a part of the Church in every generation to the present. The number and variations have been larger at various times in the history of the Church, always challenging every generation to fight the good fight by rightly handling the word of truth (2:15) for the sake of both pastor and people (1Tm 4:16).

3:2 *lovers of self.* These words indicate that problem underlying all the rest. By exalting self above all other things, the self becomes an idol. Such arrogance leads to various sinful expressions such as being *proud, arrogant . . . ungrateful, unholy.* In contrast to this self-centered sinfulness, Luther reflected on the humility of Christ, the prophets, and the apostles:

> Christ was spiritually the highest on the earth, for He taught everybody as a teacher and master, but He did not exalt His person over any man, but served them with all that he had and could [cf. Mark 10:45]. The prophets and apostles undoubtedly were also the highest on the earth spiritually, for they were the light and teachers of the world; but when did one of them ever set his person, goods, and affairs over others, to say nothing of over kings and princes? (LW 76:140–41)

3:3 *unappeasable.* This is a term often associated with a war or conflict between two parties. It refers to a brutal attitude that demands everything and is unwilling to make any kind of truce for less than everything. It calls for unconditional surrender. This attitude is perhaps best expressed in an absolute "my way—all the way—or the highway." Mercy is not to be found in such individuals.

3:4 *lovers of pleasure rather than lovers of God.* Not being lovers of what is good (v. 3), (i.e., not loving that which is beneficial to others), these people lived according to the power of sin that totally turned them in on themselves. They were under the power of sin, in which the love of what pleased and pleasured them ultimately controlled them. Such pleasures destroy godly love that seeks the welfare of others because they are totally devoid of any reverence of God. This is the opposite of the very thing a pastor is to be (Ti 1:8).

3:5 *appearance of godliness.* Everything such people said and did publicly (i.e., everything that could be seen) looked exactly like the godliness of believers. Yet when it came to their private lives and choices, none of it flowed from faith in Christ. They were, in fact, unbelievers who, like Ananias and Sapphria (Ac 5:1–11), believed that since they could deceive other people, they could deceive God too. Jesus described the hypocritical Pharisees of His day this way, calling them whitewashed tombs. "You also outwardly appear righteous to others, but within you are full of hypocrisy and lawlessness" (Mt 23:27–28). *Avoid.* As Paul tells Timothy to be constantly aware of such people, he also tells Timothy to constantly turn away from such people, lest he give credence to them, their teaching, and their godless self-indulgence (cf. 2Jn 9–11). Timothy, like Paul and every pastor, was still a sinner. This command to keep avoiding such people was also a caution against the opportunity to be tempted by such people and their teachings.

3:6 While the husband was away, religious charlatans would visit homes and try to persuade the women to accept their false teachings. *weak women.* In the Greek, this is one word, *gynaikarion*, which comes from the Greek word *gynē* that means "a little woman." This is not in reference to size but maturity. To refer to a woman by this term was to identify her as "a foolish/immature woman." These are the kind of women Paul is describing contemptuously by this term because they believe themselves to be wise, yet under the strains of unforgiven sin, and being lovers of pleasure, they fall victim to the religious charlatans. It is important to note that the *various passions* these charlatans prey upon are not necessarily sexual. This simply refers to any assortment of sinful desires they did not seek to be free from. Many charlatans would prey upon the guilt they had for such desires and likely sanction them for such women, as a means of endearing themselves to such women through deception. Such immature women have been found throughout time, from Eve to the present. Those taken captive by the Gnostic heresy and the spread of their heresy were referred to by the same Greek word Paul uses here. Nicolas of Antioch, Marcion, Montanus, and others used women as their prime instruments for spreading their cultic and condemnable heresies.

3:7 Such women were those who were lovers of pleasure. As such, they could not love God because the love of pleasures puts self before God. Such love lacks any real reverence for God because it is a rejection of Him. They may well have wanted to learn of God and His Word, but what they were willing to learn had to conform to what their sinful desires taught them was good. As such, these women never come to a saving knowledge of the truth. They kept learning but never came to a saving knowledge of Jesus Christ, who is the truth (cf. Jn 14:6).

3:8 *Jannes and Jambres.* These were likely Egyptian magicians called upon by Pharaoh to oppose and refute the message and miracles the Lord did through Moses that ultimately led to the exodus. While neither of these is mentioned in the Old Testament, their names were likely handed down through unwritten Jewish tradition or history. While Paul was an expert in the Scriptures, he would also have been familiar with the Jewish tradition/histories from which these names likely came. In the ancient Abyssinian language, the name "Jannes" refers to a "trickster," and Jambres refers to a "juggler." It is possible that over time these titles took the form of names. *these men.* The men include the babblers, like Hymenaeus and Philetus (2:17), those mentioned in v. 6, and all those opposed to the full truth of the Gospel in Jesus Christ. *disqualified.* Literally "cast away as unapproved." These are disqualified as those who are saved by grace through faith because, though they claim a knowledge of God, or even faith in Christ, they are openly rebellious in regard to the will of God and are unrepentant (Ti 1:16). As such, they have, by their unrepentant actions, disqualified or cast out themselves. Luther wrote:

> The tyrants among God's people have the appearance and act as if they were the true saints. Thus they hinder and hold back the simple, so that they cannot get free, for they are weak in conscience and cannot clearly distinguish between appearance and reality, between glittering and truth. . . . Thus the Magi were held back at Jerusalem by Herod, who pretended to search the Scriptures. (LW 76:161)

3:1–9 in Devotion and Prayer Here Paul foretells a more detailed exposition of what he foretold in his First Letter to Timothy (4:1–3). Paul is not speculating, as an apostle of our Lord, but by divine inspiration expounds upon what Christ Himself said would take place (Mt 24:11–12). How much of this Timothy will be exposed to Paul does not say, but by this prophecy, he prepares Timothy, and every pastor throughout the ages, for such times of difficulty. It is such lovers of pleasure that Christ came to save because such is what we all are conceived in sin to be. Christ does this because it was the good pleasure of God the Father to save us. Christ suffers the displeasure of man and God on the cross, so that everyone might come to knowledge of God and His saving love for us. It is now Christ's pleasure to daily save and rescue all who believe in Him through the forgiveness of sin. • Lord, my love for You and my neighbor is never free from my love of my own pleasure; save me according to Your love that I may know the pleasure of our heavenly Father. Amen.

"Continue in What You Have Learned" (3:10–17)

ESV	KJV
[10]You, however, have followed my teaching, my conduct, my aim in life, my faith, my patience, my love, my steadfastness, [11]my persecutions and sufferings that happened to me at Antioch, at Iconium, and at Lystra—which persecutions I endured; yet from them all the Lord rescued me. [12]Indeed, all who desire to live a godly life in Christ Jesus will be persecuted, [13]while evil people and impostors will go on from bad to worse, deceiving and being deceived. [14]But as for you, continue in what you have learned and have firmly believed, knowing from whom you learned it [15]and how from childhood you have been acquainted with the sacred writings, which are able to make you wise for salvation through faith in Christ Jesus. [16]All Scripture is breathed out by God and profitable for teaching, for reproof, for correction, and for training in righteousness, [17]that the man of God may be complete, equipped for every good work.	[10]But thou hast fully known my doctrine, manner of life, purpose, faith, longsuffering, charity, patience, [11]Persecutions, afflictions, which came unto me at Antioch, at Iconium, at Lystra; what persecutions I endured: but out of them all the Lord delivered me. [12]Yea, and all that will live godly in Christ Jesus shall suffer persecution. [13]But evil men and seducers shall wax worse and worse, deceiving, and being deceived. [14]But continue thou in the things which thou hast learned and hast been assured of, knowing of whom thou hast learned them; [15]And that from a child thou hast known the holy scriptures, which are able to make thee wise unto salvation through faith which is in Christ Jesus. [16]All scripture is given by inspiration of God, and is profitable for doctrine, for reproof, for correction, for instruction in righteousness: [17]That the man of God may be perfect, thoroughly furnished unto all good works.

3:10 *my.* In the Greek text, "my" is used once. While Paul is contrasting everything about his apostolic ministry with those previously mentioned, he does this in terms of the fact that Timothy has actually followed it. What Paul is therefore teaching and preaching is what Paul and Timothy have been living. Paul is not putting himself forth before the Gospel, but is setting forth what the Gospel has wrought in him and Timothy. Note what comes first in the sequence: *teaching.* Only after teaching (that is, the Word of God put forth) does all the conduct of the faith follow. This is no accidental sequence but a clear cause (the spoken Word of God) and its effect. Cf. exposition of 2:8.

3:12 *persecuted.* This is true for all who believe in Jesus Christ, not just apostles and pastors. After facing the three persecutions mentioned above, Paul states this: "Strengthening the souls of the disciples, encouraging them to continue in the faith, and saying that through many tribulations we must enter the kingdom of God" (Ac 14:22). Paul's words to Timothy, like his words to the saints in Lystra, Iconium, and Antioch, all echo the promise of our Lord, "In the world you will have tribulation. But take heart; I have overcome the world" (Jn 16:33b). While Paul's persecution took the form of lies, beatings, and condemnation, it was never limited to these. Believers in every generation all face various forms of persecution for their faithfulness to Christ.

3:13 *impostors.* The Greek word Paul uses (*goēs*) is found only here in the New Testament. In classical Greek, this word was used to refer to a "juggler," a "cheat," or an "enchanter." Paul uses this term to refer to those who serve to further people in their evil, as the Egyptian magicians served to further Pharaoh in his evil and impenitence (cf. vv. 6–9). *from bad to worse.* While the progression of these impostors will not go far in terms of others, it will progress steadily within themselves. As Paul says, they will deceive, but the greater deception will come from them becoming more deceived within themselves. Such is the orientation of the sinful nature: we are all turned in upon ourselves. Those caught in the illusions of sin will constantly turn within and become progressively more and more deceived in their attempts to deal with the fragments of the Law's judgment still written on their hearts. Lord, have mercy!

3:14 *from whom you learned it.* The Gospel as conveyed to Timothy through his mother, grandmother (1:5), and Paul (vv. 10–11).

3:15 *from childhood.* As Timothy's mother was Jewish, she would have taught him and had him schooled in the Old Testament Scriptures from a young age (today celebrated at bar mitzvah or confirmation ceremonies). The word used (Gk *brephos*) denotes an infant. He had been taught the faith from the earliest age. *sacred writings.* Literally "sacred letters" or "learning," likely referring to the Old Testament. *wise for salvation.* Paul singles out the Scriptures as the sole source by which we may be made aware of the sum and substance of salvation through faith in Jesus Christ. For people to know what salvation is, how it was accomplished for everyone in Jesus Christ, and how this is received for their salvation, they must hear the Word of God. Only the Scriptures are able to inform in these matters. It is through this informing that people are brought to faith in Christ and strengthened in that faith. And it is through this faith that they are made wise unto salvation. Such is the performative nature of God's Word. While it informs the hearer, it actually produces an effect. God promises to work through the Scriptures (cf. Ti 1:1).

3:16 *All Scripture.* This teaching is not limited to parts of the Bible (e.g., the New Testament or the red-letter words of Jesus). The entire Bible is inspired by God and is His Word. *breathed out by God.* This can also be translated "inspired" by God (cf. KJV). When we speak, the words have their origins in our minds and then are given expression by breath. So also, the words of Scripture have their origin in God and are given breath by His Spirit, who first breathes into the prophets and apostles the revelation of God, and then exhales them out in spoken and written words. St. Peter explains the same teaching in different words, saying, "For no prophecy was ever produced by the will of man, but men spoke from God as they were carried along by the Holy Spirit" (2Pt 1:21). This is a passive participation on the part of the prophets, apostles, and even believers. In English, we say the "Holy Spirit," but the Greek might also be read "Holy Air," "Wind," or "Breath." The Holy Spirit is the Breath of God. Christ Himself breathed on the apostles to give them the Holy Spirit (Jn 20:22). It is through the Holy Spirit that the prophets and apostles spoke and wrote what God wanted revealed and heard from Him. Even the believer can confess Jesus Christ is Lord only by the Holy Spirit (1Co 12:3). *teaching.* Imparting of knowledge or doctrine that had not been known or understood, so that the hearer may be made wise for salvation that cannot be found anywhere else.

reproof. This refers to the disproving of falsehoods, myths, and all such ideas that obscure, shade, or reject the full truth of the Gospel in Jesus Christ. *correction.* This ought always follow reproof because it is a setting forth of the truth so as to call people back from their sin, falsehood, and unbelief, that they might repent and believe the Gospel. The goal is the restoration of the sinner. *training.* The Greek word is *paideia* and refers to the exercising of a child through both instruction and discipline. *training in righteousness.* Literally "exercised in righteousness." The Scriptures are used for exercising those who have been declared righteous. This exercise is twofold. It is first an exercise in receiving the Word through faith, and only then can it be exercised in the second step of responding, through faith, in good works according to our vocations (cf. Heb 12:4–11). This passage receives comparably little comment from the reformers and their heirs, for whom the inspiration of Scripture was never in doubt. Chemnitz provides an example of the issue they discussed from this passage:

> [God] willed that the doctrine [of good works] be repeated in many statements of Scripture, because it is a means and instrument through the hearing of which and the meditation on which He might stir up, kindle, preserve, confirm, increase, and cause to grow a zeal for the Spirit of renewal, or as Paul says, a zeal for good works in the hearts of the regenerate. (8:1179)

3:17 *man of God.* This phrase is consistently applied to those men who were prophets in service of God. As such, Paul is referring to those whom God has called into the pastoral office. Having said this, it has to be said that Scripture is able to make all believers competent and equipped for every good work of their varied vocations through faith in Christ. *complete, equipped.* God does not call the competent, the self-sufficient, the complete, or the equipped; He makes complete and equips through His Word and Sacraments. Everyone has natural gifts and abilities that God has given, yet apart from Christ, these gifts all lack the completeness to overcome the sin they are captive to, and thus, to be pleasing and acceptable to God. Apart from faith, one's natural gifts are equipped by sin for oneself alone and not for one's neighbor. Only in Christ is a man's personal aptitude taken captive to Christ and enlightened by the Holy Spirit, so that he is made complete and equipped to serve in the pastoral office.

3:10–17 in Devotion and Prayer In the face of such false and destructive teachers, Paul sets the stage for what is likely to come, as Timothy continues to follow Paul's teaching, conduct, and aim of life. He promises Timothy, every pastor, and every believer that following Christ through faith, in a godly life, will bring persecution. In light of this, every believer, be it a prophet, apostle, pastor, or layperson, often wonders how to live through such times. Paul then identifies the only means and way to live through such times of persecution and suffering for the faith: "continue in what you learned" (v. 14). Only through the Word of God are we made competent and equipped by God to endure such times through faith. • I am trusting Thee for power; Thine can never fail. Word which Thou Thyself shalt give me Must prevail (*LSB* 729:5).

Final Charge to Timothy (4:1–5)

ESV	KJV
4 ¹I charge you in the presence of God and of Christ Jesus, who is to judge the living and the dead, and by his appearing and his kingdom: ²preach the word; be ready in season and out of season; reprove, rebuke, and exhort, with complete patience and teaching. ³For the time is coming when people will not endure sound teaching, but having itching ears they will accumulate for themselves teachers to suit their own passions, ⁴and will turn away from listening to the truth and wander off into myths. ⁵As for you, always be sober-minded, endure suffering, do the work of an evangelist, fulfill your ministry.	4 ¹I charge thee therefore before God, and the Lord Jesus Christ, who shall judge the quick and the dead at his appearing and his kingdom; ²Preach the word; be instant in season, out of season; reprove, rebuke, exhort with all long suffering and doctrine. ³For the time will come when they will not endure sound doctrine; but after their own lusts shall they heap to themselves teachers, having itching ears; ⁴And they shall turn away their ears from the truth, and shall be turned unto fables. ⁵But watch thou in all things, endure afflictions, do the work of an evangelist, make full proof of thy ministry.

4:1 *charge.* Literally, "I am testifying." The full understanding of this has to be drawn from the words of Paul that both precede and follow it. There is an implied "therefore" attached to this word. Because of all false teachers and teachings Timothy was facing, and because he would train other pastors to face and refute them, Paul "testifies" in the presence of God and Christ that pastors are to do the following things. With this word, Paul makes it clear that his command to Timothy, and to every pastor, to preach the Word is not his will or his own concept of ministry, but rather it is the divine will and the substance of the pastoral office that Christ created for the sake of the Church. As such, it is not subject to alteration by addition or subtraction. *judge the living and the dead.* Paul reminds Timothy of the final judgment of the world that will take place at the return of Christ, not as a threat to Timothy, but to identify the reason for the perpetual and unaltered preaching of God's Word. This judgment is coming, and nothing can stop it. As God would have all men to be saved (1Tm 2:4), so God establishes the preaching office of the pastor so the Gospel may be heard and people may be saved from this coming judgment. The "living and the dead" refers to those who will be alive at the coming of Christ and those who have died prior to that moment at the end of time. *appearing.* The end of time when Christ's return will be visible in the flesh on the last day for the purpose of the final judgment of all people throughout time. *kingdom.* This describes every time, place, and person where Christ reigns as Savior. Wherever the crucified and risen Christ rules by His grace through faith, there is His kingdom. This Kingdom spans all of time through the Old and New Testament Church.

4:2 Here Paul sets forth five imperatives of the pastoral office, the final four of which are some of the fruit and purpose for always preaching the Word for believer and unbeliever. While each of the final four may take different forms in how it is carried out for the sake of the hearers, the substance of each must always be the Word of God. *in season and out of season.* This is Paul's way of telling Timothy, and every pastor, that he is always to be ready to speak the Word of God when the opportunity arises. "In season" refers to those times when things appear favorable for preaching the Word. "Out of season" refers to those times when it might seem as if preaching the Word of God would be of no effect. The issue for every pastor, and Timothy, is not the favorability of the situation or outcome, but the opportunity. Therefore, the pastor is to seize every season, never skipping any of them. The outcome in either is the responsibility and work of God through His Word, not of the pastor. Said another way, Paul is saying, "Be always ready and never let anything or anyone keep you from preaching the Word." *reprove.* The first part of any attempt to call another person to repentance and faith. This refers to the process of making another person aware of his or her sin by showing it to the person in light of both his or her actions and God's Word (cf. 3:16). The goal of this is that the hearer may have a sound, healthy faith (cf. Ti 1:13). This might be analogous to a physician diagnosing a cancerous tumor for a patient. *rebuke.* This is the second part in the call to repentance. At this point, debate ends. The authority of God's Word of Law is brought to bear on the sin and the sinner. To continue the medical analogy, this might be thought of as a surgeon cutting the cancerous tumor out of a patient. *exhort.* Having given the people the opportunity to repent and receive the forgiveness of sins, pastors are to boldly set before the forgiven the assurance of God's favor in Christ and the will of God for them as the forgiven and justified (Eph 2:10). This may be thought of as a doctor medicating and bandaging the surgical wound from which the cancerous tumor was removed so that the patient is free to go back to life healthy and whole. *complete patience and teaching.* Here, Paul sets forth the two key components to accomplishing the previous three imperatives of reproving, rebuking, and exhorting. Each must be done by "teaching." The Greek word (*didachē*) is also translated as "doctrine," which refers to the process of setting forth all divine truths or facts as found in God's Word, so that the hearer might learn, know, and believe them. While the substance of what the pastor is to teach is fixed, the time required to bring his hearers to the knowledge and faith is not. Therefore, Timothy, and every pastor, is to be patient, leaving room for the Holy Spirit to work through the Word when and where He will in the hearts of the hearers (Jn 3:8).

4:3 Paul now turns to the reason for the charge he gives to Timothy and every pastor. *itching ears.* The people had a desire—an itch that they wanted scratched through what they heard. Such an itch is born of their passions, rather than Christ's passion for them. It is a sinful desire that the Word of God will not allow them to have satisfied. Thus they go looking for someone to say it is okay to satisfy that desire. They did not want the faithful and proper use of Law and Gospel. God's Word would not scratch the sinful itch, but rather kill it, and then resurrect, heal, and strengthen the new life within them through the forgiveness of their sinful desire. *teachers to suit their own passions.* Having rejected the Word of God in regard to their desires, they turn elsewhere; namely, to false teachers, who under the guise of spirituality and religiosity, provide them with the teaching and preaching that approves and sanctions their own sinful desires. Despite the voices of these false prophets approving of what they desire, the Law, though imperfectly written on their hearts, continues condemning and accusing them. This is why Paul says they *accumulate*, literally "heap up stacks" of these false teachers. Yet no matter how many voices of supposed spiritual authority they gather, they are unable to quiet the accusing word of the Law. Only the Gospel can deal with the Law through repentance and faith, which they have already rejected.

4:4 *myths*. The Greek text has the definite article "the" before this word—"the myths." In this way, Paul is referring to the whole spectrum of empty humanistic, religious, and spiritual inventions of mankind. By using the term "myth," Paul is stating that all such human teachings, like the sinful desires they sanction, arise from and are sustained by mankind, not by God. Cf. exposition of 1Tm 1:4.

4:5 *sober-minded*. Peter calls this girding or building up the "loins" or muscles of the mind (1Pt 1:13). Paul is not calling Timothy merely to be sober-minded when necessary, but to continuously be sober-minded and ready—a "continuing to be" so. By this, Paul tells Timothy and every pastor to have continuous clarity of thought and sound judgment. Pastors, even Paul and Timothy, are still sinners and subject to the same temptation and passions that carry others away. Only with a mind exercised in thought and judgment based on the Word of God can any of them attend to their calling to preach and teach the Word for the sake of those inside and outside the Church. *evangelist*. This is not to be understood as some kind of revivalist or missionary. This is used in the general sense and refers to one who is a "good news giver." As such, an evangelist is one who teaches and preaches the Law and Gospel of salvation to all, through faith in Jesus Christ. *fulfill your ministry*. From the charge (v. 1) forward, Paul has been putting forth essential imperatives for the work of every pastor. This final imperative is not set down because Timothy has been failing to do this, but in light of those who would turn away from his pastoral ministry; he is not to let this hinder his faithful service as a pastor. Paul is telling Timothy that he must sobermindedly leave nothing lacking when it comes to fulfilling the previous imperatives, even if it may seem as if it is turning people away. Whether it be reproving, teaching, or exhorting, Pastor Timothy was to faithfully serve for the sake of his hearers both inside and outside of the Church.

PART 3

PAUL'S FAREWELL (4:6–22)

Paul's Impending Martyrdom (4:6–8)

ESV	KJV
⁶For I am already being poured out as a drink offering, and the time of my departure has come. ⁷I have fought the good fight, I have finished the race, I have kept the faith. ⁸Henceforth there is laid up for me the crown of righteousness, which the Lord, the righteous judge, will award to me on that Day, and not only to me but also to all who have loved his appearing.	⁶For I am now ready to be offered, and the time of my departure is at hand. ⁷I have fought a good fight, I have finished my course, I have kept the faith: ⁸Henceforth there is laid up for me a crown of righteousness, which the Lord, the righteous judge, shall give me at that day: and not to me only, but unto all them also that love his appearing.

4:6 *poured out as a drink offering.* While Paul is referring to his impending death sentence, he is employing a figure connected with Jewish sacrifices where wine was poured out next to the altar, not on it (cf. Ex 29:38–41). Paul likens the pouring forth of his blood, when he is put to death, to the pouring forth of wine in the sacrifice. He sees his life and his death as offerings God has called forth from him. The fact that Paul refers to this in the past tense, "already being poured," means that he sees his imprisonment and the events that have followed since as the tipping of the glass from which the drink offering will finally pour at his execution. *departure.* Literally, the "season of my departure is present." While Paul is referring to his death, note that Paul is not referring to the exact moment but the "season" in which it will finally take place. This is a reference to that time period in which one begins preparation to leave on a trip or to move. It has been revealed to Paul that he will die soon, so he is using this time to get ready to leave. This letter to Timothy is a part of what Paul does during the season of his departure.

4:7–8 Bengel wrote: "Paul, in accordance with the actual moment of his departure, looks to his three states: 1. the past, 'I have fought'; 2. the immediate present, 'there is laid up'; 3. the future, 'the Lord shall give'" (313).

4:7 *good fight.* The Greek word (*agōn*) is often translated as "fight." Since Paul uses other military terminology (e.g., 1Tm 1:18; 6:12), this may seem like another example. But this does not fully express the meaning of *agōn*. This word was used to refer to various kinds of competitions and contests. Since in this context Paul immediately makes reference to a finishing of a race, this would be better translated here as the "good contest." In sum, this is the fulfilling of the apostolic ministry, to which Christ Himself called Paul, in the places and the times chosen for him by the Lord. He calls the contest "good" because the Lord who has called Paul to this is good, He makes Paul good, and He works through Paul to accomplish His good will through the preaching of the Gospel—the salvation of all who believe. He refers to this as the "holy calling" (1:9) and "upward call in Christ Jesus" (Php 3:14). *race.* Literally, the "course." With this, Paul refers to the physical and spiritual journey his earthly life had taken along the course that God had chosen and laid out for him. *kept the faith.* Since Paul is using the definite article "the," he is referring to the substance of the Christian faith, rather than to his personal faith. Paul begins this verse with the contest chosen for him, then moves to the course upon which this contest has taken place. Through all this, he concludes by stating that he has faithfully proclaimed the substance of the Christian faith. Despite the conflicts, beatings, imprisonments, and temptations, he never yielded any part of the Gospel and the fullness of salvation by the grace of God through faith in Jesus Christ alone (Eph 2:1–10).

4:8 *the crown of righteousness.* This might be better rendered "the crown of the righteous." This crown belongs to the righteous and is a sign of the righteousness that is theirs in Christ. This righteousness is imputed to believers and is ours through faith in Christ. Note that Paul does not say that this crown is being laid up, but that it has already been laid up for him in Christ. Melanchthon wrote of this:

The justified are due the crown because of the promise. Saints should know this promise, not that they may labor for their own profit, for they ought to labor for God's glory. But saints should know it so they may not despair in troubles. They should know God's will: He desires to aid, to deliver, and to protect them. (Ap V 242–43)

Calvin wrote:

As soon as God has received us into favour, he likewise accepts our works, so as even to deign to give them a reward, though it is not due to them. Here two blunders are committed by the Papists; first, in arguing that we deserve something from God, because we do well by virtue of free-will; and secondly, in holding that God is [indebted] to us, as if our salvation proceeded from anything else than from his grace. But it does not follow that God owes anything to us, because he renders righteously what he renders; for he is righteous even in those acts of kindness which are of free grace. And he "renders the reward" which he has promised, not because we take the lead by any act of obedience, but because, in the same course of liberality in which he has begun to act toward us, he follows up his former gifts by those which are afterwards bestowed. (262)

that Day. The day of the resurrection, when Christ will return and separate the sheep and the goats (Mt 25:31–46). It is the day when all those who have believed, and who love the appearing of Christ, shall say, "Behold, this is our God; we have waited for Him, that He might save us. This is the LORD; we have waited for Him; let us be glad and rejoice in His salvation" (Is 25:9). *loved.* These are believers throughout time who have prayed, "Your kingdom come" (Mt 6:10), and "Amen. Come, Lord Jesus!" (Rv 22:20). They have and still love His promises, His appearing in the flesh, and His death and resurrection for them through faith in all of these. Thus believing it is all for them and their salvation, they love the purpose of His coming again. *His appearing.* Paul is referring to that moment of Christ's returning in the flesh when the trumpet will sound and the dead shall be raised imperishable (1Co 15:52). Yet for the believer to love this moment would be impossible without loving also His first appearing in flesh as an infant and all that He accomplished for us before our eyes. Wesley wrote:

Only a real Christian can [love His appearing]. . . . The word Christian necessarily implies whatsoever is holy, as God is holy. Strictly speaking, to join real or sincere to a word of so complete an import, is grievously to debase its noble signification, and is like adding long to eternity or wide to immensity. (554–55)

4:1–8 in Devotion and Prayer Fully aware of the fact that his death is imminent, Paul lays upon Timothy, and every pastor in the Church, the awesome responsibility of faithfully handling the Word of God for the sake of those inside and outside the Church. Such faithful preaching and teaching is no guarantee of belief in, and support for, what they have preached and taught. Nothing will be more essential to the faithful handling of the Word of God than understanding its two essential doctrines of Law and Gospel. It is in the application of these that the greatest care must be taken in reproving, correcting, and exhorting everyone. The Law will bring the sting of sin and guilt so that each may repent, and hear and receive the healing of the Gospel through the forgiveness of sins. • Lord of the prophets and of the prophets' sons, bless those whom You have called into the pastoral office with conviction and faithfulness in preaching and teaching Your Word. Grant that by the power of Your Word, those who hear might believe and receive the crown of righteousness through Jesus Christ, our Lord. Amen.

Final Greetings and Requests (4:9–22)

ESV	KJV
[9]Do your best to come to me soon. [10]For Demas, in love with this present world, has deserted me and gone to Thessalonica. Crescens has gone to Galatia, Titus to Dalmatia. [11]Luke alone is with me. Get Mark and bring him with you, for he is very useful to me for ministry. [12]Tychicus I have sent to Ephesus. [13]When you come, bring the cloak that I left with Carpus at Troas, also the books, and above all the parchments. [14]Alexander the coppersmith did me great harm; the Lord will repay him according to his deeds. [15]Beware of him yourself, for	[9]Do thy diligence to come shortly unto me: [10]For Demas hath forsaken me, having loved this present world, and is departed unto Thessalonica; Crescens to Galatia, Titus unto Dalmatia. [11]Only Luke is with me. Take Mark, and bring him with thee: for he is profitable to me for the ministry. [12]And Tychicus have I sent to Ephesus. [13]The cloke that I left at Troas with Carpus, when thou comest, bring with thee, and the books, but especially the parchments.

he strongly opposed our message. [16]At my first defense no one came to stand by me, but all deserted me. May it not be charged against them! [17]But the Lord stood by me and strengthened me, so that through me the message might be fully proclaimed and all the Gentiles might hear it. So I was rescued from the lion's mouth. [18]The Lord will rescue me from every evil deed and bring me safely into his heavenly kingdom. To him be the glory forever and ever. Amen.

[19]Greet Prisca and Aquila, and the household of Onesiphorus. [20]Erastus remained at Corinth, and I left Trophimus, who was ill, at Miletus. [21]Do your best to come before winter. Eubulus sends greetings to you, as do Pudens and Linus and Claudia and all the brothers.

[22]The Lord be with your spirit. Grace be with you.

[14]Alexander the coppersmith did me much evil: the Lord reward him according to his works:

[15]Of whom be thou ware also; for he hath greatly withstood our words.

[16]At my first answer no man stood with me, but all men forsook me: I pray God that it may not be laid to their charge.

[17]Notwithstanding the Lord stood with me, and strengthened me; that by me the preaching might be fully known, and that all the Gentiles might hear: and I was delivered out of the mouth of the lion.

[18]And the Lord shall deliver me from every evil work, and will preserve me unto his heavenly kingdom: to whom be glory for ever and ever. Amen.

[19]Salute Prisca and Aquila, and the household of Onesiphorus.

[20]Erastus abode at Corinth: but Trophimus have I left at Miletum sick.

[21]Do thy diligence to come before winter. Eubulus greeteth thee, and Pudens, and Linus, and Claudia, and all the brethren.

[22]The Lord Jesus Christ be with thy spirit. Grace be with you. Amen.

Introduction to 4:9–22 Though imprisoned and facing a death sentence, Paul faithfully continues to exercise his apostolic office. In these closing words, Paul sets his situation and his need for assistance to continue to coordinate the mission work of many.

4:9 *come to me soon.* There are two possible reasons for Paul's instruction to come quickly. First, imprisoned and facing the likelihood of death at a time he did not know, Paul wanted to see Timothy in person. While Paul will be greatly comforted by Timothy, he is mindful of his departure and of what this will mean for the church when he is gone. Timothy has served as a faithful representative of Paul in some difficult situations. Paul knew that he could count on Timothy to be one of those who would continue to lead and further establish the Church in her mission according to the apostolic Word of God. Face-to-face discussions would serve to both encourage Timothy and better inform him of the wide and varied mission work that Paul was directing. The second reason for the request for a quick arrival could have been the time of the year and weather concerns. In v. 21, Paul wants Timothy to arrive before winter, a season when travel by boat was limited, if not discontinued.

4:10 *Demas.* Prior to Paul's current situation, Paul identified Demas as his co-worker (cf. Col 4:14; Phm 24). Other than this, and what Paul says of him here, nothing further is known about this man. *deserted me.* More poignantly put, Demas "abandoned" Paul. The time of this desertion is not known. While it might be surmised that this took place when persecution arose, Paul had been imprisoned before and suffered other persecutions. The fact that Paul identifies the reason for his desertion was being "in love with this present world" would indicate that Demas left for love or want of something worldly and therefore temporal, something that he could get in Thessalonica. The fact that Paul mentions Demas and his reason for leaving leaves no room to put the best construction on what Demas has done. In contrast to loving the Lord's appearing, Paul sets forth Demas's loving of the worldly things and going after them to the abandonment of Christ. *Crescens.* Clearly another one of Paul's faithful co-workers who has left on a mission trip to Galatia in furtherance of the Gospel. This is the only mention of him in the Bible. *Titus.* A co-worker of Paul whom Paul had sent to Dalmatia, a city on the eastern coast of the Adriatic Sea. As to Titus himself, very little is known. We know that he also served in Crete and Nicopolis. He is the one to whom Paul addressed the pastoral letter titled by his name. (See introductory material to Titus.)

4:11 *Luke.* Luke was the only faithful servant still with Paul during his imprisonment in Rome. This means that Luke likely sent this letter to Timothy. Luke had been with Paul on his voyage to Rome (Ac 27:1; 28:11, 16). He was with Paul when he wrote the letters to the Colossians (4:14) and Philemon (24). He is the author of the Gospel account in his name, and the account of the Acts of the Apostles, which he wrote during Paul's two-year imprisonment. *Mark.* Since Timothy is to bring Mark with him, Mark must have been assisting Timothy in his ministry with the churches of Ephesus and greater

Asia. Mark had accompanied Paul and Barnabas on a mission trip, but had withdrawn from them in Pamphylia, refusing to do the mission work. Because of that, Paul did not want Mark going with them on their trip to revisit all the cities to which they had first gone. So set was Paul against Mark coming along that he and Barnabas split up, with Mark going with Barnabas (Ac 15:37–40). Under Peter's instruction, and Barnabas's supervision in the Word of God and the mission work, Mark had matured and had reconciled with Paul, and was clearly beneficial to him and to the Church. Mark is the writer of the Gospel account that bears his name. *useful*. Mark drafted his Gospel account from what he heard Peter preaching and teaching over and over again during Mark's long service with him. Mark had been in Rome with Paul (Col 4:10; Phm 24), and then later with Peter. He knew the city of Rome and many of the Christians who were still there. As such, Mark could and would be most useful to Paul in his current circumstances.

4:12 *Tychicus*. He had traveled much with Paul and had been Paul's pastoral emissary, delivering his letters and personal information to the Ephesians (6:21) and the Colossians (4:7). Paul was likely to send him to Ephesus to take over for Timothy while he was away in Rome.

4:13 When one was imprisoned for a capital crime in Rome, as Paul was, nothing was provided by the state, apart from water and something that might be called food. The only means for having anything else was through the provision of family and friends. With winter approaching and the length of his imprisonment uncertain, Paul wanted a warm cloak and the means to continue his apostolic work while time remained. *Carpus*. Likely someone in Troas, with whom Paul stayed and whom he trusted enough to leave his cloak, books, and parchments with for safe keeping. *books*. The Greek word is *biblia*, which in English is translated "book." It is the term for the Scriptures—the "Bible." In the Greek usage, *biblia* were rolls of papyrus, what we in English call "scrolls." *parchments*. These were also scrolls, but they were made of animal skin. The reason Paul stresses the importance of having these is that they were likely copies of the Old Testament Scriptures in the Greek language. This translation is called the Septuagint.

4:14–15 *Alexander the coppersmith*. While the name would have been among the most common, Paul identifies this Alexander by his trade to warn Timothy when he arrives in Rome. It is unlikely that this is the same man Paul mentions in 1Tm 1:20 because he was in Asia Minor and would have needed to travel to Rome to further trouble Paul. While we cannot be sure what he did, Paul does say that it harmed him. This suggests that, in his opposition to the Gospel, he either had Paul physically assaulted or assaulted Paul himself in an attempt to stop the Gospel.

4:15 *message.* The Greek word (*logos*) is often translated "word." It is used in John's Gospel to refer to Christ (cf. Jn 1:1, 14).

4:16 *first defense.* This refers to what might best be described as a preliminary hearing where a legal indictment was officially brought against Paul. On this occasion, Paul, as the defendant, was to answer the indictment with some kind of defense. If an adequate defense could not be made, he would be bound over to trial before Nero. As everyone had left him, he is bound and awaiting trial before Nero.

4:17 *the Lord stood by me.* The Greek word for "stood" (*paristēmi*) means more than merely standing by someone, being with them or in their presence. It carries the understanding of standing by for the purpose of helping or benefiting someone. In a legal context, it can mean "represent before a judge." Though his earthly companions, who could have come to his defense, had fled, the Lord was with Paul for more than mere companionship. In the context of having to defend himself, it might be thought that the Lord was with Paul to influence the judge and his decision. Yet what the Lord does to help Paul is to put strength and resolve into his heart in the face of all he was about to go through so that he could fulfill his God-given mission of bringing the message of Christ before kings (cf. Ac 9:15); namely, Caesar. As a servant of God's Word, Paul trusted the Lord's promise that He is always with His people (Mt 28:20). *message.* The Greek term is *kerygma,* which means "preaching" or "proclamation." This was Paul's shorthand way of referring to the message of the Gospel of salvation in Jesus Christ that Paul spoke during his first defense. In this way, all the Gentiles who would have been gathered at such an event heard the Gospel of Jesus Christ. Even in his defense, Paul was able to fulfill his apostolic mission of preaching the Word of God wherever he was. *lion's mouth.* Here, Paul echoes what the Lord had done according to his prayer, which was likely taken from Ps 22:21: "Save me from the mouth of the lion!" Paul is referring to God saving him from execution at the time of his first defense.

4:18 *His heavenly kingdom.* As a baptized child of God, Paul had been born again of God into His kingdom of grace here on earth. In this Kingdom, Christ rules and reigns with His grace through the Gospel, keeping and preserving the saints who still live in this sinful world. Here, Paul refers not to a different kingdom, but a different location in which the same kingdom is found—heaven. In His heavenly kingdom, Christ rules and reigns with His heavenly and unfiltered glory. Paul was trusting in Christ's promise to come and take all believers to be with Him in the place that He has prepared for him and for all who live and believe in Christ (Jn 14:3). *glory.* As Paul concludes testifying to all that the Lord has done and would do for him, he keeps it completely focused on the Lord. Everything, from the desire to do all this, the doing of all this, the praise, the credit, and the thanks for it all—for him and every believer—always belongs to God. As such, our Lord should be glorified by telling all this to everyone we meet.

4:9–18 in Devotion and Prayer As Paul concludes his letter, he urges Timothy to come to him as soon as possible and lays out his reasons. When we read of the great exploits of Paul in his apostolic ministry, we might imagine him to be the bravest of the brave, able to stand alone. Yet in truth, no one was born—or born again in Baptism—to be alone. We are the Body of Christ, and we each have need of one another. Paul was no different. He needed both the encouragement of Timothy as well as Timothy's faithfulness to help carry on the mission of the Church. When our sin left us alone and helpless, Christ came to us and met us in our aloneness, to save us from our sin. By grace, He has brought us into His kingdom, and He is with us in all things—ready to rescue and to save all who believe in Him.
• Holy Savior, strong to save, make us to stand in You that we may stand in the evil day, so that, being found faithful in Your kingdom of grace, we may at last be found in Your kingdom of glory. Amen.

4:19 *Prisca and Aquila.* A Jewish wife and husband who had been forcibly exiled from Rome. Paul met them in their exile while on his trip to Corinth (Ac 18:2). Paul sent his greeting to them in the closing verses of his Letter to Rome, calling them "fellow workers" in Christ (Rm 16:3). They were likely in Ephesus when he wrote this, fleeing Rome and Nero's persecution of Christians. *Prisca.* This is a diminutive variation of the name Priscilla.

4:20 *Erastus.* He was identified as one of Paul's helpers, sent with Timothy into Macedonia about the time a riot was started by tradesmen who opposed Paul and the Gospel (Ac 19:22). He is identified as the treasurer of Corinth (Rm 16:23), which was likely his home and the reason he returned there. *Trophimus.* He was an Ephesian that had accompanied Paul in his journeys to Troas and Miletus, and then went with him when he returned to Jerusalem. The Jews once accused Paul of taking Trophimus, a Gentile, into the temple, which was forbidden (Ac 20:4; 21:29).

4:21 *come before winter.* Due to the winter winds and storms on the Adriatic, sea travel would have been impossible for Timothy (cf. Ac 27:9–12). It might also be that Paul's hearing before Nero was anticipated to take place prior to Nero leaving Rome for a warmer climate. Thus he would want Timothy there in time to assist in his defense, but also to make sure things were set for the continuation of the Church and her mission. *Eubulus . . . Pudens . . . Linus . . . Claudia.* All we know of these fellow saints is that they were acquaintances of Paul who had contact with him through Luke. It is likely that these were key leaders of the Church in Rome. These names are not mentioned elsewhere in the Bible, but Irenaeus and Eusebius identify Linus as the first bishop of Rome who led the church there. *all the brothers.* While this might seem like a reference to all the Christians in Rome, it is much more likely that these were all those who also had contact with Paul through Luke. Paul had not really had much contact with the whole congregation in Rome, as he had been brought there under arrest and was kept in prison.

4:22 *with your spirit.* Paul is concluding a grave letter to his young friend and fellow servant of Christ. He gives this blessing to Timothy to encourage him in both his travels to be with Paul and in all that lay ahead for him. *Grace be with you.* Paul also sends his blessing to all those who are with Timothy and those he served. "Your spirit" is singular as it is addressed to Timothy. Here, Paul broadens the blessing of grace, making the "you" plural. This is directed toward all believers who would read this letter. This plural "you" also serves to indicate that this letter was to be read to all the congregations in the area of Ephesus.

4:19–22 in Devotion and Prayer Paul concludes his Second Letter to young pastor Timothy by sending His greetings to those he knew personally, the greetings of those with him in Rome, and his blessing upon Timothy and the saints in Ephesus. While these were the last recorded words of the apostle Paul before he was put to death, they are God's Word to the Church, and they carry the same blessing as Timothy and the saints at Ephesus first heard and received by them. • Blessed Lord, thank You for Your servant Paul, his fellow servant Timothy, and all the saints who stood faithful in the days of persecution, so that we might have the Word of God and the doctrine of our salvation. May every pastor and each believer be ever so faithful in all things pertaining to our salvation and that of the world. Amen.

TITUS ✦

Introduction to
Titus

Overview

Author
Paul the apostle

Date
AD 68

Places
Crete; Nicopolis

People
Paul; Titus; Artemas; Tychicus; Zenas; Apollos

Purpose
To guide Titus's teaching and administration for the Christians on Crete

Law and Sin Themes
Be above reproach; rebuke; the pure and the defiled; submissiveness; devotion to good works

Grace and Gospel Themes
Election; soundness; God's grace; redemption; washing and renewal; justification

Memory Verses
Redeemed and purified (2:14); renewal by the Holy Spirit (3:4–7)

Reading Titus

The rich man grips his belly in pain, pleading for the physician to explain what is wrong. "Too much rich food! Too much wine!" the physician complains. "Excesses will kill you. No wonder your body is not sound."

Like a sincere physician, the apostle Paul warns Titus about the excesses that afflict the congregation of Cretans, who were proverbial for gluttonous excess (1:12) and who craved new and different doctrines (1:10, 13–14; 3:9). Paul teaches that soundness (1:9, 13; 2:1–2, 8) comes from modest living in accordance with the truth. The wholeness of the Gospel brings salvation and leads to self-controlled living.

Luther on Titus

This is a short epistle, but a model of Christian doctrine, in which is comprehended in a masterful way all that is necessary for a Christian to know and to live.

In chapter 1 he teaches what kind of man a bishop, or pastor, ought to be, namely, one who is pious and learned in preaching the Gospel and in refuting the false teachers of works and of man-made laws, those who are always warring against faith and leading consciences away from Christian liberty into the captivity of their own man-made works, [as if these works,] which are actually worthless, [should make them righteous before God.]

In chapter 2 he teaches the various estates—the older, the younger, wives, husbands, masters, and slaves—how they are to act, as those whom Christ, by his death, has won for his own.

In chapter 3 he teaches Christians to honor worldly rulers and to obey them. He cites again the grace that Christ has won for us, so that no one may think that obeying rulers is enough, since all our righteousness is nothing before God. And he forbids association with the obstinate and with heretics. (LW 35:389–90)

For more of Luther's insights on this Book, see *Lectures on Titus* (LW 29:1–90).

Calvin on Titus

Paul, having only laid the foundations of the church in Crete, and hastening to go to another place, (for he was not the pastor of a single island only, but the Apostle of the Gentiles,) had given charge to Titus to prosecute this work as an Evangelist. It is evident from this Epistle that, immediately after Paul's departure, Satan laboured not only to overthrow the government of the Church, but likewise to corrupt its doctrine.

There were some who, through ambitious motives, wished to be elevated to the rank of pastors, and who, because Titus did not comply with their wicked desires, spoke unfavourably of him to many persons. On the other hand, there were Jews who, under the pretence of supporting the Mosaic law, introduced a great number of trifles; and such persons were listened to with eagerness and with much acceptance. Paul therefore writes with this design, to arm Titus with his authority, that he may be able to bear so great a burden; for undoubtedly there were some who fearlessly despised him as being but one of the ordinary rank of pastors. It is also possible that complaints about him were in circulation, to the effect that he assumed more authority than belonged to him, when he did not admit pastors till he had made trial and ascertained their fitness.

Hence we may infer, that this was not so much a private epistle of Paul to Titus, as it was a public epistle to the Cretans. It is not probable that Titus is blamed for having with too great indulgence raised unworthy persons to the office of bishop, or that, as an ignorant man and a novice, he is told what is that kind of doctrine in which he ought to instruct the people; but because due honour was not rendered to him, Paul clothes him with his own authority, both in ordaining ministers and in the whole government of the Church. Because there were many who foolishly desired to have another form of doctrine than that which he delivered, Paul approves of this alone—rejecting all others—and exhorts him to proceed as he had begun. (Commentaries, pp. 277–78)

Gerhard on Titus

Titus, to whom this Epistle was written, was bishop of the church of Crete, a faithful minister and dear friend of the apostle (2 Cor. 2:13; 7:6). The apostle sent him this Epistle from Macedonia. It has nearly the same theme as 1 Timothy.

It consists of three chapters and the same number of parts. The first teaches what sort of persons should be elected to the episcopate and diaconate. The second prescribes to individuals their duties. In the third he gives Titus advice about his office.

But yet, at one time, Marcion rejected these entire Epistles to Timothy and Titus, according to Epiphanius (Haeres. 42) and Jerome (commentary on Titus); however, they have always been considered canonical by the common approval of the entire Church. Augustine, De doctor. Christ., bk. 4, c. 16: "Paul wanted him on whom the persona of a teacher has been imposed in the Church to have always before his eyes these three apostolic Epistles." (E 1.268)

Bengel on Titus

See Bengel's comments on 1 Timothy, pp. 5–6.

Wesley on Titus

Titus was converted from heathenism by St. Paul, Gal. [2:3], and, as it seems, very early, since the apostle accounted him as his brother at his first going into Macedonia. And he managed and settled the Churches there, when St. Paul thought it not good to go thither himself. He had now left him at Crete, to regulate the Churches; to assist him wherein, he wrote this epistle, as is generally believed after the first, and before the second to Timothy. The tenor and style are much alike in this [epistle] and in those, and they cast much light on each other; and are worthy [of] the serious attention of all Christian ministers and Churches in all ages. (Wesley 556)

Challenges for Readers

Paul's Authorship. Because Paul's other letters do not mention a mission to Crete, and because word choices in Titus differ somewhat from those in Paul's earlier letters, some critics have concluded that Paul did not write this Letter to Titus. However, there was time for a mission to Crete after Paul's imprisonment at Rome and before his martyrdom (see the timeline above). Also, authors often adapt their style based on the intended recipient. Paul typically worked through a scribe, which could also affect the letter's style (see note, Rm 16:22). The Early Church unanimously received Titus as a letter from Paul.

Relation to 1 Timothy. See "Relation to Titus," pp. 6–7.

Faith and Works. In Titus, Paul places special emphasis on the relationship between faith and works, explaining that our works result from God's saving action. When Paul describes the Christian life (2:1–10; 3:1–2), he also provides the theological basis for the life of faith (both passages are introduced by Gk *gar*, "for") as he emphasizes God's saving action (2:11–14a; 3:3–7). Finally, he provides a summary statement that explicitly states how Christians are to do good works, springing from God's work in Baptism (2:14b; 3:8).

Blessings for Readers

As you read Titus, reflect on the excesses in your life. Our world today offers excesses of every variety. Yet, as Paul demonstrates, the basics in life and in doctrine are God's greatest gifts. The simple purity of the truth is the hope of our salvation.

Outline

I. Opening Salutation (1:1–4)
II. Body (1:5–3:11)

A. Appointment and Qualifications of Elders (1:5–9)

B. Elders' Duty to Refute False Teaching in Crete (1:10–16)

C. Instructions to Various Groups regarding Christian Living (2:1–10)

D. Theological Basis for This Christian Living (2:11–15)

E. General Instructions about Living as Christians in Society (3:1–2)

F. Theological Basis for This Christian Living Grounded in Holy Baptism (3:3–8)

G. Final Instructions about Dealing with False Teaching and Teachers (3:9–11)

III. Closing (3:12–15)

A. Personal Instructions (3:12–14)

B. Greeting (3:15)

PART 1

OPENING SALUTATION (1:1–4)

ESV	KJV
1 ¹Paul, a servant of God and an apostle of Jesus Christ, for the sake of the faith of God's elect and their knowledge of the truth, which accords with godliness, ²in hope of eternal life, which God, who never lies, promised before the ages began ³and at the proper time manifested in his word through the preaching with which I have been entrusted by the command of God our Savior; ⁴To Titus, my true child in a common faith: Grace and peace from God the Father and Christ Jesus our Savior.	*1* ¹Paul, a servant of God, and an apostle of Jesus Christ, according to the faith of God's elect, and the acknowledging of the truth which is after godliness; ²In hope of eternal life, which God, that cannot lie, promised before the world began; ³But hath in due times manifested his word through preaching, which is committed unto me according to the commandment of God our Saviour; ⁴To Titus, mine own son after the common faith: Grace, mercy, and peace, from God the Father and the Lord Jesus Christ our Saviour.

1:1 *servant.* The Greek word is *doulos,* which means "slave." While it could be rightly said that Paul, like all Christians, is not his own, for we all have been purchased for a price (1Co 6:19–20), his point is not about bondage but about serving God according to his call to be an apostle. This is why "servant" is a good rendering of the word. In the cultural context of the people of Crete, the people hearing the apostle Paul identify himself as a "slave" would immediately see that he is the same as they, and that he and Titus are bound under the same Word of God and instruction that they both preach and teach. *apostle.* While Paul places himself under the Word of God with the Christians on Crete, he makes it clear by this title that he has been called to an office in service to God. Paul uses this term in the narrower sense to refer to himself as one whom the Lord Jesus Christ

Himself personally called and sent with His full authority (1Co 1:1) as His gift to the Church (Eph 4:11–12). It is according to this office that Paul will proceed with the divine instruction that follows in this letter. The very meaning of the word "apostle" ("sent one") excludes any idea that it is an office people takes on themselves and of their own authority. This identifies the purpose of Paul's apostleship. He was called to preach and teach for the sake of God bringing people to faith in Christ (Rm 10:17), as well as informing, confirming, and strengthening the substance of the faith of those whom He had already brought to faith. In this way, Paul set down the divine doctrines that are the substance upon which saving faith in Jesus Christ rests. This letter, and the two to Timothy, are essential in the understanding of the pastoral office, as God established it, for the sake of calling people to faith and nurturing those who believe. *elect.* This refers to all believers, throughout all of time, chosen by God before the foundation of the world so that they should be holy and blameless before Him (cf. Eph 1:4). *accords with godliness.* Faith comes from hearing the true Gospel, and by the faith given, a knowledge of the truth. God gives this faith according to this truth for a purpose, that we live this faith according to the truth of His Word. We are not saved for ourselves but for Christ and the good works which God prepared in advance for us to do (Eph 2:10). Such good works are not left to speculation but flow from the Ten Commandments, and particularly from the Great Commandments—love God and love your neighbor (Mt 22:37–40). While the doing of such good works accords with what is godly, the doing of them does not make one godly. Godliness flows only from faith. The good works of godly living, which faith produces, are for the sake of our neighbor.

1:2 *God, who never lies.* Here, Paul sets forth something that might be taken for granted, but the Cretans were new converts to the faith. Since their former pagan religions were the creation of man, they proved false on many levels. They worshipped false gods and their teachings were lies. In contrast to what they had experienced, Paul sets forth the fact that the God who saves is also a God who does not lie. He is not a man, or like men, that He has reason to lie (Nu 23:19). The fact that God speaks promises and keeps every one of these promises in Jesus Christ (2Co 1:19–20) means that His Word is the living truth for us. It is the arbiter of all truth. Thus He can be trusted in all things and above all things. This was a favorite verse for Luther, who said: "God's Word cannot err" (LC IV 57). *promised before the ages began.* First-century Greek had no word for "eternal," so Paul uses *pro chronōn aiōnōn*, which is translated "before the times of ages past." In this way, he is stating that God had made the promise of salvation through faith in the hope of eternal life prior to all the ages, seasons, or epochs of mankind—in other words, before time in eternity (cf. Eph 1:3–6).

1:3 *proper time.* See exposition of 1Tm 2:6. *command of God our Savior.* Paul here again affirms that everything he preaches, teaches, or writes in this letter is done according to the command of Christ, who called him to be an apostle. In this way, he sets down the authority upon which and with which he does all things, even the sending of instruction to Titus and to those he served in the pastoral office. Cranmer corrected Henry VIII's *Institution* by referring to this passage, noting:

> [The apostles] did in all places and at all times open and inculcate the [resurrection], as a principle and a chief article of Christ's doctrine: wherein should depend and rest the great comfort and solace of all true and faithful believers in Christ. (Cranmer 2:35)

1:4 *Titus.* Unlike Timothy, Titus was a Gentile. He was converted through Paul's proclamation of the Gospel and was further instructed by Paul. Though he is not mentioned by name in Acts, Titus was one of Paul's companions and collaborators in the ministry. Paul left Titus to serve in the Church at Corinth for a time. Later, Paul took Titus with him to Crete, where they began the mission and ministry of the Gospel. As Paul moved on, he left Titus to oversee the continued organization of the Church and her work over the whole island. Later, Titus served in Dalmatia (2Tm 4:10), which is present-day Croatia and Montenegro. *my true child.* The same designation as Paul used in referring to Timothy (1Tm 1:2), by which Paul expresses the dearness of his relationship to Titus. Unlike Timothy, Titus was brought by the Lord to faith in Christ through Paul's preaching and teaching. As such, Paul acknowledges Titus as his spiritual child in Christ. Cf. exposition of 1Tm 1:2. *common faith.* Referencing the faith, Paul is referring to both the substance of the biblical doctrine of salvation in Jesus Christ, and the gift of saving faith they both had been given in Christ through it. In using the adjective "common" to describe the faith they both shared, Paul is emphasizing that their differing ethnicities had no bearing on the fullest unity and communion they shared in Christ. It is in the context of this common faith that the instructions that follow are to be taught and applied, as an instruction and aid to this unity and communion in the mission and ministry of the Church. *Christ Jesus our Savior.* Paul referred to Christ Jesus as "our Lord" in 1Tm 1:2 to emphasize Christ as the Head of the Church (Col 1:18; Eph 4:15). Here, Paul refers to Christ as "our Savior" to emphasize the basis by which both Jew and Gentile are bound forever in unity through the saving work of Christ, whom God the Father sent to save the world.

1:1–4 in Devotion and Prayer From the opening verse to the end of his greeting, Paul asserts that what is written and set down in this letter is from an apostle of Christ. It is for the sake of the faith and the living of their faith by those who would first read it and those who would yet be brought to faith. In this greeting, Paul totally removes the issue of ethnicity when it comes to all matters of salvation and the response or consequence of our salvation. Everything follows from God's Word and is to be done in service of sharing that Word. Sin is the result of following anything and everything other than God's Word. Christ comes as God's incarnate Word to meet us in all the places of sin we have been led to by the words of others. He comes not to condemn us but to be and give us a new word—forgiveness—and from this, a host of new words by which we are made one with Christ and with all other believers. • Thanks and praise to You, O Christ our Lord, for You look upon us in all that we are, in all the times of our lives, and in looking, embrace us as Yourself and make us children of God for all eternity. Amen.

PART 2

BODY (1:5–3:11)

Appointment and Qualifications of Elders (1:5–9)

ESV	KJV
⁵This is why I left you in Crete, so that you might put what remained into order, and appoint elders in every town as I directed you—⁶if anyone is above reproach, the husband of one wife, and his children are believers and not open to the charge of debauchery or insubordination. ⁷For an overseer, as God's steward, must be above reproach. He must not be arrogant or quick-tempered or a drunkard or violent or greedy for gain, ⁸but hospitable, a lover of good, self-controlled, upright, holy, and disciplined. ⁹He must hold firm to the trustworthy word as taught, so that he may be able to give instruction in sound doctrine and also to rebuke those who contradict it.	⁵For this cause left I thee in Crete, that thou shouldest set in order the things that are wanting, and ordain elders in every city, as I had appointed thee: ⁶If any be blameless, the husband of one wife, having faithful children not accused of riot or unruly. ⁷For a bishop must be blameless, as the steward of God; not selfwilled, not soon angry, not given to wine, no striker, not given to filthy lucre; ⁸But a lover of hospitality, a lover of good men, sober, just, holy, temperate; ⁹Holding fast the faithful word as he hath been taught, that he may be able by sound doctrine both to exhort and to convince the gainsayers.

Introduction to 1:5–16 What Paul writes to Titus is similar to what he wrote to Timothy, except for the order of instruction. In First Timothy, Paul began by addressing the issue of false teachers and troublemakers, then moved on to the issue of elders and their qualifications. In this letter, Paul reverses the order and begins with elders, then moves to the false teachers. The reversal of the order is likely due to the context. Crete was a relatively new mission field, as compared to Ephesus, and the greater need was to find and train qualified men for the pastoral office. Both Titus and Timothy had been given basically the same responsibility of further establishing and strengthening the congregations already started.

1:5 *I left you in Crete.* Paul visited here with Titus on his way to Ephesus after his first imprisonment. There were congregations on Crete, which were either started by Paul or already started, that needed pastors. Titus was not only to appoint them but also to finish setting things in place for the divine organization of the churches. He would also instruct these pastors in the faith so they in turn could nurture the saints in the faith and further the sharing of the Gospel. There is no indication that this was a permanent assignment to Titus, as Paul requested that he join him at Nicopolis (3:12). *appoint elders.* Paul uses the term "elder" to refer to the office of leadership within the Church—what we know today as the pastoral office. These men, when appointed, were charged with the responsibility of caring for and nurturing souls through the faithful teaching and preaching of the Word of God and administration of the Sacraments. Paul also uses the word "overseer" (v. 7) to refer to the same office. Based on the fact that Paul uses these two different words to refer to the same office, he is speaking to different aspects of it. The Greek term for elder (*presbyteros*) literally means "older" or "old man." Paul uses the word "elder" in regard to qualifications of the office. In the context of vv. 7 and 9, Paul uses the word "overseer" (Gk *episkopos*) in regard to the responsibilities of the pastoral office. With regard to the use of the word *appoint*, Paul is not referring to Titus choosing who will serve in this or that place. As in Acts 14:23, which implies a selection by vote of the congregation, Titus was to identify qualified men, based upon what is described here, and then put them before the congregation for approval (cf. 2Co 8:19). God, through the congregation, would choose the man He would have to serve as their elder or pastor. Titus was then to appoint them through the laying on of hands (1Tm 4:14), by which these men were then installed in the pastoral office. Melanchthon described the duties of those who hold this office, regardless of title, saying:

> The Gospel assigns those who preside over Churches the command to teach the Gospel [Matthew 28:19], to forgive sins [John 20:23], to administer the Sacraments, and also to exercise jurisdiction (i.e., the command to excommunicate those whose crimes are known and to absolve those who repent). Everyone confesses, even our adversaries, that this power is common to all who preside over churches by divine right, whether they are called pastors, elders, or bishops. (Tr 60–61)

every town. Crete, though a small island, was well known for its hundred cities. Christianity had spread across the island in the various cities where people were gathering. Each of the churches in these cities needed a pastor, for the Christ who created the Church and is its Head also instituted the pastoral office (Eph 4:11, 12; 1Co 12:28; Ac 20:28) to provide for the preaching and teaching of God's Word and the administration of the Sacraments on behalf of, and for the sake of, that Church, as she lives out her mission and ministry (Mt 28:19–20).

1:6–9 The lists of qualifications in 1 Timothy and Titus are not identical, but they cover the same central themes. The differences suggest some degree of flexibility to meet the needs of the local church. For example, 1Tm 3:6 requires that elders not be recent converts, but Titus does not mention this constraint, perhaps because all Cretan Christians were relatively recent converts. These standards in the list reflect God's expectations for those who serve as leaders in His Church.

1:6 *above reproach.* See exposition of 1Tm 3:2. *husband of one wife.* See exposition of 1Tm 3:2. Luther wrote:

> Despite everything that has been said about celibacy, an apostolic bishop elected by God can have a wife. . . . [Papists] take it to mean that a diocesan, a parish priest, can have many vicars but cannot have two parishes, and that a bishop cannot have two dioceses at the same time. Are these not shocking and obvious monstrosities? (LW 29:18)

children are believers. This more literally says "children are faithful." Since Paul directed Titus to appoint older men to the pastoral office, it was essential that such men's children were also faithful believers. To have a pastor whose child refused to believe, or left the Christian faith, would serve to raise questions as to the quality of his teaching and any number of other issues. While such a man could faithfully proclaim the Word of God, his family situation would tend to undermine his own personal credibility in the ears of his hearers. *debauchery.* This refers to an undisciplined self-indulgent lifestyle, which included drunkenness and any other sensuous intoxication. Such things were public displays of immorality that were completely contrary to what their fathers would be preaching, teaching, and practicing. *insubordination.* The Greek for this word is *anypotaktos* and means "not made subject." Here Paul is referring to children who totally refuse to honor their fathers (Ex 20:12) by submitting to the parental authority God has given them. We might say "out of control." Does this mean the pastor's children must be perfect? No, for Christ did not come to make perfect people but to save the imperfect through humble repentance and faith. The kind of children Paul is referring to are not insubordinate here and there, falling into sin as every believer does, but these continue in their insubordination and are unrepentant. May God have mercy on such children in every family of every time and of every place. Amen.

1:7 *overseer.* See expositions of v. 5 and 1Tm 3:1. *God's steward.* A pastor is a servant whom God has called from among all His servants to serve as the manager of His estate, as found in the local congregation. He is to manage the wealth of Lord (i.e., His Word and Sacraments) for the sake of the Lord's estate, the body of believers that are His Church. In this local congregation, the Lord will raise up other servants who will serve under the pastor's guidance to feed, nurture, and strengthen believers in faith, through other ministers, the words of elders, boards of education, and the like. The sweep of the pastor's stewardship responsibilities is limited to the care and nurture of souls through His Word and Sacraments.

1:8 *self-controlled.* The very opposite of what Paul forbids in a candidate for the pastoral office in v. 7. This refers to the ability to stop oneself from refusing to do what God commands and from doing what is contrary to God's Word. While this sounds like an impossibility, a good illustration of this would be found in the life of Joseph (Gn 37; 39–40). Self-control is one of the fruits of the Holy Spirit given to work in believers as they live out their lives of faith (Gal 5:22–23).

1:9 *as taught.* Paul is making it clear to Titus that every pastor, those whom Titus would appoint and those whom God would call until the time of Christ's return, must himself cling to the entire Word of God as it has been taught to him from the Word of God. He cannot, in any point or place, delete this or that part of this trustworthy Word, but he must cling to the whole for his sake and for the sake of his hearers. Only by clinging to the whole Word of God—as taught by the prophets, Christ, and the apostles—will the pastor be able to preach and teach sound or healthy doctrine. *sound doctrine.* Healthy teachings as opposed to false teachings that bring eternal death. See exposition of 1Tm 1:10. Cf. Ti 1:13; 2:1. Calvin wrote:

This is the chief gift in a bishop, who is elected principally for the sake of teaching; for the Church cannot be governed in any way than by the word. . . . In a pastor there is demanded not only learning, but such zeal for pure doctrine as never to depart from it. (295)

rebuke those who contradict it. This refers to the responsibility that every pastor has of putting forth sound doctrine, in an attempt to convict those who oppose it of their error. While it is not the responsibility of any pastor to get such false teachers to admit their error, it is his responsibility to faithfully make the case, by way of sound doctrine, as to why their teaching is false and that of Christ alone is true, for their sake and the sake of believers, lest they be seduced by their errors.

Elders' Duty to Refute False Teaching in Crete (1:10–16)

ESV	KJV
[10]For there are many who are insubordinate, empty talkers and deceivers, especially those of the circumcision party. [11]They must be silenced, since they are upsetting whole families by teaching for shameful gain what they ought not to teach. [12]One of the Cretans, a prophet of their own, said, "Cretans are always liars, evil beasts, lazy gluttons." [13]This testimony is true. Therefore rebuke them sharply, that they may be sound in the faith, [14]not devoting themselves to Jewish myths and the commands of people who turn away from the truth. [15]To the pure, all things are pure, but to the defiled and unbelieving, nothing is pure; but both their minds and their consciences are defiled. [16]They profess to know God, but they deny him by their works. They are detestable, disobedient, unfit for any good work.	[10]For there are many unruly and vain talkers and deceivers, specially they of the circumcision: [11]Whose mouths must be stopped, who subvert whole houses, teaching things which they ought not, for filthy lucre's sake. [12]One of themselves, even a prophet of their own, said, the Cretians are alway liars, evil beasts, slow bellies. [13]This witness is true. Wherefore rebuke them sharply, that they may be sound in the faith; [14]Not giving heed to Jewish fables, and commandments of men, that turn from the truth. [15]Unto the pure all things are pure: but unto them that are defiled and unbelieving is nothing pure; but even their mind and conscience is defiled. [16]They profess that they know God; but in works they deny him, being abominable, and disobedient, and unto every good work reprobate.

1:10 *empty talkers.* These were individuals, and possibly groups, whose talk and teaching likely sounded godly, holy, and religious but did nothing to lead and point their hearers to Christ and the goal of salvation by grace through faith in Him. *circumcision party.* Literally "those of the circumcision." These people are one example of the empty-talking deceivers. This was Paul's way of referring, not to Jews, but to Jewish converts to Christianity who were constantly teaching that, in addition to faith in Christ, the observance of Jewish circumcision and other ceremonial laws was necessary for salvation (Ac 15:1, 5). This group's denial of free salvation by grace through faith in Christ alone was one of the most persistent and difficult opponents Paul and the first-century Church faced. In his letters to the Galatians, the Philippians, Timothy, and now Titus, Paul presses the need for sound doctrine to expose and refute those of this party. Whenever requirements on the part of mankind are added to the Gospel, as necessary for one to be saved, there is empty talk and a total deception. It is easy to understand why this happens: to add something I can do allows me to have my faith rest on what I know and can do, rather than on God, His merciful knowledge of me, and His gracious Word of promise given to me. While this boosts a person's ego, it does so to the person's peril, as only God can save.

1:11 *silenced.* Best understood as stopping or muzzling the mouth of the circumcision party (v. 10). What this meant for Titus and for the pastors he would appoint was that they were to preemptively stop such deceivers from speaking in the Church or any worship service. It means the same thing today. While many in Titus's day, as today, might call for an open hearing of all such teachings, God, through the apostle Paul, makes clear that there is to be no such open hearing of any teaching that is contrary to sound doctrine in the Church. The reason for this is that there is absolutely nothing to be gained in faith, and the life of faith, from hearing what is contrary to sound doctrine. *whole families.* By their deception, one or more members of a household plies the rest of the household with deception, pitting them one against another (Mt 10:35–36), creating chaos in both faith and family. Titus, and every pastor, is to silence these deceivers for the sake of the Church and the family. *shameful gain.* The Greek for this is *aischrou* meaning "disgraceful, horrible, or shameful" and *kerdous* meaning "gain." Everything these empty talkers and deceivers said and did was done for the sake of their own personal and financial gain, but it was not an honest wage but a shameful want of gaining for themselves. Based upon the next verse, this kind of shameful behavior may not have been far beyond the norm. God's instruction through Paul in this matter proves that while the Gospel is freely offered to all ethnicities, it makes one people and ethic (that is, Christ and living through faith in His Word).

1:12 *Cretans, a prophet.* Paul is referring to Epimenides, a Cretan philosopher born in Knossos (c. 600 BC). Paul cites one of their own notable spokesmen as the basis for understanding. This is an apologetic tool in which Paul uses one of their own authorities as a starting point. In this way, what he says is based not upon his observations of them but upon the observations of one of their own. Paul likely applies the title "prophet" to Epimenides because those of the circumcision party fashioned themselves as prophets. *Cretans are . . . gluttons.* The origins of this charge come from a treatise Epimenides had written concerning supposed prophetic oracles and those who wrote them. This charge was directed against the Cretans because they claimed that Zeus (of Greek mythology) was buried on the island. Paul uses this quote as a charge, not against the Cretans as a whole but against those deceivers and false teachers, who fashioned themselves as prophets to the Cretans. The first charge Epimenides makes against the Cretans is that they are "liars." He does this because it is the basis or means by which they became "evil beasts" and "lazy gluttons." Paul does not miss this fact when using this quote against the deceivers and false teachers. Bengel wrote, "The Cretans had the sepulcher of Jupiter; therefore they were called liars by the poets" (4:320).

1:13 *testimony is true.* Paul uses this quote (v. 12) against all deceivers and false teachers, especially those Cretan Jews of the circumcision party (v. 10). *rebuke . . . sharply.* Paul charges Titus and the pastors of Crete to bring the full testimony of God's Word to bear, first on the false teaching that it might be proved wrong, and second on those who were teaching it. The fact that Paul states that they are to be rebuked "sharply" means it was to be done without delay and without concession on any point of doctrine. *them.* The circumcision party that had been teaching what is false and deceptive did have a knowledge of Christ. Certainly, the goal was to stop their deceptive teachings; however, the greater goal is that these false teachers might fully know the Word of God, and through it, know Christ and all that He is for them. Through the faithful and full application of God's Law and Gospel, those who were lost in their own deceptions would have the opportunity to repent and finally believe fully in the Gospel. *sound.* The Greek word used here literally means "healthy." Paul uses this in terms of a body. A "healthy" body is a "sound" body. Faith must be healthy or sound. As healthy food serves to make a body healthy, so also faith must be fed and nourished only on what is healthy—the Word of God.

1:14 *Jewish myths.* See exposition of "myths and endless gene-alogies" at 1Tm 1:4. *commands of people.* These were religious cere-monies, rituals, and ascetical practices that all make for a great show of religiosity and spirituality but lack both because they come from man and not from God. Yet they distort and pervert the pure gift of God's grace in Jesus Christ. Jesus speaks woes, or curses, upon the Jewish scribes and Pharisees, and even calls them serpents for setting aside the commands of God and replacing them with the traditions and commandments of men (Mt 15:1–9; 23:1–36).

1:15 *To the pure, all things are pure.* To understand this, we need to take hold of the second part before the first. All things in creation, apart from fallen mankind, are good. While all is bound under the curse that God placed upon it (Gn 3:17), no created thing, in and of itself, is sinful or evil. Having been purified by God's grace in Bap-tism, through faith in Jesus Christ, believers have been reborn in the purity of Christ. As a new creation in Christ, we find that everything is clean and good and is to be used for the good of our neighbor. Je-sus declares "there is nothing outside a person that by going into him can defile him" (Mk 7:15). Melanchthon wrote, "[Everything is pure] to those who believe in Christ and are righteous by faith" (Ap XXIII 34). *minds . . . consciences are defiled.* Jesus says, "out of the heart of man, come evil . . . . All these evil things come from within, and they defile a person" (Mk 7:21–23). What Paul describes is the condi-tion of an unregenerate heart. A heart that is conceived in sin and brought forth in iniquity (Ps 51:5) is defiled and defiles the whole life and conscience of the sinner. As such, sinners came up with all kinds of religious and spiritual rituals, and the like, by which they thought they could remove their defilement. They tried to get others to join them in their false religion because, in the sinful mind, the more followers you have, the more right you must be. Such an idea always appeals to those who have their sinful hearts still bound by the power of sin. It is only through a faithful application of the Law and the Gospel that they shall have any chance for God to create in them a clean heart and give them a right spirit (Ps 51:10). Luther wrote:

> In a pure man, . . . the conscience has faith, and vice versa. Therefore faith is the purity of conscience, which believes that it is pleasing to God in Christ; on the other hand, a conscience which seeks to please God otherwise and does so without the Word is always uncertain and polluted. On the Last Day its works, vows, and the creatures will all accuse it. (LW 29:46)

1:16 *profess . . . deny.* These false teachers publicly claim not only that they know God, but also that they are more fully informed of God than anyone else. Yet their lifestyles and actions, which ought to reflect God since they know Him so well, do not reflect God as He reveals Himself to be in His own Word. Thus by their actions they not only deny any knowledge of Him, they also deny that they have any real faith in Him (cf. Mt 7:15–20). *unfit.* Good works flow from one who has been saved by grace through faith in Jesus Christ (Eph 2:8–10). Hypocrites have no such faith; everything they do, no matter how great it is, will be only "a noisy gong or a clanging cymbal" (1Co 13:1). They will still be "nothing" (1Co 13:2), and they will have "gained nothing" (1Co 13:3), because none of it flows from the love of God that is given and shared in faith. Everything a person does, be it a believer or an unbeliever, is tainted by the sin that is still in us. The only thing that makes the work of a believer fit or good is that it is cleansed by the blood of Christ through faith. The unbeliever can do the same work, yet the work remains unfit and not good, because it has not been cleansed through faith in Christ. Hus wrote: "He is lacking in faith . . . unbelieved things are as holes, and thus he has a shield of faith which is full of holes. . . . He is lacking in faith who lacks in use of this shield" (*The Church*, p. 70).

1:5–16 in Devotion and Prayer Paul clearly sees the threat to the Cretan Christians, and immediately addresses both the means of combating this threat—the appointment of qualified elders in every city—and the nature of the threat—the circumcision party. Paul has seen this same threat constantly challenging the Gospel in the Church throughout the Mediterranean. As the Cretan churches are young, they need to be nurtured in the faith through faithful teaching and preaching of God's Word. Thus Titus is to appoint elders or pastors in every city so that when and where the deceivers speak, there the Word is to be spoken to protect the faithful and, hopefully, convert the deceived. Paul does something else for Titus that is essential: he provides a clear understanding of the threat, the motive for it, and the nature of those who perpetuate it. This is essential for Titus to rightly apply the Law and Gospel to all his hearers for their sake. How often can any of us be deceived by some teaching that allows us to indulge our sinful ideas and desires? Thanks be to God that Christ met us as we are in our deceptions of sin with the truth of God's love, not to condemn us but to save us and to create in us clean hearts that might, through faith, know and believe in Him alone for our salvation. • Give me ears to hear and a heart to believe Your appointed pastor for me, O Lord, that I may rightly know the Word of God, be saved from all deceptions, and strengthened in the true faith unto life everlasting. Amen.

Instructions to Various Groups regarding Christian Living (2:1–10)

ESV	KJV
2 ¹But as for you, teach what accords with sound doctrine. ²Older men are to be sober-minded, dignified, self-controlled, sound in faith, in love, and in steadfastness. ³Older women likewise are to be reverent in behavior, not slanderers or slaves to much wine. They are to teach what is good, ⁴and so train the young women to love their husbands and children, ⁵to be self-controlled, pure, working at home, kind, and submissive to their own husbands, that the word of God may not be reviled. ⁶Likewise, urge the younger men to be self-controlled. ⁷Show yourself in all respects to be a model of good works, and in your teaching show integrity, dignity, ⁸and sound speech that cannot be condemned, so that an opponent may be put to shame, having nothing evil to say about us. ⁹Bondservants	2 ¹But speak thou the things which become sound doctrine: ²That the aged men be sober, grave, temperate, sound in faith, in charity, in patience. ³The aged women likewise, that they be in behaviour as becometh holiness, not false accusers, not given to much wine, teachers of good things; ⁴That they may teach the young women to be sober, to love their husbands, to love their children, ⁵To be discreet, chaste, keepers at home, good, obedient to their own husbands, that the word of God be not blasphemed. ⁶Young men likewise exhort to be sober minded. ⁷In all things shewing thyself a pattern of good works: in doctrine shewing uncorruptness, gravity, sincerity,

are to be submissive to their own masters in everything; they are to be well-pleasing, not argumentative, [10]not pilfering, but showing all good faith, so that in everything they may adorn the doctrine of God our Savior.

[8]Sound speech, that cannot be condemned; that he that is of the contrary part may be ashamed, having no evil thing to say of you.
[9]Exhort servants to be obedient unto their own masters, and to please them well in all things; not answering again;
[10]Not purloining, but shewing all good fidelity; that they may adorn the doctrine of God our Saviour in all things.

Introduction to 2:1–10 Here Paul builds upon a divine foundation to explain special emphases for teaching different groups within the churches. These exhortations are not as complete as the requirements for elder and overseer in ch. 1, but both aim to encourage growth in areas of personal behavior that are important to individuals and their roles in the Christian community. Paul urges older men and women to be dignified and reverent; these virtues are important as positive models for the younger men and women. Many of the qualities asked of the younger men and women focus on a godly life. These exhortations have both Law and Gospel applications, in that they represent God's expectations and urge behaviors that God will enable, use, and bless through the Gospel.

2:1 *sound.* See exposition of 1Tm 1:10. Paul here identifies for Titus and every pastor, as he did for Timothy, the primary responsibility in which they are to be constantly engaged for the sake of the Church, her mission, and her ministry in this fallen world.

2:2 *Older men.* Paul here addresses not the elders/pastors, but the older men in the congregations, as they ought to serve as examples and mentors to the younger men and youth. What follows is the implied responsibility of all parents and grandparents before their children in the Fourth Commandment (Ex 20:12). *sound.* See exposition of 1:13. As examples, these older men were to be living billboards of spiritual health and vitality for all to see. This health and vitality was nurtured by pastors who did as Paul commanded Titus in v. 1.

2:3 *Older women.* As the younger women who are addressed in the next verse have children, these older women are likely those whose children are grown and no longer dependent upon them. It is difficult to grasp the age here since the average age a woman died in the first century was 34 years. *slaves to much wine.* This is Paul's way of referring to being addicted to alcohol. Wine was a common beverage at meals, social gatherings, and the like (e.g., Jn 2:9–10), because often the water was not sanitary. Wine was also used for medicinal purposes, for which Paul told Timothy to drink a little wine (1Tm 5:23). Yet when one is enslaved to the excess of wine, senses are dulled and self-control is lost. There are many factors that could have contributed to the excessive use of wine and ultimately to their addiction. The cultural context and pagan practices could have supported such excess. Due to their age, the absence of their children, or perhaps the loss of their husbands, they could easily have been dealing with some kind of depression, for which wine might have been used to lift their spirits. As result of their conversion, Christ was, and still is, the believer's gladness in the midst of all circumstances and situations of life. *teach what is good.* As the older men were to be living billboards of spiritual health and maturity for the younger, so also were the older women. These older women, just like older men, were to teach the younger ones with their behavior as well as their words. Behavior is a confession of the faith of the heart through what one actually does. Christian behavior in the presence of an unbeliever creates confusion that calls for explanation, and thereby provides an opportunity to share the Word of Christ.

2:4 *young women.* These were women who were old enough to marry, those married, and those married with children. Under Roman law, the legal age for marriage was 12 years. Paul has Timothy himself teach and admonish the young women in Ephesus. Here in Crete, he has Titus charge the older women with this responsibility. *love.* The Greek root word Paul uses here is *philos*, which refers to the kind of love or devotion that may be found in the context of every healthy family. While this is a natural kind of love, it is exercised by sinners in relation to other sinners. As sin always separates, so this kind of love is not immune to sin's power to separate the most basic unity of love in the family. Notice the glorious fact that Paul directs these young women to exercise this love in the context of their vocations found in the relationships God has given them in marriage and motherhood. Here, Paul tells these young Christian women what their ministry is and where their mission field is. That's what Christ does in redemption; He meets us in our context, redeems and rebirths us in Himself, and then gives us back to those in our context as His gift.

2:5 *working at home.* Inasmuch as women in the first century were not allowed to work outside the home in which they lived, it is evident that Paul is referring to the management of their homes (1Tm 5:14). Here again, while the husband and the children are those to whom these young women are to minister, the home is the mission field. The seven things Paul lists here are various behaviors through which they are to witness their faith in God's Word for them. *submissive.* Having addressed these women according to their vocations as wife and mother, Paul here reaffirms that, as believers, they have been returned in Christ to the original created order in which God has given the husband headship over the woman (Eph 5:21–22). Having said this, it is by no means an authorization of the neglect or abuse of any wife. When this was brought up in a Bible study I lead, a woman asked, "Can a man point to this and say, 'See, I can tell my wife to do anything I want and she has to do it'?" To which I told her, "Yes, any man could say this, but not a Christian man. The reason a wife is to submit to her husband is that he is charged with making all decisions according to what is best for her and her welfare." *word of God . . . reviled.* See exposition of 1Tm 6:1.

2:6 *younger men.* This refers to all who are younger than the older men because there is no age range affixed to either designation. Here, Paul is likely referring to those who were in their upper teens through grand-parentage. Not that one ever reaches an age where self-control isn't an issue, but when younger, when passions and pride are most active, self-control is most challenged in men.

2:7–8 These expectations reflect Titus's role as pastor, or head elder, as he leads young men into mature Christian discipleship and service.

2:7 Like Pastor Timothy (1Tm 4:12), Pastor Titus is to be a living billboard of what a pastor is to be to those he will appoint and teach to be pastors, as well as to those he will minister to personally. In this way, Titus will set before pastors and laity alike that every believer, no matter his or her vocation or station in life, is to be a model of good works flowing from faith in Christ. See exposition of *example* at 1Tm 4:12. Cf. 1Pt 5:3.

2:8 While Paul is concerned about Titus's credibility, he is more concerned about the need for his preaching and teaching to be faithful, healthy, spiritual food to nourish the faith of the people. Having done this, Titus will have been a living billboard and pattern of how to teach to their pastors, their older men and women, and to every parent.

2:9 *Bondservants.* This can also be translated as "slaves." See exposition of "yoke as bondservants" at 1Tm 6:1. *submissive.* Voluntarily submitting to the will of their masters. See exposition of *worthy of all honor* at 1Tm 6:1. Cf. 1Pt 2:18–25. *masters.* Any Christian or pagan who owned or managed a Christian slave or bond servant. See exposition of *masters* at 1Tm 6:1. *in everything.* This is best understood as "in all respects." When slaves were given something to do, the doing of it was to be done in all aspects for the sake and benefit of the master. In this, they would prove themselves trustworthy (v. 10) to their masters, and a witness of their faith in Christ their Savior.

2:10 *all good faith.* What Paul says here is best explained by Paul in Col 3:22: "Bondservants, obey in everything those who are your earthly masters, not by way of eye-service, as people-pleasers, but with sincerity of heart, fearing the Lord." In this way, they would gain the trust of their master, which could afford them opportunities to share the Word of the Gospel that inspires and enables their earthly faithfulness to their master. *adorn the doctrine.* Such faithful behavior would put flesh on the divine teachings/doctrine and show it as more than mere words, but life and living itself in Jesus Christ. Rather than disgracing the teachings of Christ, the behavior of every believer, slave or free, serves to let the love of Christ become real in simple ways, so that others might hear the Gospel and be called by the Holy Spirit to life and salvation. Luther wrote:

> We are to show a certain gratitude toward the Word that in turn it may be well heard and glorified in the sight of men, in the sight of God and of the holy angels. . . . We are to live a good life, not in order to attain salvation, but in order that more people may be converted. (LW 29:64)

Theological Basis for This Christian Living (2:11–15)

ESV	KJV
[11]For the grace of God has appeared, bringing salvation for all people, [12]training us to renounce ungodliness and worldly passions, and to live self-controlled, upright, and godly lives in the present age, [13]waiting for our blessed hope, the appearing of the glory of our great God and Savior Jesus Christ, [14]who gave himself for us to redeem us from all lawlessness and to purify for himself a people for his own possession who are zealous for good works. [15]Declare these things; exhort and rebuke with all authority. Let no one disregard you.	[11]For the grace of God that bringeth salvation hath appeared to all men, [12]Teaching us that, denying ungodliness and worldly lusts, we should live soberly, righteously, and godly, in this present world; [13]Looking for that blessed hope, and the glorious appearing of the great God and our Saviour Jesus Christ; [14]Who gave himself for us, that he might redeem us from all iniquity, and purify unto himself a peculiar people, zealous of good works. [15]These things speak, and exhort, and rebuke with all authority. Let no man despise thee.

Introduction to 2:11–14 Here Paul summarizes the substance of the teaching and doctrine Titus is to preach and teach, and by which he is to train pastors to do likewise.

2:11 *salvation for all.* This whole verse is a shorthand version of John 3:16. This states the universality and objective justification of all people—of all times, ethnicities, social and economic conditions—by God's grace in Jesus Christ. Here, Paul states the divine basis upon which he told Timothy that God our Savior "desires all people to be saved" (1Tm 2:3–4). Cf. Gal 3:28; Col 3:11.

2:12 *renounce.* As the baptized, we are put to death as God unites us to the death of Christ (Rm 6:3–4), so that there is a complete break from sin and all its various forms of ungodliness and sinful passions (Rm 6:7). Through this divine act of God's grace, we have been born again to live in newness of life (Rm 6:4). The grace of God that trains us is nothing other than the means by which God gives us His grace: His Word and Sacraments. Through these, the Word of God not only educates us in godliness through faith, but it also actually works godliness in us through faith, so that we not only say ungodliness is wrong, we also refuse to have any part in what is ungodly. Only through the renunciation of ungodliness will we be able to be devoted to good works (3:8). Paul's rhetorical question states the reality of the baptized in regard to ungodliness. "How can we who died to sin still live in it?" (Rm 6:2). *present age.* While this refers to the time between Christ's bodily ascension and His bodily return on the Last Day, it also refers to what kind of an age it is. It is a sinful age that is under the curse of God (Gn 3:17), in which everyone is conceived and born in sin (Ps 51:5) and is in need of being saved from sin and death. It is an age in which the Church is commissioned to go into all the world, in all this present age, with the Gospel of salvation in Jesus Christ. It is an age in which the Church is to baptize all people for the forgiveness of their sin and to teach everything that Christ has commanded (Mt 28:19–20). That this might be accomplished in this age by the Church, the grace of God trains the very believers it has saved to renounce all ungodliness.

2:13 *the appearing of the glory.* Now we behold the glory of Christ through faith. Here, Paul is speaking of the return of Christ on the Last Day when everyone, believer and unbeliever, will behold Him in all His glory with resurrected physical eyes. Luther wrote, "Deliver Your servants by Your glorious return!" (SA Preface 15). See expositions of "appearing" at 2Tm 4:1; and "His appearing" at 2Tm 4:8. *our great God and Savior Jesus Christ.* Here, Paul states the fact that Jesus Christ is both God and Savior. With these words, Paul identifies the blessed hope, and therefore the confident expectation, of every believer—namely, the appearing of the divinity of Jesus Christ. This is not the verification of our faith but the physical manifestation of what we do believe about Jesus Christ. When mankind last looked upon Christ, He was bodily resurrected from the dead, yet even then, the greatness of His divinity was still hidden from the human eye. Paul uses "great" as testimony to how all the fullness of God and His salvation is found in the humble Son of God and Son of Man—for us. Calvin wrote:

> Paul wishes that believers may now contemplate by faith that which shall be manifested on the last day, and therefore that God may be magnified, whom the world either despises, or, at least, does not esteem according to his excellence. (320)

2:14 *redeem.* This refers to the exchange God made of Christ, His Son, as payment for our sins to release us from the debt of sin and the wrath of God. This was the will of God the Father (Jn 3:16) and the faithful will of Christ, who offered Himself and His holy precious blood to buy us back from the power of sin and death (1Pt 1:18). Having exchanged Himself for us, to save us from the power of sin, He also has saved us from lawlessness, which is sin (1Jn 3:4). As such, we belong to Him for His purposes (1Co 6:19–20). *purify.* The Greek word is *katharidzō*, and is used here to refer to a "cleansing." Simply understood, this refers to cleansing from all sin. The fact that Paul uses the conjunction "and" to tie this cleansing to His redeeming us means both our redemption and cleansing, or purification, is for His purpose of doing good works. While "purify" refers to making us clean, it also carries the reality of being consecrated, or set apart, for His holy use in good works. *His own possession.* When God created man and woman, they belonged to Him. They were His possessions. In their sin, they sought to own themselves, only to lose not only themselves as they hid but also God. God in His great love made His Son the ransom through whom we are bought back, not from ourselves but from the sin to which we have sold ourselves in slavery (Jn 8:34). Titus and every pastor must constantly proclaim this glorious truth that we belong to Christ. They must also remind believers when tempted, "You are not your own, for you were bought with a price. So glorify God in your body" (1Co 6:19–20).

2:15 *these things.* Every precept in this chapter that accords with the teaching and practice of sound doctrine (v. 1). *exhort and rebuke.* This refers to both the encouraging of the saints in all that is good, and the reprimanding and correcting of anything that is not good, through the faithful application of both God's Law and Gospel. These are present imperatives, which indicate that Titus is doing both already. This is Paul's way of telling him to "continue in the very thing you've been doing with my full support and blessing." See exposition of "rebuke" at 2Tm 4:2. *all authority.* The only authority Titus and every pastor throughout time has is that which belongs to the Word of God. Because Titus has been appointed a pastor, Christ has given him and every pastor the authority to teach and preach God's Word, as binding upon all people. The authority of the pastor lies solely in what God says in His Word. Therefore, when the pastor speaks the Word of God, it cannot be disregarded, no matter how young, old, feeble, or infirm the pastor might be. Bengel wrote:

> The minister of the Divine word, defenseless, unwarlike, is certainly despised by those who do not submit themselves to the

word of God, but think that it is only political defenses that are of any avail. (4:323)

Ch. 2 in Devotion and Prayer Redeemed and purified to be Christ's own people, and zealous for good works, Paul would have Titus teach and preach God's Law and Gospel to educate and train baptized believers in the new life and living they have received in Christ. This education and training is for the blessing and benefit of their families, fellow believers, and those who are yet apart from Christ. Such faithful teaching and preaching of God's Word to the baptized reminds them that these works flow from faith and are a confession of their salvation in Christ. Thanks be to God that in Christ, He makes us zealous for good works. He also Himself is at work within us to will and to do according to His good pleasure (Php 2:13). • Take my life and let it be Consecrated Lord to Thee; take my moments and my days, Let them flow in ceaseless praise. Amen (*LSB* 783:1; *H82* 707:1; *TPH* 391:1; *TUMH* 399:1).

General Instructions about Living as Christians in Society (3:1–2)

ESV	KJV
3 ¹Remind them to be submissive to rulers and authorities, to be obedient, to be ready for every good work, ²to speak evil of no one, to avoid quarreling, to be gentle, and to show perfect courtesy toward all people.	*3* ¹Put them in mind to be subject to principalities and powers, to obey magistrates, to be ready to every good work, ²To speak evil of no man, to be no brawlers, but gentle, shewing all meekness unto all men.

3:1 *submissive.* This refers to the act of putting oneself under another authority. Paul identifies the daily path of faith toward all authorities that God has established for the sake of order and our neighbor (1Pt 2:13–14). Here, he points to the civil authorities that God has established for the sake of His creation. Neither the quality of people in any office of authority, nor their actions, can ever void the believer's responsibility to submit to the authority of the office. To do so is to rebel against God Himself (Rm 13:1–7). Christ Himself did not rebel against the false and corrupt Pharisees when they condemned Him to death in a mock trial. Neither did He refuse to be subject to the unjust death sentence conveyed by a cowardly governor. The redemption that saves us from the corruption of sin and death does not free us from God's created order but puts us back into that order, as examples and witnesses of Christ. Paul here begins a brief listing of every believer's obligation as a citizen to those in authority and to fellow citizens. *every good work.* This echoes Christ's command to "render to Caesar the things that are Caesar's" (Mt 22:21). All good works are done in the context of the various vocations God has called us to. Here, Paul considers each believer's vocation of citizenship. Good works, in this context, would be those lawful things that are commanded by rulers and authorities for citizens to do (Rm 13:4). Of course, this has its limits when such commands violate the Word of God. The calling to good works would certainly include Paul's urging that prayers and intercessions be made for kings and all in authority (1Tm 2:1–3).

3:2 *speak evil of no one.* Cursing, slander, denunciations, and the like against anyone, those in authority or fellow citizens, is not to be heard from the lips of believers. Every person, no matter his or her character, condition, or actions, is one whom God loves and for whom Christ has died, so that the person might be saved and be one with every believer. *perfect courtesy toward all people.* The Greek word here is *prautēs* and is often translated "meekness" or "gentleness." This refers to dealing with people, not according to how they may have dealt with you, whether good or bad, but gently, according to their needs. Perfect courtesy works because one is warmly welcoming to all so as to offer oneself to their blessing or benefit. Whatever they may have done prior to our offer is for Christ to deal with, as is what they may do after our offer of courtesy. Luther wrote:

> The law can deal only with the general situation. The head of a household decides that his family should get up at the third hour. This is a general law. But a special case arises if someone in his family has a headache and cannot do this. If [the head of the household] is foolish, he pushes his way through and does not observe epieikeia [Gk: gentleness]. He does not soften the rigor of the law. (4:323)

Theological Basis for This Christian Living Grounded in Holy Baptism (3:3–8)

ESV	KJV
[3]For we ourselves were once foolish, disobedient, led astray, slaves to various passions and pleasures, passing our days in malice and envy, hated by others and hating one another. [4]But when the goodness and loving kindness of God our Savior appeared, [5]he saved us, not because of works done by us in righteousness, but according to his own mercy, by the washing of regeneration and renewal of the Holy Spirit, [6]whom he poured out on us richly through Jesus Christ our Savior, [7]so that being justified by his grace we might become heirs according to the hope of eternal life. [8]The saying is trustworthy, and I want you to insist on these things, so that those who have believed in God may be careful to devote themselves to good works. These things are excellent and profitable for people.	[3]For we ourselves also were sometimes foolish, disobedient, deceived, serving divers lusts and pleasures, living in malice and envy, hateful, and hating one another. [4]But after that the kindness and love of God our Saviour toward man appeared, [5]Not by works of righteousness which we have done, but according to his mercy he saved us, by the washing of regeneration, and renewing of the Holy Ghost; [6]Which he shed on us abundantly through Jesus Christ our Saviour; [7]That being justified by his grace, we should be made heirs according to the hope of eternal life. [8]This is a faithful saying, and these things I will that thou affirm constantly, that they which have believed in God might be careful to maintain good works. These things are good and profitable unto men.

3:3 *once foolish.* In contrast to what Christ has redeemed and re-created us to do, Paul here describes for Titus and the Cretans how every believer was, toward God and others, prior to conversion. Such is how those yet unredeemed still are, apart from Christ. Paul's vision of how we were, prior to conversion, is also a glimpse into how our sinful nature still is and how it continues to work within us. This is especially helpful for the proper use of Law and Gospel by Titus and every pastor in the care of souls who constantly struggle against the sin that still adheres within them until death (Rm 7:18–25).

3:4 *when.* Paul refers to God's timing in a twofold sense. First, he refers to Christ's coming in human flesh as the Son of God and the

Son of Man to save all mankind (Jn 3:16). Second, Paul is referring to this same Christ appearing to them, personally and individually, in His Word and Sacraments, through which He has saved them. Paul's reference to timing serves as a good reminder to Titus and all pastors that conversion of the heart, as the work of God alone, takes place according to His timing. This is a warning against attempting to force the conversion of someone. The pastor's charge is to preach and teach God's Word of Law and Gospel; it is God's work to bring hearers to faith, as it is His to make them new creations in Christ. *God our Savior.* See exposition at 1Tm 1:1.

3:5–7 Cranmer held that Baptism was a sacrament "in which we would be regenerated and pardoned of our sin by the blood of Christ" (2:100). Wesley saw in this passage "a delightful view of our redemption" including its (a) cause, (b) effects, being justification and sanctification, and (c) its consummation, "that we might become heirs of eternal life, and live now in the joyful hope of it" (Wesley 559).

3:5 *not because of works.* With these words, Paul makes it clear that God's saving of us was not in any way a consequence or result of anything we did or might have done (Eph 2:8–10). In the midst of such admonitions to all kinds of good works and service, Paul severs all of these from having any role in any aspect of our salvation (2:11–14; 3:4–7), or in our abiding in this salvation through faith in Christ. Good works are always the result of faith; they do nothing to strengthen faith or better secure the favor of God, both of which come purely through the receiving of Christ in His Word and Sacrament. Bengel wrote:

> The negative belongs to the whole sentence: we had not been in a state of righteousness; we had not done works in righteousness; we had no works by which we could be saved. (4:324)

according to His own mercy. Literally, "in accord with His mercy." This means that the source of the mercy by which He has saved us is God Himself. The standard, the quality, the quantity, the extent, the depth, the fullness, the source, and the reason for this mercy being given to us is found in God alone. It can be known only by the receiving of it through faith as He speaks to us in His Word and gives Himself in the Sacraments. *washing of regeneration and renewal.* Far more than a symbol for the eye, Paul uses a grammatical form that shows possession (regeneration is a genitive). This means that God's work of "regeneration" belongs to the "bath" or "washing." Thus this might be better said, "washing effecting regeneration." Water alone cannot accomplish this, but water with the Word of God is the means by which God cleanses and saves us (Eph 5:26). Here, we are shown again that Baptism is a work of God that is worked upon us by the Holy Spirit, through which we are saved and renewed. As each person is saved passively by the mercies of God in Jesus Christ, so also in Baptism, God the Holy Spirit unites each person to Christ in all that He is. As a result, all that belongs to us God unites to Christ, and all that belongs to the resurrected Christ is given to us, so that we might be born again and walk in newness of life (Rm 6:3–11). Luther wrote, "Baptism may certainly be called a divine, blessed, fruitful, and gracious water. Such power is given to Baptism by the Word that it is a washing of new birth" (LC IV 27). Cyprian said: "The blessed apostle sets forth and proves that Baptism is that wherein the old man dies and the new man is born" (*ANF* 5:388). Calvin wrote, "Paul, while he speaks directly about the Holy Spirit, at the same times alludes to Baptism" (334).

3:6 *poured.* The same Greek word (*ekcheō*) is used to describe how the Holy Spirit was first given at Pentecost (Ac 2:17). This word is used to state how God gives His Holy Spirit, because the image carries the understanding that God is in complete control of the giving, and our part is totally and completely one of reception. Prior to the giving of the Holy Spirit through the Word of God, we are dead in sin (Eph 2:5; Col 2:13). No one can even ask for the Holy Spirit until after the Holy Spirit has made them alive through the Word. Using this word to describe how God gives the Holy Spirit is a beautiful illustration, another glorious aspect of God's mercy that saves us.

3:7 *justified by His grace.* Paul uses what might be called judicial language to state the result of the believer's regeneration and renewal of the Holy Spirit. To be "just" is to be righteous, or right with the Law, before God. Here, Paul states that believers are made "just" or "righteous" before God by the grace of God, which always does for us what we cannot do to be "just" and "right" with Him. Like Baptism and regeneration, believers are totally passive. I remember being taught in my catechism class that to be justified by God's grace means that God has made me "just as if I'd never done anything wrong." The Lutheran reformers wrote, "Justification before God is regeneration" (FC SD III 19). Cf. Rm 3:24. *heirs.* This is what God makes believers through His washing and regeneration as He causes each of us to be born of Himself (Jn 1:12–13) into His family, and makes us coheirs with Christ (Rm 8:17). Thus we shall inherit the same eternal life in glory that Christ shall inherit when He returns in glory. As an heir, each believer owns this inheritance of eternal life now, although we cannot fully enjoy it as it has not fully come. *hope.* Unlike the common "hopes" anyone may have for "what might be," Paul here differentiates Christian hope as that which "shall be," based on the promises of God in Christ Jesus. Christian hope is always a confident expectation of what shall be, because God Almighty has promised it to us, Jesus Christ has accomplished it for us, and the Holy Spirit is giving and working it in every believer through faith. This hope is wonderfully expressed by the apostle John: "Beloved, we are God's children now, and what we will be has not yet appeared; but we know that when he appears we shall be like him, because we shall see him as he is" (1Jn 3:2).

3:8 *The saying.* Paul is referring to everything in every aspect of what he has just stated in vv. 4–7. See exposition at 1Tm 1:15. *devote themselves.* Here, we see the intended consequence or result of what God has done (vv. 4–7) for each believer in Jesus Christ. The goal here is not merely that we have a new and eternal life in Christ, but that this new life be lived in this world through faith, so that we might be conformed to the image of Christ (Rm 8:29), who came not to be served but to serve (Mt 20:28). This active devoting of oneself is not by way of a maintenance program of good works, but as a matter of always zealously taking the lead in doing and getting them done (2:14). Such is what each believer has been regenerated in Christ Jesus to do (Eph 2:10). In this way, the believers will be better able to avoid what ought to be avoided (v. 9).

Titus Article

Sacraments as Ladders: Up or Down?

In 1549, John Calvin believed that he reached an important agreement on the doctrine of the Sacraments that would satisfy Protestants in French-speaking Switzerland, German-speaking Switzerland, and perhaps even in Germany. But when the Zurich Agreement (*Consensus Tigurinus*) was published in 1551, the opposite came true. Further controversy erupted.

Joachim Westphal, a Lutheran pastor in Hamburg, published a tract against the agreement. Calvin expected Melanchthon to come to his side, but Melanchthon remained silent such that persons on both sides tried to claim him or denounce him. (See F. Bente, *Historical Introduction to the Lutheran Confessions* [St. Louis: CPH, 2005 edition], 417.) Reformed leaders in Geneva and Zurich complained that Calvin wrote his defense of the agreement too harshly in some respects but too gently in others, leading Calvin to complain that he would never again publish in Geneva. (See Wulfert de Greef, *The Writings of John Calvin, Expanded Edition* [Louisville: Westminster John Knox Press, 2008], 178–79.) What was the problem?

In this exchange, Calvin learned, and we may see in his writings, that unreconciled differences existed among the reformers. One of Calvin's comparisons, described by Randall C. Zachman, helps to illustrate the problem. (See *John Calvin as Teacher, Pastor, and Theologian: The Shape of His Writings and Thought* [Grand Rapids, MI: Baker Academic, 2006], 222.) Zachman notes that Calvin describes the Sacraments as "ladders." Calvin wrote:

> In the present day, when bidding pious minds rise up to heaven, [we do not] turn them away from Baptism and the holy Supper. Nay, rather, we carefully admonish them to take heed that they do not rush upon a precipice, or lose themselves in vague speculations, if they fail to climb up to heaven by those ladders which were not without cause set up for us by God. We teach, therefore, that if believers would find Christ in heaven, they must begin with the word and sacraments. (*Tracts containing Treatises on the Sacraments*, Henry Beveridge, trans. [Edinburgh: Calvin Translation Society, 1849], 2:296)

Calvin's thought on this point may depend on the medieval mystics who described Christian contemplation and life as "The Journey of the Mind to God" beginning with bodily and temporal things (e.g., Bonaventure, *Late Medieval Mysticism* in The Library of Christian Classics [Philadelphia: Westminster Press, 1957], XIII:132–35).

The Lutherans responded that the mind of believers should focus on the Lord's promise and "be directed to the present action, by which Christ, as with out-stretched hand, brings us his body" (*Tracts* 2:443; compare this with the common statue of Christ on Lutheran altars, where He spreads out His nail-printed hands to welcome the congregation to the chancel). Calvin wrote:

> I admit that any one who passes by the external sign cannot be benefited by this sacrament. But how can we reconcile the two propositions, that the sacraments are a kind of ladders by which believers climb upwards to heaven and yet that we ought to stop at the elements themselves, or remain fixed, as if Christ were to be sought on earth? It is preposterous in them to pretend that Christ holds out his hands to us, while they overlook the end for which he does it, viz., to raise us upwards. (*Tracts* 2:443)

But when looking at the Sacraments, the Lutherans were seeing something different: they were not climbing the ladders! In mercy, God and His heaven came down the ladders to them. Luther taught in just this way while explaining Jacob's ladder in Genesis 28.

> Wherever that Word is heard, where Baptism, the Sacrament of the Altar, and absolution are administered, there you must determine and conclude with certainty: "This is surely God's house; here heaven has been opened.". . . He sets up a heavenly habitation and the kingdom of God at that place on the earth." (LW 5:244) ❧

Final Instructions about Dealing with False Teaching and Teachers (3:9–11)

ESV	KJV
9But avoid foolish controversies, genealogies, dissensions, and quarrels about the law, for they are unprofitable and worthless. 10As for a person who stirs up division, after warning him once and then twice, have nothing more to do with him, 11knowing that such a person is warped and sinful; he is self-condemned.	9But avoid foolish questions, and genealogies, and contentions, and strivings about the law; for they are unprofitable and vain. 10A man that is an heretick after the first and second admonition reject; 11Knowing that he that is such is subverted, and sinneth, being condemned of himself.

3:9 *law.* The Mosaic Law, as found in the first five books of the Old Testament. See exposition on "teachers of the law" at 1Tm 1:7 for insight to who these were and what they were doing with the Law.

3:10–11 Here Paul directs Titus and the Church as to how to deal with those who unrepentantly teach, preach, and demand that which is contrary to sound doctrine. Unchecked by the Word of God and repentance, such false teachers harden themselves in their heresy and create divisions within the Church. Where one is unrepentant to the rebuke of the pastor, that person must be brought before the Church, and if still unrepentant, must be put out of the Church. This means far more than merely not letting them in the building. This process is known as excommunication. It happens when a person, after proper admonition (Mt 18:15–18), refuses to repent of teaching, preaching, and actions that continue contrary to the biblical doctrines he confesses to believe. Because of their unrepentance, such persons are publicly judged as separated from the Church, because their actions are willfully contrary to the biblical faith of the Church. The key in this is not that they have sinned, but that they refuse to repent, and willfully continue in their sin to their detriment and that of the Church. The goal is not to get rid of such a person but to awaken this person to the real and dire condition he has placed himself in through lack of repentance and unbelief in the Word.

3:10 *who stirs up divisions.* This descriptive phrase is a single word in Greek: *hairetikos,* from which we get our English word "heretic." This is the only use of this word in the New Testament, though it is known in other Greek literature. Wesley wrote:

This is the only place in the whole Scripture where this word heretic occurs; and here it evidently means a man that obstinately persists in contending about foolish questions, and thereby occasions strifes and animosities, schisms and parties in the Church. (560)

after warning . . . have nothing more to do with him. Every pastor who is called to the care of souls through preaching and teaching of God's Word, like Titus, must deal with all false teaching and teachers. Here, Paul sets down the path and pattern Christ Himself commanded (Mt 18:15–17). While this is for the sake of that person, it is also for the sake of the Church lest pastor or people be tempted (Gal 6:1). With regard to having nothing to do with them, John states that if believers receive such false teachers into their homes or greet them, those believers are taking part in their wicked works (2Jn 1:10–11). Cf. Rm 16:17. Through the centuries, the Church has acknowledged the importance of these matters. Irenaeus said: "Such was the horror which the apostles and their disciples had against holding even verbal communication with any corrupters of the truth" (*ANF* 1:416). Melanchthon reiterated: "Paul commands that godless teachers should be avoided and condemned as cursed" (Tr 41). Calvin also wrote about the importance of dealing with false doctrine while urging care lest these teachings be misapplied:

There is a common and well-known distinction between a heretic and a schismatic. But here, in my opinion, Paul disregards that distinction: for, by the term "heretic" he describes not only those who cherish and defend an erroneous or perverse doctrine, but in general all who do not yield assent to the sound doctrine which he laid down a little before. Thus under this name he includes all ambitious, unruly, contentious persons, who, led away by sinful passions, disturb the peace of the Church, and raise disputings. . . . But we must exercise moderation, so as not instantly to declare every man to be a "heretic" who does not agree with our opinion. (341–42)

3:11 *warped.* Literally "turned out from." Paul uses this word to describe such persons according to what they have done. Such persons have, by their turning away from the truth of biblical doctrine, become separated from Christ and thus His Body, the Church. *self-*

condemned. This happens not because heretics simply believe something that is false, but because they have heard the truth multiple times, and still have the biblical truth that refutes their error, so that they might repent and be saved; yet they willfully refuse to believe it, preferring their own erroneous and false ideas.

3:1–11 in Devotion and Prayer Paul sets before Titus the realities of the new life that all believers have been given in Baptism by the work of God the Holy Spirit. These realities include the work of God for us and for our salvation, that we might be heirs of eternal life, and the good work of God through us in faith, for the sake of our neighbors. We have been saved by the mercies of God for His purposes, and those are intimately related to our service as new creations in the various vocations God has given us. Both our salvation through faith and the response of faith cannot in any way be corrupted by false teachers or lack of living the faith. Where this happens, those who do such things must be confronted with gentleness, that they might repent and be restored to the Church. Yet where they will not, they must be put out from the Church, lest they divide the Church. How great is the love of God for us, sinners who were by nature perverted and turned from God in sin, yet He turned to us in Christ so that we might be forgiven and born anew, completely justified by God's grace. • Come, holy Light, guide divine, Now cause the Word of life to shine. Teach us to know our God aright And call Him Father with delight. From ev'ry error keep us free; Let none but Christ our master be That we in living faith abide, In Him, our Lord, with all our might confide. Alleluia, alleluia! Amen (*LSB* 497:2).

PART 3

CLOSING (3:12–15)

Personal Instructions (3:12–14)

ESV	KJV
¹²When I send Artemas or Tychicus to you, do your best to come to me at Nicopolis, for I have decided to spend the winter there. ¹³Do your best to speed Zenas the lawyer and Apollos on their way; see that they lack nothing. ¹⁴And let our people learn to devote themselves to good works, so as to help cases of urgent need, and not be unfruitful.	¹²When I shall send Artemas unto thee, or Tychicus, be diligent to come unto me to Nicopolis: for I have determined there to winter. ¹³Bring Zenas the lawyer and Apollos on their journey diligently, that nothing be wanting unto them. ¹⁴And let our's also learn to maintain good works for necessary uses, that they be not unfruitful.

3:12 *Artemas or Tychicus.* Co-workers with Paul. Artemas is never mentioned again in the NT. We can surmise that he and Tychicus were thought of highly enough by Paul that he could send them to replace Titus. The fact that he mentions Tychicus being available to come tells us that this letter was written prior to Paul's Second Letter to Timothy, where Paul states that he sent Tychicus to Ephesus to take Timothy's place. Tychicus is mentioned in a few other places in the NT (Ac 20:4; Eph 6:21; Col 4:7). *Nicopolis.* A city on the west coast of Greece. Paul had not yet arrived at Nicopolis, as he was likely still in Macedonia. Yet this would be the best place for Paul to winter because it was near Apollonia, whose harbor sets across from Brindisum in Italy. This would have been Paul's most direct route to Rome. This location is in good proximity to Dalmatia where Paul would send Titus (2Tm 4:10). *spend the winter.* As ships did not travel during these months due to the rough seas from the winter storms, Paul would go to Nicopolis to rest and prepare for his trip to Rome and for the mission work that needed to be done around Nicopolis and Dalmatia. This cannot be the same winter Paul references in his Second Letter to Timothy (4:21), as Paul was in prison in Rome when it was written. For winter travel conditions, see exposition on "come before winter" at 2Tm 4:21.

3:13 *Zenas . . . Apollos.* Co-workers in the Gospel well known by Paul and sent by him to Titus with Apollos. Zenas is a shortened version of "Zenodorus." While he was a lawyer, it cannot be known whether he was a Jewish or Roman lawyer. Apollos was a Jew from Alexandria, an eloquent speaker, who was further instructed in the faith by Aquila and Priscilla in Ephesus (Ac 18:24–26). He taught and proclaimed the Gospel in Corinth and was likely the one who brought this letter to Titus. *lack nothing.* The verb here refers to the complete outfitting for the purpose of travel. Paul is telling Titus and the churches of Crete to supply, prepare, and pack up whatever funds, clothing, and the like that would be needed for Zenas and Apollos to set off on their way, to destinations like Alexandria (Apollos's home). Such outfitting would likely include Titus, or someone else, traveling with them as far as they could. All of this fell under the banner of contributing to the needs of the saints and the showing of hospitality (Rm 12:13).

3:14 *devote themselves.* See exposition of v. 8.

Greeting (3:15)

ESV	KJV
[15]All who are with me send greetings to you. Greet those who love us in the faith. Grace be with you all.	[15]All that are with me salute thee. Greet them that love us in the faith. Grace be with you all. Amen.

3:15 *All who are with me.* This refers to all those traveling with Paul through Macedonia, as well as those who were gathered with him from Macedonia. *to you.* As "you" is singular, this is a personal greeting to Titus. *with you all.* This "you" is plural; this is meant for the entire Church. Paul closes his letter with this blessing of God's grace. This blessing is not given as a mere closing salutation but to convey and give the blessing of God's grace to Titus and all the churches of Crete. The fact that he speaks this blessing upon all would indicate that Paul expected this letter to be shared with all churches in Crete.

3:12–15 in Devotion and Prayer It is fascinating to hear how Paul closes his Letter to Titus, and the churches of Crete, by talking about the good works they have all been baptized and regenerated in Christ to do for the sake of their families, their churches, and their communities, but also by telling them how they can do good works for the larger Church. In this closing, Paul tells the Cretans how they can let their good works bless the Church beyond the island of Crete. Here, we see the exhortation to help the Church in her international mission and ministry by aiding the missionaries on the way to their various fields of service. Christ, who has made us to be members of His Body the Church, blesses us with the ability to support the rest of the Body, so that the whole Church is built up. • Spread Your kingdom, oh Christ, our Lord. As we lack nothing by Your grace, may we supply all that may be needed for mission and ministry of Your Church here at home and around the world. Amen.

PHILEMON

INTRODUCTION TO
PHILEMON

Overview

Author
Paul the apostle

Date
c. AD 60

Places
Likely written in Rome

People
Paul; Timothy; Philemon; Apphia; Archippus; house church members; Onesimus; Epaphras; Mark; Aristarchus; Demas; Luke

Purpose
To reconcile Philemon to his runaway slave, Onesimus, who had become a Christian

Law and Sin Themes
Usefulness; imprisonment; service; debt; partnership

Grace and Gospel Themes
Comfort/refreshment; reconciliation; forgiveness

Memory Verses
Receive your brother (17–18)

Reading Philemon

With trembling hands, the dying master folds the papyrus and presents it to his chief slave. "Upon my death, this frees you, trusted friend, as well as your family and three others. Yet be diligent in your final duties." The chief slave welcomes his master's kindness but, on the way out of the house, he reaches for a whip. Not all the slaves would be set free and, for them, the master's will commands punishment.

Roman slavery is confusing for us today because it was different from the types of slavery we know best. As you reflect on the circumstances of Paul's Letter to Philemon, be prepared to rethink this important aspect of first-century culture and to consider closely what Bible passages about slavery teach about the Christian life.

Luther on Philemon

This epistle gives us a masterful and tender illustration of Christian love. For here we see how St. Paul takes the part of poor Onesimus and, to the best of his ability, advocates his cause with his master.

He acts exactly as if he were himself Onesimus, who had done wrong.

Yet he does this not with force or compulsion, as lay within his rights; but he empties himself of his rights in order to compel Philemon also to waive his rights. What Christ has done for us with God the Father, that St. Paul does also for Onesimus with Philemon. For Christ emptied himself of his rights [Phil. 2:7] and overcame the Father with love and humility, so that the Father had to put away his wrath and rights, and receive us into favor for the sake of Christ, who so earnestly advocates our cause and so heartily takes our part. For we are all his Onesimus's if we believe. (LW 35:390)

For more of Luther's insights on this Book, see *Lectures on Philemon* (LW 29:91–105).

Calvin on Philemon

The singular loftiness of the mind of Paul, though it may be seen to greater advantage in his other writings which treat of weightier matters, is also attested by this Epistle, in which, while he handles a subject otherwise low and mean, he rises to God with his wonted elevation. Sending back a runaway slave and thief, he supplicates pardon for him. But in pleading this cause, he discourses about Christian forbearance with such ability, that he appears to speak about the interests of the whole Church rather than the private affairs of a single individual. In behalf of a man of the lowest condition, he demeans himself so modestly and humbly, that nowhere else is the meekness of his temper painted in a more lively manner. (*Commentaries*, pp. 347–48)

Gerhard on Philemon

The apostle calls Philemon his "fellow worker" (v. 1), namely, in preaching the Gospel. From this it appears that he was the minister of the church at Colosse (v. 17). Anselm calls him a bishop; Jerome, an evangelist. The occasion for the writing of this Epistle was this: Onesimus, Philemon's servant, had secretly escaped from his master and had stolen some things from him. He went to Rome, was there converted to the Christian faith, and became a faithful servant to Paul in his imprisonment (Col. 4:9). Wanting to repay this faithfulness, the apostle earnestly intercedes for him with Philemon.

This treatise is divided into the proposition or explanation of his petition, the confirmation of his petition, and the confutation in which he removes the charge against Onesimus and promises that he himself will make satisfaction for him.

The Anomoeans held this Epistle in contempt as "written in human fashion," as Epiphanius relates (Haeres. 76). The devout ancients, however, who list the canonical books of the New Testament, do not omit this Epistle. (E 1.269)

Bengel on Philemon

A familiar and exceedingly courteous . . . epistle, concerning a private affair, is inserted among the books of the New Testament, intended to afford a specimen of the highest wisdom, as to the manner in which Christians should manage civil (social) affairs on more exalted principles. . . . This epistle (ver. 22) was written before the second Epistle to Timothy. (Bengel 327)

Wesley on Philemon

Onesimus, servant of Philemon, an eminent person in Colosse, ran away from his mater to Rome. Here he was converted to Christianity by St. Paul, who sent him back to his master with this letter. It seems Philemon not only pardoned, but gave [Onesimus] his liberty; seeing Ignatius makes mention of him as succeeding Timotheus, at Ephesus. (Wesley 561)

Blessings for Readers

As you read Philemon, reflect on the roles of Law and Gospel in your relationships with church members and with colleagues. God calls us to extend His mercy toward every repentant heart and to build up one another in His love. The difficult circumstances for Philemon illustrate how God in Christ can transform our service and relationship to one another.

Outline

I.   Opening Salutation (vv. 1–3)
II. Thanksgiving for Philemon's Faith and Love (vv. 4–7)
III. Appeal to Philemon on Behalf of Onesimus (vv. 8–20)
IV. Concluding Remarks and Greetings (vv. 21–25)

PART 1

OPENING SALUTATION (VV. 1–3)

ESV	KJV
1 ¹Paul, a prisoner for Christ Jesus, and Timothy our brother, To Philemon our beloved fellow worker ²and Apphia our sister and Archippus our fellow soldier, and the church in your house: ³Grace to you and peace from God our Father and the Lord Jesus Christ.	*1* ¹Paul, a prisoner of Jesus Christ, and Timothy our brother, unto Philemon our dearly beloved, and fellowlabourer, ²And to our beloved Apphia, and Archippus our fellowsoldier, and to the church in thy house: ³Grace to you, and peace, from God our Father and the Lord Jesus Christ.

Introduction to 1–25 The Geneva Bible's introduction spiritualizes this letter by stating, "Far passing the baseness of [Paul's subject] matter, he flees as it were up to heaven, and speaks with a divine grace and majesty." Wesley wrote:

> This single epistle infinitely transcends all the wisdom of the world. And it gives us a specimen, how Christians ought to treat of secular affairs from higher principles. (Wesley 561)

1 *prisoner for Christ Jesus.* Paul was under house arrest in Rome (cf. Ac 21–28). He uses this title, rather than his usual official title of apostle, to identify himself in his relationship to Christ. Since Paul is making his appeal on behalf of a slave, he does so by identifying himself in similar circumstances, in the hopes of gaining a favorable compliance with his request. *Timothy our brother.* Timothy was Paul's assistant in Ephesus; he likely met Philemon there during the time of his conversion. Timothy likely visited the Church in Colossae where he would have gotten to know Philemon better. Timothy had become one of Paul's closest and most trusted fellow servants. *Philemon.* A man of wealth who was converted by Paul (v. 19) while in

Ephesus during Paul's three years there. He lived in Colossae at the time of this letter and owned a slave named Onesimus. *fellow worker.* Philemon was a supporter of the Church's mission and ministry, in that his home served as the meeting place for the Church of Colossae. No doubt he used his wealth to support Paul in his missionary journeys. Paul calls Philemon a fellow worker, as part of a basis of his plea for the slave Onesimus, whom Paul essentially calls a fellow worker on Philemon's behalf (vv. 10–14).

2 *Apphia our sister.* Paul refers to Apphia as "the sister," which carries the sense of a mutual relationship to both Philemon and Paul. This is reflected in the addition of the word "our." As this is a personal letter to Philemon, and Paul immediately includes her and Archippus in his greeting, she is likely Philemon's wife. Further support for this is found in the fact that she is addressed individually, separately from the church, which is also addressed. *Archippus our fellow soldier.* While this could possibly be Philemon's son, Paul's reference to him as a "fellow soldier" suggests he is the pastor serving the church in Philemon's home. He was also shown as one fighting against the Judaizers in Colossae during the absence of Epaphras (Col 4:17). *church in your house.* As there were no church buildings, many of the congregations of the first century met in Christian homes (Ac 12:12; 1Co 16:19; Col 4:15). The meager beginnings of these churches made the use of homes essential for them to gather for the preaching and teaching of God's Word, in worship and celebration of the Sacraments. Later, as persecutions began to take place, homes became safe places for believers to gather for worship and prayer.

3 The first part of Paul's salutation, *grace to you and peace,* indicates what God offers to all in Christ. The second part, *from God our Father and the Lord Jesus Christ,* refers to the relationship that only believers have as those born of God in Baptism. Here, Paul subtly sets before Philemon the reality of his equality to Paul and to Onesimus, for they all have the same Father and Savior.

1–3 in Devotion and Prayer Unlike many of his other letters, Paul begins his personal letter humbly, emphasizing his equality to Philemon under the same grace and peace from God and Christ. As Paul has not referenced his office of apostle, the contents of his letter and his appeal to Philemon will be on a personal basis, according to their friendship in Christ. Such friendships are a great blessing to us all, yet even in these, our sinful nature would still seek to divide us from those Christ has given to us. As great as the blessings are in these friendships, the blessing of God's grace and peace in Jesus Christ unites us, even in the midst of temptations and trials. By His grace and peace, the Holy Spirit leads us beyond ourselves to others with whom we share the mutual good we can offer one another in the faith. • Blessed Lord, You have come as the friend of sinners. Grant that, as You faithfully befriend us all our days, we may in faith be faithful to every friend in faith. Amen.

PART 2

THANKSGIVING FOR PHILEMON'S FAITH AND LOVE (vv. 4–7)

ESV	KJV
⁴I thank my God always when I remember you in my prayers, ⁵because I hear of your love and of the faith that you have toward the Lord Jesus and for all the saints, ⁶and I pray that the sharing of your faith may become effective for the full knowledge of every good thing that is in us for the sake of Christ. ⁷For I have derived much joy and comfort from your love, my brother, because the hearts of the saints have been refreshed through you.	⁴I thank my God, making mention of thee always in my prayers, ⁵Hearing of thy love and faith, which thou hast toward the Lord Jesus, and toward all saints; ⁶That the communication of thy faith may become effectual by the acknowledging of every good thing which is in you in Christ Jesus. ⁷For we have great joy and consolation in thy love, because the bowels of the saints are refreshed by thee, brother.

4 *my prayers.* This must be read carefully lest it be heard unrealistically, as if Paul is always praying and giving thanks for Philemon. I have had numerous Christians ask, "How could anyone always be praying and giving thanks for someone? It's impossible." To which I would say "Amen!" What Paul says is that "when" he remembers Philemon in his prayers, then he thanks God for Philemon. This sets a pattern to our prayers for others. Whenever we ask anything of God for others, we ought to also give thanks to God for them.

5 As Paul leads up to his appeal to Philemon, he sets down the unyielding connection between the acts of love and the faith in Christ from which they flow, which has been manifested by Philemon. *saints.* In the Greek, this is *tous hagious*, which literally means "the holy ones." This references the status believers enjoy by virtue of their Baptism, in which the Holy Spirit regenerated them as holy and righteous before God, through faith in Christ (Ti 3:4–7). While this title bespeaks the condition of believers through faith in Christ, it also speaks of our calling to be holy (1Pt 1:15–16).

6 *sharing of your faith.* Paul is praying for Philemon to actively be sharing all he has received in Christ with all others who are in Christ. This sharing includes the Word of God through the confession of faith and all good works that flow from the faith. Paul states this glorious activity another way in Gal 6:10: "As we have opportunity, let us do good to everyone, and especially to those who are of the household of faith." *sharing.* The Greek for this is *koinonia*, which can be translated as "fellowship," "partnership," "communion," or "sharing." It denotes things held in common. Paul uses it to refer to that activity of fellowship, which is the sharing in all things equally. No one is more or less guilty in sin or more or less forgiven of sin. No one has more or less of Christ than anyone else. The reality or basis of our fellowship in Christ is the sharing in all things that are Christ, and this includes every believer. With this word, Paul is informing or reminding Philemon that, though he is master and Onesimus is his slave, they are equal in Christ. *knowledge of every good thing.* This refers to the knowledge, understanding, and appreciation of all the good things that are given to all believers in Christ. It is according to this knowledge, given through faith in the Word, that believers see and know themselves in Christ to be His good gift, who shares all these good things of salvation freely with others. Bengel wrote:

> "Every good thing" is all the riches which Jesus procured for us by His poverty, when he lived as a poor man upon the earth. He briefly intimates to his friend what he lays down more expressly in 2 Cor. [8:9]. (Bengel 4:328)

for the sake of Christ. What is given to us, through faith in Christ for our salvation, is given also for the sake of Christ's work of salvation for all people. Thus everything we do and speak is for the sake of furthering the Gospel, that believers grow in faith and the lost might be brought to faith in the Gospel. The doing of all this is, therefore, done to the glory of Christ, and in it all, Christ is glorified.

7 The word *for* could be substituted with the word "because." Here, Paul states his personal reasons for his prayers and thanksgiving to God for Philemon. His reference to Philemon as *my brother* reminds Philemon of the basis upon which he did all things for Paul.

The fact that Philemon was known for refreshing the hearts of the saints sets the stage for Paul's appeal to do the same for Onesimus.

4–7 in Devotion and Prayer Consider what Paul is about to ask Philemon. Paul's glowing words of thanks could easily be seen as a buttering up of his friend before he makes his appeal. Such could not be further from the truth, for everything Paul states about Philemon is true. Paul is not a con man; he is most grateful for his friend's faithfulness and generosity, which has blessed him and many others. Paul states the truth, and his gratitude for it, in order to make his appeal based on that truth of Christ in Philemon, through faith. As dear as Philemon was to Paul, and our dearest friend is to us, Christ alone is the truest of friends. While, like many of our friends, He helps us, He alone saves us in all things and never leaves us nor forsakes us.

• Blessed Lord, grant that I may have a right knowledge of the truth, and live that truth to all around me so that, by my words and deeds, the Gospel is shared, Your kingdom blessed, and You may be glorified. Amen.

PART 3

APPEAL TO PHILEMON ON BEHALF OF ONESIMUS (VV. 8–20)

ESV	KJV
⁸Accordingly, though I am bold enough in Christ to command you to do what is required, ⁹yet for love's sake I prefer to appeal to you—I, Paul, an old man and now a prisoner also for Christ Jesus—¹⁰I appeal to you for my child, Onesimus, whose father I became in my imprisonment. ¹¹(Formerly he was useless to you, but now he is indeed useful to you and to me.) ¹²I am sending him back to you, sending my very heart. ¹³I would have been glad to keep him with me, in order that he might serve me on your behalf during my imprisonment for the gospel, ¹⁴but I preferred to do nothing without your consent in order that your goodness might not be by compulsion but of your own accord. ¹⁵For this perhaps is why he was parted from you for a while, that you might have him back forever, ¹⁶no longer as a bondservant but more than a bondservant, as a beloved brother—especially to me, but how much more to you, both in the flesh and in the Lord. ¹⁷So if you consider me your partner, receive him as you would receive me. ¹⁸If he has wronged you at all, or owes you anything, charge that to	⁸Wherefore, though I might be much bold in Christ to enjoin thee that which is convenient, ⁹Yet for love's sake I rather beseech thee, being such an one as Paul the aged, and now also a prisoner of Jesus Christ. ¹⁰I beseech thee for my son Onesimus, whom I have begotten in my bonds: ¹¹Which in time past was to thee unprofitable, but now profitable to thee and to me: ¹²Whom I have sent again: thou therefore receive him, that is, mine own bowels: ¹³Whom I would have retained with me, that in thy stead he might have ministered unto me in the bonds of the gospel: ¹⁴But without thy mind would I do nothing; that thy benefit should not be as it were of necessity, but willingly. ¹⁵For perhaps he therefore departed for a season, that thou shouldest receive him for ever; ¹⁶Not now as a servant, but above a servant, a brother beloved, specially to me, but how much more unto thee, both in the flesh, and in the Lord?

my account. ¹⁹I, Paul, write this with my own hand: I will repay it—to say nothing of your owing me even your own self. ²⁰Yes, brother, I want some benefit from you in the Lord. Refresh my heart in Christ.

¹⁷If thou count me therefore a partner, receive him as myself.

¹⁸If he hath wronged thee, or oweth thee ought, put that on mine account;

¹⁹I Paul have written it with mine own hand, I will repay it: albeit I do not say to thee how thou owest unto me even thine own self besides.

²⁰Yea, brother, let me have joy of thee in the Lord: refresh my bowels in the Lord.

8 *command.* To do what Paul is about to request of Philemon is the right thing to do in Christ. Paul, as an apostle, could bluntly order Philemon to receive Onesimus, as he would receive Paul (v. 17), but Paul makes no mention of his apostleship (v. 1). If Philemon received Onesimus by command, the reception would not be of the heart or of faith. Paul knows the good and loving things Philemon has done, yet many of these were likely not yet as personally challenging as receiving a runaway slave, who has likely also stolen from him to get away. Yet Paul challenged his dear friend and brother in Christ to step out in faith and love, as Philemon never had before. Luther wrote, "A man is more easily drawn than pushed, and compulsion brings with it a rebellious will" (LW 29:99).

9 *old man.* Paul identifies himself this way, and as a prisoner, to speak of himself objectively, independent of the fact that he is an apostle. He places his appeal on the same level as any other old man in Christ, who was in prison for Christ. *prisoner.* Here, Paul references the cost he is willing to pay for the sake of the faith and the faithfulness to Christ, in contrast, not to the cost but to the blessing of receiving Onesimus back.

10 *my child . . . father.* By some means the Lord brought Onesimus to Paul during his imprisonment, and through this contact, Paul led Onesimus to faith in Christ through his teaching and preaching of Christ. Thus Paul claimed that he and Onesimus had been given the spiritual relationship of father and son. *Onesimus.* The name means "profitable" and was common among the Greeks. He was a slave of Philemon's who had run away and wronged him (v. 18), and had probably also stolen from him. Somehow, Onesimus made his way to Rome. Then, by the grace of God, he was brought into contact with Paul, upon which followed his conversion and blessed service to Paul.

11 *useless.* Literally, "of no benefit," this is the exact opposite of what his name means! Having run away, Onesimus was of no use to his master. It cannot be said whether Onesimus really was useless while he was with Philemon. To attempt further explanation would be to go way beyond the text. *useful to you.* With this 180-degree change in what Onesimus was to Philemon, Paul basically portrays the reality of resurrection that takes place in all believers through Baptism. Onesimus, who once lived for himself, now in Christ was living for Christ and, through faith in Him, for others (2Co 5:15). Paul knows him to be profitable to him in his ministry, and believes that Onesimus will be useful and profitable to Philemon and the church in his house. Calvin wrote:

> This must be understood to mean, that it was done by his ministry, and not by his power. To renew a soul of man and form it anew to the image of God—is not a human work, and it is of this spiritual regeneration that he now speaks. . . . Moreover, because the word of God preached by man is the seed of eternal life, we need not wonder that he from whose mouth we receive that seed is called a father. (Calvin 353–54)

12 *sending him back.* Literally, "I sent back to you." The verb "sent" is an epistolary aorist and is a matter of timing. With these words, Paul is telling Philemon that the moment he is reading this letter is the moment Onesimus returned to him in a condition of usefulness. Paul sent Onesimus with Tychicus, who delivered this letter, to resume his vocational responsibilities as Philemon's slave. *my very heart.* Here, Paul is not speaking so much about his affection for Onesimus as he is of sending his own heart and all of his most tender affections, centered in Onesimus, to Philemon. Onesimus is a living expression of Paul's affection for Philemon.

13 *on your behalf.* Literally, "in your place." Paul knew if Philemon had known he needed an aide or servant during his imprisonment, Philemon would have likely sent Onesimus to serve Paul immediately. *imprisonment for the gospel.* While this is the third time Paul mentions his imprisonment, this time he states the reason for it—the proclaiming of the Gospel. Paul identifies how much he was

213

willing to sacrifice in faithful service of the Gospel, in hopes that Philemon will follow suit in regard to receiving Onesimus.

14 *compulsion.* While Paul wanted Onesimus to stay in his service, he resolved not to ask or compel anything of Onesimus, no matter how good it might have been, without Philemon's approval. *accord.* Literally, "willingly." As Paul told the Corinthians that God loves the cheerful giver (2Co 9:7), he wanted whatever service Philemon might render to him, through Onesimus, to be freely and willingly given from the heart. The Lutheran reformers wrote, "Truly good works should be done willingly, or from a voluntary spirit, by those whom God's Son has made free" (FC SD IV 18).

15 Paul presents the events concerning Onesimus in terms of what he told those in Athens about God determining the times and places of our lives, so that we might search for Him and find Him (Ac 17:26–27).

16 *in the flesh and in the Lord.* Paul speaks of what Onesimus has become to him, and now, most important, to Philemon in Christ. Because of his union to Christ, Onesimus returned to serve Philemon—not because he is a slave but because Philemon is now his brother in Christ. Does he return to take up his task he once had as a slave? Probably, but now he takes it up out of a desire to serve his master in whatever way is needed. Whether Philemon freed Onesimus cannot be known, but Philemon had gained a brother in Christ and a servant by his return. What we can know about Onesimus is that, even though he was a slave, in Christ he was a freedman of the Lord. Thus as a freedman, he makes himself a slave and servant of all for the sake of Christ (1Co 7:22).

17 *your partner.* The Greek word is *koinōnos,* which is related to *koinonia,* often translated "fellowship." Here, Paul appeals to the reality of their fellowship—namely, that they share in the same Christ, the same salvation, the same grace, the same Holy Spirit, the same faith. Because they share in all things, through faith in Christ, they were partners in Christ and therefore in His mission and ministry. Paul wants Philemon to take Onesimus back to himself in faith, as if he were receiving Paul, because they are partners.

18 Paul realizes that whether Onesimus stole something or not, Philemon suffered the debt of his lost services, and these might stand as obstacles to his favorable reception. *If.* Paul doesn't debate whether there has been loss but leaves it up to Philemon to tally the loss.

Whatever it is, Paul tells Philemon that he has assumed the debt Onesimus has created in his running away. As a father is responsible for the debts of his child, so Paul assumes the debt of his child, Onesimus (v. 10).

19 *with my own hand.* Literally, "I, Paul, did write it with my own hand." The tense of the verb used here is that which is used on documents or accounts (cf. v. 18) when signatures are affixed as pledging oneself. To show how serious he was about assuming the debt Onesimus owed, Paul points to the fact that this letter is written in his own hand. In this way, his promise in this letter was a promissory note. *to say nothing of your owing me your own self.* Paul is not trying to shame Philemon by this statement, but he seeks to show that his whole goal is to ease any personal debt to Philemon. Paul is telling Philemon, "I will assume this debt, knowing that I do not have to appeal to the great debt you owe me." As Paul did not want to live off his service of the Gospel (1Co 9:15), so he didn't want Philemon's response to rest on what Paul might deserve from the Gospel ministry he had done for Philemon.

20 *benefit.* While Paul seeks some benefit, he seeks it in the Lord. This can refer only to the benefit that is the joy of knowing that two men, both of whom he loves, are reconciled in Christ and enjoy the blessing of Christian fellowship. With such a reconciliation of Onesimus, Philemon would be truly profitable to Paul in the Lord. *Refresh.* Paul here petitions Philemon for this benefit of joy by actually crediting any debt to his account, and warmly reconciles Onesimus to himself. Philemon was skilled in refreshing the saints by his works of love and sacrifice for countless saints through the ministry of the church in his home (v. 7).

PART 4

CONCLUDING REMARKS AND GREETINGS (VV. 21–25)

ESV	KJV
²¹Confident of your obedience, I write to you, knowing that you will do even more than I say. ²²At the same time, prepare a guest room for me, for I am hoping that through your prayers I will be graciously given to you. ²³Epaphras, my fellow prisoner in Christ Jesus, sends greetings to you, ²⁴and so do Mark, Aristarchus, Demas, and Luke, my fellow workers. ²⁵The grace of the Lord Jesus Christ be with your spirit.	²¹Having confidence in thy obedience I wrote unto thee, knowing that thou wilt also do more than I say. ²²But withal prepare me also a lodging: for I trust that through your prayers I shall be given unto you. ²³There salute thee Epaphras, my fellowprisoner in Christ Jesus; ²⁴Marcus, Aristarchus, Demas, Lucas, my fellowlabourers. ²⁵The grace of our Lord Jesus Christ be with your spirit. Amen.

21 *obedience.* Paul has commanded nothing of Philemon. Paul's reference to Philemon doing what he asks as "obedience" must be put in the context of faith, in which we are guided in all things by the law of Christ, which is love. Paul believes Philemon will do as he asks because Philemon lives by faith, and through this faith, the love of Christ would compel him to this and much more for Onesimus.

22 *guest room.* There is nothing to confuse the understanding here. Paul states his actual hope and therefore, his desire to visit his friend. So great is his desire and hope that he tells Philemon not just to expect him but to get things ready for him. While Paul may have intended to go to Spain from Rome, plans can and do change, as the time may not have been right for his venture to Spain at the time of this letter. This would also serve as added inducement to the favorable reception and reconciliation with Onesimus. *given to you.* Paul knew that he was not his own (1Co 6:19); called to be an apostle and set apart by God for the Gospel, he was at the Lord's disposal. If he came to Philemon in Colossae, he would come as God's gift to Philemon and the saints there.

8–22 in Devotion and Prayer In the context of their fellowship in Christ, and the blessed change Christ had brought to Onesimus in his Baptism, Paul pleads for Philemon to receive his former slave in the same fellowship, with all the grace and mercies afforded them all in Christ. Paul pleads, and is willing to assume the debt owed by Onesimus, to free him of his guilt, as Christ pled for us and did pay our debts with His own body and blood to set us free from our slavery to sin. • Lord, grant that in all things I may plead for welfare of others through the Gospel, as You have pled and even now plead and intercede before the Father for my welfare and salvation. Amen.

23 *Epaphras.* He is a Christian from Colossae (Col 4:12). While he was a fellow prisoner with Paul, he is likely mentioned first because he was the founder of the Church in Colossae and the surrounding churches in Phrygia. While all those listed would have been known to Philemon, it is likely that Epaphras was better known and dearer to him. *fellow prisoner.* Paul would refer only to Epaphras this way because he was imprisoned with Paul. Whether he was in the same house during this time or one nearby, he had stayed faithful to the Gospel and was now suffering for it.

24 These were co-workers with Paul that likely ministered to him and Epaphras during their imprisonment. Each of them is also known to Philemon. *Luke.* He is the author of both the Gospel according to Luke and the Book of Acts. He was a physician by trade, who traveled and worked with Paul on some of his journeys (Col 4:14). He would also be the faithful one who remained with Paul during his final imprisonment in the dungeon in Rome until his execution (2Tm 4:11). See exposition of Luke at 2 Tm 4:11.

25 *with your spirit.* As flesh and blood cannot receive the things of the Spirit (Gal 3:2), Paul blesses his beloved friend according to the new life he has been given in Christ through Baptism. It is through this grace that Philemon would respond favorably in faith to Paul's request, and go forward in fellowship with Onesimus. Paul closes his personal letter, written out of love for, and in love with, his friend Philemon. What could possibly be a better expression of this love than the blessing of God's grace?

23–25 in Devotion and Prayer Paul's letter written in and about love, mentions five others whom Philemon knew and equally loved. In these early days of the Church, the work was hard, dangerous, and often lonely, as Paul's imprisonment testifies. The mention of these near to Philemon's heart is done for the purpose of comforting him and consoling him in the absence of these friends, who once served with him in Colossae. Jesus came as the friend of sinners and on the cross never left us when, by our sins, we deserved to be friendless. Even now, He companions us in all our journeys of life through faith. What a blessing to receive His personal visit in the Lord's Supper, as He feeds us with His body and blood, so that we might be comforted in His peace. • Lord God, heavenly Father, You sent Onesimus back to Philemon as a brother in Christ, freeing him from his slavery to sin through the preaching of the apostle Paul. Cleanse the depths of sin within our souls and bid resentment cease for past offenses, that, by Your mercy, we may be reconciled to our brothers and sisters and our lives will reflect Your peace; through Jesus Christ, our Lord. Amen (1146).

Biographical Sketches

The following brief sketches introduce preachers and commentators cited or referenced in this volume. They appear in chronological order by the date of their death or era of influence. Although some of them are Ancient and Medieval Church Fathers respected by the reformers, they are primarily writers of the Reformation era and heirs of the Reformation approach to writing biblical commentary. This approach includes

(1) interpreting Scripture in view of Scripture and by faith, so that passages are understood in their literary and in their canonical contexts;

(2) emphasis on the historic and ordinary meaning of the words and literary expressions;

(3) careful review of manuscripts and texts in search of greater accuracy;

(4) faith in the canonical Scripture as divinely inspired, truthful, and authoritative;

(5) respect for the ancient, ecumenical creeds (Apostles', Nicene, and Athanasian) as touchstones of faithful interpretation and application of Scripture; and most important

(6) focus on Christ and justification through Him as the chief message of Holy Scripture (e.g., the distinction of Law and Gospel or sin and grace in interpretation and application).

For more information about these figures, see Edward A. Engelbrecht, gen. ed., *The Church from Age to Age: A History from Galilee to Global Christianity* (St. Louis: Concordia, 2011).

Ancient and Medieval Fathers

Irenaeus. (c. 130–c. 200) Bishop of Lyons, in what is now France. He opposed early heresies and was the first dogmatic theologian.

Cyprian. (d. 258) Bishop of Carthage, North Africa. One of the earliest Latin Church Fathers, known for his dedication and pastoral care.

Ambrose. (c. 339–97) Governor of Milan who was suddenly made bishop, though only a catechumen at the time. He became a great preacher and defender of orthodoxy, influencing the conversion of Augustine.

John Chrysostom. (c. 347–407) Bishop of Constantinople and a key figure in the early Christological controversies. He was called "golden-mouthed" because of his brilliant oratory style. His commentaries on Scripture are sermons, valued by the Church from ancient times.

Bernard of Clairvaux. (1090–1153) Cistercian abbot and preacher. Bernard's sermons often beautifully proclaim Christ and God's grace, which made him a favorite medieval Father in the eyes of the reformers.

Hus, John. (c. 1372–1415) Priest and martyr. Lecturer and rector at the University of Prague, an enormously popular preacher and writer, greatly influenced by Augustine's theology and John Wycliffe's writings. Hus was falsely accused of heresy and condemned at the Council of Constance when the Medieval Church was sorely divided. His efforts heralded the Reformation.

Reformers

Luther, Martin. (1483–1546) Augustinian friar and preeminent reformer, lecturer on the Bible at the University of Wittenberg. Luther's preaching, teaching, and writing renewed biblically based piety in Western Christendom. His translation of the Bible influenced the work of Bible publication throughout Europe, notably William Tyndale and the King James translators.

Cranmer, Thomas. (1489–1556) Archbishop of Canterbury and martyr. Cranmer served as a writer and editor for the Book of Common Prayer, one of the most influential works of the Reformation.

Mill, Walter. (d. 1558) Scottish pastor and martyr. Mill was ordained as a priest. He later traveled to Germany where he adopted Protestant views. After returning to Scotland, he married. In April 1558, Scottish bishops tried him for heresy and burned him at the stake.

Melanchthon, Philip. (1497–1560) Lecturer on classical literature and languages at the University of Wittenberg. Melanchthon's *Commonplaces* and the Augsburg Confession laid the foundation for all subsequent works of Protestant dogmatic theology. He also wrote significant biblical commentaries.

Calvin, John. (1509–64) Preacher and lecturer on theology, founder of the Academy of Geneva. Calvin organized reformation efforts for Swiss, French, Dutch, and English Protestants. Calvin's *Institutes of the Christian Religion* and his extensive commentaries on Scripture are the most influential works of the second-generation reformers.

Knox, John. (c. 1513–72) Scottish preacher and reformer. Knox edited the Book of Common Order used in Scottish churches and wrote a history of the Reformation in Scotland.

Chemnitz, Martin. (1522–86) Pastor and theologian at Brunswick, Germany. Chemnitz was largely responsible for the Formula of Concord that unified churches in Lutheran territories following the deaths of Luther and Melanchthon. His *Examination of the Council of Trent* equipped Protestant churches for responding to the Roman Catholic Counter-Reformation.

Heirs of the Reformation

Gerhard, Johann. (1582–1637) Professor of theology at Jena and devotional writer. Gerhard wrote the most extensive dogmatic of the Protestant age of orthodoxy, the *Theological Commonplaces*, and was widely regarded for his knowledge of biblical Hebrew.

Bengel, Johann Albrecht. (1687–1752) New Testament scholar and professor. Bengel wrote the first scientific study of Greek New Testament manuscripts. His *Gnomon* on the New Testament is an influential, succinct commentary of enduring value.

Wesley, John. (1703–91) Missionary preacher. Wesley preached throughout England, Scotland, Ireland, and the American colonies. His *Explanatory Notes upon the New Testament* is a classic evangelical commentary, which drew upon principles and emphases of the reformers.